SPAIN TO ENGLAND

Spain to England

A Comparative Study
of Arabic, European, and English Literature
of the Middle Ages

ALICE E. LASATER

UNIVERSITY PRESS OF MISSISSIPPI

JACKSON

Library of Congress Catalog Card Number 73-94277
ISBN 0-87805-056-6
Manufactured in the United States of America
Printed by Heritage Printers, Inc., Charlotte, N. C.
Designed by J. Barney McKee

THIS VOLUME IS AUTHORIZED
AND SPONSORED BY
THE UNIVERSITY OF SOUTHERN MISSISSIPPI
HATTIESBURG, MISSISSIPPI

contents

Foreword

Dealing in English with languages having sounds for which there is no English equivalent is always a problem. Some writers simply use the closest English approximation, which can be confusing—as in the case of *t* for the two *t* sounds in Arabic, ت and ط. For accuracy, the latter should be distinguished from a regular *t* in English since it has a separate character in the Arabic alphabet. T. E. Lawrence, in his correspondence with the publisher who was concerned about his erratic English spellings of Arabic names in *The Seven Pillars of Wisdom,* remarked that Arabic sounds could not be represented in the English alphabet. That is nonsense. They can be, and there is a standard manner of representing them. I have therefore followed the transliteration system recognized by the United States Library of Congress, with one exception: for ظ, instead of ẓ, I use ḍh since it is a closer approximation of the sound in Classical Arabic. In the dialect which I learned to speak, that of Cyrenaica (Eastern Libya), the ظ is not always slurred into a *z* sound as it is in other dialects which are less close to the Classical pronunciation. For those readers not familiar with Arabic, the alphabet and the standard English transliteration can be found in most large dictionaries, such as the new *American Heritage Dictionary.*

Many Arabic works have been translated into French and a few into English. Where an English translation of either primary sources or critical discussions was available, I have used that translation; where the only available translation of works was French, I used the French. I have also either summarized or tacitly translated comments from those critical studies written in French, German, and Spanish which I have cited. I have not, however, translated or modernized the Middle-English passages cited, since there are numerous modern versions, including paperback editions, of the works from which I quote.

In the research and preparation of this study, I am deeply indebted to Professor Thomas B. Irving of the University of Tennessee, who rendered invaluable assistance in the Spanish and Arabic languages, literature, and history. In addition to providing bibliographical guidance, he has given me countless hours of his time and expert help with literary Arabic, without which I could not have written the Hispano-Arabic portions. It has been a privilege to work with him and to know him as a friend as well as a scholar. To Professor Neil D. Isaacs of the University of Maryland, I am indebted for the encouragement and guidance he provided in my early research and for an enthusiasm for Middle-English literature in general. Any merits this study may have can be attributed to the influence of these two scholars. Its faults are, of course, my own.

SPAIN TO ENGLAND

CHAPTER I

introduction

The Moving Finger writes, and, having writ,
Moves on; nor all your Piety nor Wit
  Shall lure it back to cancel half a Line,
Nor all your Tears wash out a Word of it.
Edward Fitzgerald
The Rubáiyát of Omar Khayyám

It is surely one of the ironies of history that the remains of our one English saint were found to have been clothed in a robe which bore the Islamic creed woven into its fabric. When Saint Cuthbert's relics were disinterred in 1827, scraps of a strange, foreign garment were still visible. The garment was of purple silk brocade, bearing the fish design of Persian royalty. Embroidered into it, in gold thread, in Kufic (a stylized Arabic) script was the *kalima* or saying "There is no god except The [one] God" (Āllah), the first half of the Islamic Profession of Faith, the second part of which is "and Muḥammad was the Messenger of God."

The mystery of Cuthbert's robe was solved in 1931 with the tracing of the historical events leading up to the appearance of such a robe on the English saint.[1] These events began in 765 when Pippin of France sent a mission to the ʿAbbāsid caliph, al-Maʾmūn, in Baghdad. Three years later his representatives returned, accompanied by Saracens bearing many presents. Pippin's successor, Charlemagne, later dispatched a mission consisting of three ambassadors (one of whom was Jewish and served as interpreter) to al-Maʾmūn's successor, Hārūn-al-Rashīd in 797 and a second one between 802 and 806. On both occasions,

[1] F. W. Buckler, *Harunuʾl-Rashid and Charles the Great* (Cambridge, Mass., 1931), pp. 53–54. The facts on Saint Cuthbert are taken in their entirety from Buckler's monograph.

Hārūn-al-Rashīd sent representatives to France in return. The political ramifications of these diplomatic embassies involved basically Catholic interests in the East and Muslim interests in Spain. The Frankish rulers sought certain concessions in the Holy Land and an alliance against Constantinople because of the iconoclastic controversy, while the ʿAbbāsid caliphs of Baghdad sought to enlist the Franks to secure ʿAbbāsid interests in Spain against the Umayyads, who were then in power in Spain.

The two reciprocal exchanges of ambassadors between Charlemagne and Hārūn-al-Rashīd, like that between Pippin and al-Maʾmūn, involved exchanges of presents; among the items known to have arrived in France were an elephant, an ivory horn, a sword, a golden tray with colored-glass inlay, and a set of chessmen. Upon the dissolution of the Carolingian Empire in 888, the oriental treasures were distributed among the French dukes. One of them, Duke Hugh, in his suit for the hand of King Aethelstan's sister, sent various presents from the oriental collection to England.

Twelve years later, Aethelstan bestowed several gifts upon the monastery at Durham where Saint Cuthbert was buried, and included among his gifts were seven *pallia* (robes). Two centuries later, in 1104, the monks at Durham disinterred Cuthbert's relics to clothe them in what was described as a "royal ecclesiastical robe." This was the robe whose remnants were found when Saint Cuthbert was again disinterred in the nineteenth century.

But Cuthbert's robe was not the only occasion of English utilization of the Muslim profession of faith in ignorance of its meaning. In 774, a contemporary of Charlemagne, Offa, King of Mercia (757–96), had a gold coin struck on which appear the words "There is no God but Āllah." The Arabic script, the words *Offa Rex*, and the date are all still quite legible on the coin, now in the British Museum.[2]

There were other instances in history in which inadvertent Christian use of Arabic script seems a bit ironic. In orthodox

2 A. H. Christie, "Islamic Minor Arts and Their Influence upon European Work," in *The Legacy of Islam*, ed. Thomas Walker Arnold and Alfred Guillaume (Oxford, 1931), pp. 113–14. The coin is reproduced on page 106 (fig. 14).

Islam, the depicting of men or animals in paintings, sculpture, or architecture was (and still is, especially in the puritanical schools of theological thought such as those currently prevalent in Saudi Arabia and Libya) strictly prohibited to preclude any tendency towards idolatry arising within the faith from the use of icons. Consequently, Arabic letters and intricate geometric designs were adapted for ornamentation on bas relief in architecture, on borders of robes, and on sundry articles. That such ornamentation was not only familiar, but also admired artistically is evident in its appropriation by several Italian Renaissance painters who were apparently unaware of its origin. Fra Angelico and Fra Lippo Lippi employed this type of decoration even on the sleeves and borders of the Virgin's robe.[3] In Fra Lippo Lippi's *Coronation of the Virgin,* the Arabic lettering on Mary's robe, on her sleeves, and on the long, ribbon-like piece of material held by the angels in the painting is clearly discernible. Although he was no doubt totally unaware of the nature of his decoration on the Virgin's robe, it is tempting to imagine Fra Lippo Lippi having some inkling as to its origin and chuckling over such a secret in his painting—especially if Robert Browning's dramatic monologue of the good brother is a true character portrait of him.

Decorative Arabic script is also to be noted in devotional manuscript illuminations. It appears rather extensively on the robes in those miniatures of the *Très Riches Heures* of the Duke of Berry painted between 1413 and 1416 by the Limbourg brothers, who were familiar with Italian art.[4]

The instances cited up to this point intimate that the Islamic culture of the Near East and portions of southern Europe in the Middle Ages influenced the graphic arts of the more traditionally European cultures. Similar influence can be detected in another realm of art—literature, both oral and written. Like the appro-

[3] Thomas Walker Arnold, "Islamic Art and Its Influence on Painting in Europe," in *The Legacy of Islam,* pp. 151–54. Fra Lippo Lippi's *Coronation of the Virgin* at the Uffizi, Florence, is reproduced on page 154 (fig. 73) of Arnold's article.

[4] The manuscript is in the Musée Condé, Chantilly, France. The manuscript's miniatures and selections from its text pages have been reproduced in facsimile as *The Très Riches Heures of Jean, Duke of Berry,* ed. Jean Longnon and Raymond Cazelles, trans. Victoria Benedict (New York, 1969). It is one of the most beautiful works of art of the Middle Ages.

priation of Arabic decorative script, literary borrowings were sometimes inadvertent. Sometimes they were not, as in the case of Saint Thomas à Becket's being fancifully credited with Saracen ancestry because of the fame of Salāh-al-Dīn (Saladin).[5]

In a considerable amount of later medieval literature, i.e., that of the twelfth through the fifteenth centuries, the line between Christian and Islamic motifs, between European and Arab-Persian stories, was not always as distinct as it perhaps is today. The spread of tales, fables, and romances among various countries and the distribution of manuscripts among certain monastery and cathedral libraries suggest that medieval Europe—especially the higher social strata, the merchants, and the clergy—was, in spite of the time involved in travel, fairly mobile. For example, the appearance of a Persian robe in England in the late ninth century has a counterpart in the appearance of a manuscript of tenth-century Anglo-Saxon prose homilies, saints' lives, and poems in the cathedral library in Vercelli in northern Italy. No one knows, however, exactly how or when *The Vercelli Book* reached Italy. The point is that, even with limited mobility, there was naturally contact between European and Arab-Persian cultures; and, with contact, some interchange was virtually inevitable.

Unfortunately, there is a dearth of research into the interchange between medieval Arabic and European belles-lettres. One reason for the lack is the Arabic language which, like Hebrew, requires a knowledge of an alphabet different from that in which Old and Middle English, Old Provençal, Old French, Middle High German, or medieval Latin were written. So does Greek. And while there have been and are at present a number of eminent scholars of Arabic, there has not been sufficient communication between the scholars of Arabic and Islamic literature and the scholars of English and European literatures.

The language gap found among studies in medieval vernacular literatures is of course nonexistent with regard to studies involving Latin writings. For example, O. B. Hardison, Jr., rejects the

[5] Philip K. Hitti, *History of the Arabs*, 4th ed., rev. (London, 1949), p. 652, *n.* 7.

generally accepted thesis that medieval passion plays were germinated in the question-and-answer dialogue of the *quem quaeritis* of the liturgy, grew into full-length liturgical dramas, blossomed into the vernacular, and were finally excised from the church ritual.[6] In his discussion of the variations among rites in different countries, Hardison includes the Mozarabic rite of Spain, and whether or not his particular views are accepted, it can at least be said that he has taken all available and relevant materials into consideration. But by and large, the historians and orientalists of the Middle Ages have far outdistanced those of us interested in the vernacular literatures of the period, and the student of medieval European history is therefore presented with a more composite and more complete picture than is the student of medieval European literature.

A second reason for the paucity of comparative studies in medieval European and Arabic literature involves nationalistic interests and prejudices. While Old- and Middle-English scholars have understandably sought models for comparison in ancient Celtic lore, and while French scholars have been concerned with the Old-Provençal lyrics of the troubadours, such biases are justifiable and have certainly not been without merit in the results which they have produced. This cannot be said of another type of bias, such as that evident in the remarks of C. Sánchez Albornoz who in 1929 supposed that Spain's being intellectually and economically so far behind other countries of Europe in the twentieth century was caused by the centuries of Islamic rule in Spain. The best reply to this is perhaps a wry comment that the name *Albornoz* is an obvious corruption of the Arabic *al-Burnusī*, "he who wears a burnous" (a type of robe still worn in North Africa).[7]

The levels of intellectual and scientific achievement and the general economic progress in Western Europe which are superior to those in the Arabic-speaking countries of the present century cannot be compared with scientific achievements and economic

[6] O. B. Hardison, Jr., *Christian Rite and Christian Drama in the Middle Ages* (Baltimore, 1965).

[7] See J. B. Trend, "Spain and Portugal," in *The Legacy of Islam*, pp. 1–39. The observation on the derivation of *Albornoz* is Trend's.

situations in the tenth through the twelfth centuries when, under Islamic rule, the cities of Cordoba, Toledo, and Granada were major centers of learning and civilization in an otherwise relatively primitive Western Europe. The impoverishment of Spain was a consequence of active attempts following the *reconquista* to eradicate all Arab- and Moorish-Islamic influences and mores. Soon after the fall of Granada to Christian forces in 1492, Archbishop Ximénez conducted a massive burning of any and all Arabic manuscripts he could lay hold to.[8] Was there not a similar attempt in Europe in the 1930s to obliterate priceless treasures of learning because of doctrinaire opposition? Fortunately, the archbishop was not completely successful, and many manuscripts were smuggled out of the country to the libraries of mosques in Tunisia and Morocco while others were concealed within Spain not to be rediscovered until the twentieth century. Finally, with the expulsion of the Jews and Arabs, Spain in effect rid herself of her physicians, scientists, merchants, and craftsmen—in fact, of most of her intellectuals and artisans.

To read *The Canterbury Tales* with a recognition of French influences on Chaucer but with a denial of Italian influences (rationalizing that Italy was too far geographically from England for Chaucer to have been familiar with Italian writers) would be absurd. And to state that Morgan le Fay could not possibly be of Celtic origin because Celtic material was non-Christian and would therefore have been rejected by the French writers of Arthurian romance would be equally absurd. Likewise, the all-too-often-encountered opinion that there could have been little or no interchange between medieval Christian and Islamic literature in and through Arab Spain is nonsense and hints of an acceptance of the events and motives in the *Chanson de Roland* as factual.

Beginning in the late eleventh century and extending through the middle of the thirteenth century, there occurred two remarkable cultural phenomena in Western Europe. One of these was the inundation of Europe with the scientific and philosophical

[8] Reynold A. Nicholson, *A Literary History of the Arabs* (Cambridge, England, 1969), p. 435. This study was first published in 1907.

knowledge of the ancient Greeks which had been preserved by the Byzantines and further developed by the Hindus, Jews, Persians, and Arabs of the East. Concurrent with this scientific and philosophical infusion was a sudden rapid evolution of vernacular literature in the countries which were recipients of the Eastern learning.

The Arab scientific contributions to Western European civilization through the massive translation projects in twelfth-century Spain and Sicily are widely acknowledged, due in part to the extensive researches of such medievalists as C. H. Haskins, George Sarton, and Lynn Thorndike. Spain and Sicily, where the bulk of the translation was accomplished, were, as a result, major bridges over which Arab cultural elements were carried into Europe, with Spain being by far the greater of the two.[9] (Sicily, which had been conquered by the Normans by the end of the eleventh century, became under Norman rule an important center for translation by the second quarter of the twelfth century.) In spite of Spain's scientific contributions, however, belletristic literature from south of the Pyrenees is rarely given sufficient consideration in surveys of medieval European vernacular literature. In W. T. H. Jackson's guide, for example, the chapter "Literature of the Iberian Peninsula," is, even for an outline, inadequate as a representation of Spanish literature.[10]

In addition to the translations, lyric poetry of a type not native to Western Europe but which closely resembled popular poetry of Islamic Spain also sprang up in southern France during the twelfth century. There also occurred about the same time in Europe a renewed development of Oriental materials in visions of the afterlife, with the addition of new and particularly Islamic ones which were known in Spain and France. Persian and Arabic *contes* and fables proliferated all over Europe from the beginning of the twelfth century, many of them possibly having come through Spain; with the tales, the Oriental frame-story was intro-

9 Philip K. Hitti, *Islam and the West* (Princeton, 1962), p. 72.

10 See W. T. H. Jackson, *Medieval Literature: A History and a Guide* (New York, 1966), pp. 235–44. The chapter mentioned is the weak section in an otherwise excellent survey.

duced into Europe. And, borrowing from the epic, vision, poetry, and *conte* traditions, the romance developed, bringing in additional masses of Celtic and Eastern materials. All of these events suggest that the Arabic belles-lettres of Spain are relevant to the early vernacular literature of Western Europe and that they are due more recognition than they have been accorded. Some of the theories promulgated to account for the rise and development of the earlier vernacular genres point directly to Arab Spain.

Provençal lyric poetry, arising in southern France in the twelfth century, is frequently cited as having influenced, or at least having given impetus to, the development of northern-French, Middle-English, German, and Italian rimed lyric poetry. There is considerable divergence of opinion, however, as to the origins of the Provençal lyrics. The Latin theory of origin for the meters of the Provençal troubadours, as put forth by Diez and Warren, is no longer widely credited.[11] Alfred Jeanroy proposes that the poetry of Provence simply appeared and blossomed as a French phenomenon with no outside influence or inspiration, and Gaston Paris attributes it to pagan Celtic May Day festivals.[12] Theodor Frings disputes the suggestion of Provençal influence on other European vernacular poetry and states that all lyric poetry was an outgrowth of primitive dancing and chanting of women, epitomized by the early German *Frauenlieder*, in all European countries simultaneously. Curiously, Leo Spitzer sees in the discovery in 1946 of certain Judeo-Mozarabic-Andalusian strophes predating Provençal poetry a corroboration of Frings's *Frauenlieder* theory.[13] The significance of these early strophes has not yet been fully recognized since a great deal of linguistic and metrical analysis remains to be done on them.

11 Diez's theory is summarized by Robert S. Briffault in *The Troubadours*, ed. Lawrence F. Koons (Bloomington, 1965), p. 223, *n.* 22; for F. M. Warren's theory, see "The Troubadour *Canso* and the Latin Lyric Poetry," *Modern Philology*, 9 (1912), 469–87. (Briffault's work was originally published in 1945. Briffault himself translated it from the French, with the exception of the notes, which were translated by Koons.)

12 Alfred Jeanroy, *Les Origines de la poésie lyrique en France au moyen âge*, 4th ed., rev. (Paris, 1965); Gaston Paris, *La Littérature française au moyen âge*, 5th ed. (Paris, 1914); and Briffault, *The Troubadours*, pp. 21; 224, *n.* 22.

13 Leo Spitzer, "The Mozarabic Lyric and Theodor Frings' Theories," *Comparative Literature*, 4 (1952), 1–22.

An Arabic-Andalusian theory of origin for Provençal strophic forms was first supported strongly by Julián Ribera in 1926. He was followed by R. Menéndez Pidal, Robert S. Briffault, and the Arabists R. A. Nicholson and A. R. Nykl.[14] However, both Gaston Paris, a prominent French historian, and Alfred Jeanroy, perhaps the most eminent French authority on the troubadours, reject the Arabic theory. An authority on Spanish literature, Gerald Brenan, believes that verse forms of the troubadours were not derived from those of Arab Spain, but that the concept of courtly love and the high prestige which the troubadours seem to have enjoyed were so derived.[15]

Courtly love, a major theme of the troubadours, has also been attributed to a number of sources, most notably Ovid, the Albigensians, the Arab poets of Spain, and the Arab philosophers of Spain. It is possible that the concept of courtly love as it appears in Old-French and Middle-English romances owes something to each of these.

The theory of Arabic origin for both the lyric form and the ideology of courtly love has been gradually gaining adherents, notwithstanding its rejection by the French critics Jeanroy and Gaston Paris. The observations of Roger Sherman Loomis, renowned for his studies in Arthurian romance and Celtic influences on Old-French and Middle-English literature, merit quoting at length in this regard:

> Every medieval scholar recognizes the great debt which the West owed to Arabic science and philosophy, and it is increasingly realized how prosperous and refined was the society of Moorish Spain in the eleventh and twelfth centuries. And in spite of intermittent wars, and partly because of them, there was a flow of cultural influences to the north. It is therefore no accident that

14 A. R. Nykl, trans., *A Book Containing the Risāla Known as The Dove's Neck-Ring about Love and Lovers*, by ᶜAlī Ibn-Aḥmad Ibn-Ḥazm (Paris, 1931), p. lxxiii. (A more recent and less prosaic translation of *The Dove's Neck-Ring* was done by A. J. Arberry in 1953.) See also Ramón Menéndez Pidal, *Poesía arabe y poesía europea*, 5th ed. (Madrid, 1963); Briffault, *The Troubadours*; Nicholson, *Literary History of the Arabs*; and A. R. Nykl, *Hispano-Arabic Poetry and Its Relations with the Old Provençal Troubadours* (Baltimore, 1946).

15 Gerald Brenan, *The Literature of the Spanish People*, 2nd ed. (New York, 1957), p. 32.

> we find in the literature of Moslem Spain metrical forms approximating those of the troubadours, and similar conventions such as that of addressing the mistress as "my lord," in Provençal "midons." Most significant is the fact that a book called the *Dove's Neck-Ring*, written by the Andalusian Ibn-Hazm, about 1022, might almost serve as a textbook on *fin amor*, so close are its idealistic doctrines on all points except one.[16]

Scholars of medieval visions of the afterlife have attributed their origin to *Ṣūfī* (Islamic mystic) influence, to pagan Celtic influence, and to Christian patristic influence. But few of the visions can be attributed to any one of these sources to the exclusion of the other two. Sufism, along with its relevance to medieval European visions of the afterlife, has, outside of the work of Asín Palacios, scarcely been touched upon to date, and the *Ṣūfī* influence in Spain was a significant one, not only on visions, but also on other types of literature.

The diverse theories as to the origin of short tales and fables include the Aryan theory, which proposes an ultimately Indo-European source for all fables and most tales; the anthropological theory, which attributes tales involving incest, cannibalism, and savagery to the precivilized era of man's development; the theory of accidental coincidences, which assumes that the tales and fables of all countries sprang up everywhere simultaneously; and the oriental theory, which traces all fiction to an ultimately Indian origin. Joseph Bédier, who lists and discusses these theories, credits none of them and concludes that the problem of the origin and the propagation of tales is insoluble.[17] Insoluble the problem may be, but it is an intriguing one.

In the case of some tales, those which enjoyed an early and widespread popularity all over Europe, it would be difficult, if not impossible—as Bédier points out—to determine definite origins. With other tales, those containing recognizably Celtic, Scandinavian, Persian, or Arab motifs, both the origin and the approximate path of dissemination can be traced with reasonable certainty. The short tale, perhaps more than any other form of

[16] Roger Sherman Loomis, *The Development of Arthurian Romance* (London, 1963), pp. 53–54.

[17] Joseph Bédier, *Les Fabliaux*, 6th ed. (Paris, 1964), pp. 53–59, 62–75, 254.

literature, appears to have been particularly conducive to oral transmission, and crusaders returning from the East were probably responsible for the introduction of several Eastern *contes* into Europe. But when a recognizably Arabic or Persian tale suddenly appeared fully developed and written down in Old French, the chances are that it was imported through Spain. Without regard to the origins of individual tales, the frame-story, frequently embodying collections of tales and fables, is generally recognized as an Oriental, originally Indian, device which was imported into Europe between the eleventh and the thirteenth centuries. The frame story too was present in medieval Spain.

There has been little disagreement as to the origins of the matter in medieval romances. The French poet Jean Bodel, in the twelfth century, classified romance matter into that of Britain (involving Arthur and the Knights of the Round Table), of France (involving Charlemagne and his Peers), and of Rome (involving classical Greek and Roman gods and heroes). Bodel's grouping is still accepted, although most scholars tend to expand it somewhat. The addition of a classification "Matter of the Near East" to include Byzantine, Persian, and Arab heroes would not be unwarranted.

Arthurian matter seems to be ultimately Celtic, although it reached the apex of its development in France rather than in Wales or in Britain at large. The question of why Celtic materials should have received their greatest development in France has not yet been answered. Closely connected with Arthurian matter is the quest of the grail. While there is general agreement on the Celtic origin of most Arthurian matter, there is no such agreement on the origin of the grail quest. Theories proposed to account for it have suggested that it developed from Byzantine ritual, Coptic ritual, Christian mysticism, pagan Celtic lore, oriental lore, and vegetation myths. In their development in France, Arthurian and grail materials absorbed many non-Celtic motifs, both French and Eastern, the latter possibly through Spain by contact among the troubadours of Provence and Aragon and the writers of the romances.

If the theory—and it is the most plausible one—of an Arabic-

Andalusian origin for courtly love is accepted, then it is not inconceivable that other literary influences filtered north from Spain concurrent with the twelfth-century translation of scientific and philosophical manuscripts being accomplished in Spain and in some centers in southern France. Although the definitely Arabic influences on European lyrics, visions, tales, and romances are not always as patently obvious as the Arabic characters identifiable in the ornamentation of robes in European paintings of the late Middle Ages and Renaissance, they are still discernible.

Source-hunting, of course, is pointless as an end in itself, merely to "prove" that an idea, story, or theme originated in a certain locale, especially if it is motivated by a nationalistic or religious bias. But knowing the source of a piece of literature, approximately when and how it was transmitted and how it was combined with other materials, adapted, and acted upon by different mentalities working with nonnative traditions is important for a true critique of the Western European literary heritage. A realization of the literary impact of Arab Spain on European tradition is therefore essential if one is to appreciate the diversity and richness of that heritage within which our early vernacular poets worked and the extent of their accomplishments in adapting foreign traditions to their own use.

CHAPTER II

medieval spain

Spain, or part of it, was under Arab domination from 711 to 1492, a period of over seven hundred years during the first part of which the area controlled by the Arabs extended over most of the peninsula and across the Pyrenees into southern France. During the last two and a half centuries, Arab rule was confined to the kingdom of Granada in the south. The history of Islamic Spain is usually divided into six periods: (1) the viceroyalty under North Africa (711–56); (2) the independent emirate and caliphate of the Ummayad dynasty, centered in Cordoba (756–1030); (3) the period of petty kingdoms (1030–90); (4) *The Almorávid* period (1090–1146); (5) the *Almóhad* period (1127–1248); and (6) the Granada period (1230–1492).

Although often used indiscriminately to describe medieval Spain in general, the term "Moorish Spain" can be applied accurately only to the Spain ruled by the *Almorávides* and *Almóhades* for a century and a half, 1090–1248, not to the Islamic or Arab Spain of other periods. The Moors consisted of two groups who invaded Spain from North Africa and were Muslims but not Arabs. They were actually of Hamitic, rather than Semitic, ancestry. The first of these were *al-Murābiṭūn* (Spanish *Almorávides*), meaning "those who live in forts," a narrow, puritanical Islamic sect which originated in southern Morocco and along the borders of what is now Senegal. The second group of Moors, *al-Muwaḥḥidūn* (Spanish *Almóhades*), meaning "unitarians," also founded originally as a religious reform movement, was not as rigid or as puritanical as the *Almorávides*, but rather theological and philosophic. The term "Moorish" is therefore used here only to refer to the period between 1090 and 1248, when the Moors were the dominant Islamic political power in Spain.

By no means is the sketch which follows all-inclusive. The political history of Spain, fascinating as it is with the interaction of Christians and Muslims, must, of necessity, be omitted in order to concentrate on the literary history under, or as affected by, Islamic rule. And even of the literary history, only a few high points can be filled in, but they should be sufficient to give a general historical perspective to Spanish literature and to provide connections between Spain and other West European countries.[1]

The Pre-Moorish Period

The Umayyad dynasty (756–1030). It was under the Umayyads that Arab Spain reached the height of its cultural development. The dynasty was founded as an emirate or principality by ʿAbd-al-Raḥmān I (ruled 756–88), who freed Spain from North African control. He had escaped the ʿAbbāsid slaughter of the Umayyads in the East (for control of Islam) and then made his way across North Africa to Morocco and later to Spain.[2]

Under ʿAbd-al-Raḥmān II (ruled 833–52), the Vikings invaded Spain and were repelled. Spain was, incidentally, the only West European country to successfully resist the Vikings' invasions. During his reign, the Persian musician Ziryāb immigrated to

[1] For a more complete history of medieval Spain, see Carl Brockelmann, *History of the Islamic Peoples,* trans. Joel Carmichael and Moshe Perlmann (New York, 1960); Philip K. Hitti, *History of the Arabs;* W. Montgomery Watt, *A History of Islamic Spain,* Islamic Surveys, No. 4 (Edinburgh, 1967); and Reynold A. Nicholson, *A Literary History of the Arabs.* I have drawn from all of these sources in this chapter. The following works are also of interest: E. Lévi-Provençal, *Histoire de l'Espagne musulmane,* rev. ed., 2 vols. (Paris, 1950); E. Lévi-Provençal, *La Civilisation arabe en espagne: Vue générale* (Paris, 1948); Claudio Sánchez Albornoz, *La España musulmana: Según los autores islamitas y cristianos medievales,* 2 vols. (Buenos Aires, 1946); and Angel Gonzáles Palencia, *Histoire de la Literatura arábigo-española* (Barcelona, 1928). Palencia's study is well organized, but the Arabic translation of his work (from the second edition of 1945) is better because it cites examples of Arabic poems omitted in the Spanish versions. See Angel Gonzáles Palencia, *Tarīkh al-Fikr al-Āndalusī,* trans. Ḥusayn Muʾnis (Cairo, 1955).

[2] Adolfo Frederico Schack, *Poesia y arte de los arabes en españa y sicilia,* trans. Juan Valera (Buenos Aires, 1865), is an old but very good study which includes examples and illustrations of poetry by ʿAbd-al-Raḥmān I and others of pre-Moorish Spain. Another which covers major poets of the tenth through the fourteenth centuries is Emilio García Gómez, *Cinco poetas musulmanes* (Buenos Aires, 1945); and the Arabic translation, *al-Shiʿr al-Āndalusī,* trans. Ḥusayn Muʾnis, 2nd ed. (Cairo, 1952).

Spain and introduced Persian music, poetry, stories, styles of dress, and court manners, all of which became very fashionable and were widely imitated in Spain in succeeding periods.

ᶜAbd-al-Raḥmān III (ruled 912–61) declared Spain an independent caliphate and, in 921, took the title of "Caliph," a title which had up to this time been reserved for the ruler of all of Islam, then in Baghdad. He expanded Cordoba into the greatest city in Western Europe, bar none, as a center of learning and cultivation of the arts. Of particular importance during his reign were Ibn-ᶜAbd-al-Rabbihī (860–940) and Ibn-Masarra (883–931). The former compiled an anthology of Spanish-Arab poetry entitled *The Unique Necklace,* which indicated an early interest in Arabic poetry in Spain where it was to develop along different lines from the classical Arabic poetry of the East. Ibn-Masarra, an ascetic mystic, was the first Spanish-Arab scholar to go east (to Syria and Iraq) to study. He set a precedent for a great number of scholars, most of whom returned to Spain with voluminous collections of manuscripts of Greek, Arab, and Persian astronomy, astrology, medicine, mathematics, and philosophy.

Under Ḥakam II (ruled 961–76), interest in the science and literature of the East continued to grow. Ḥakam amassed some 400,000 volumes in his library and subsidized Abū-al-Faraj al-Isfahānī in the work on his *Kitāb-al-Aghānī (Book of Songs)* in the East, because he wanted to receive the first copy of it. During or shortly after the reign of Ḥakam, one of the scholars returning from the East, Maslamah of Madrid, thus called al-Majrīṭī, "the man from Madrid" (d. ca. 1006), introduced into Spain Khwarīzmi's tables with Arabic numerals and the zero, which were subsequently disseminated all over Europe, and the *Rasāʾil Ikhwān al-Ṣafā (Epistles of the Brethren of Sincerity),* which were an encyclopedic compilation of science, philosophy, and mysticism. The *Epistles,* with their mystic content, were to influence later mystic poetry and vision literature in Spain.

The mulūk al-ṭawāʾif period (period of petty kings) (1030–90). These sixty years were characterized by struggles for power among the Arab nobles and by conflicts between the Christian north and the Islamic south. Years of political decline for the Arabs, they were at the same time an era of brilliance in poetry and the arts.

An outstanding figure during the *mulūk al-ṭawā'if* was Ibn-Gabirol (Latin *Avicebron,* ca. 1021–ca. 1070), the philosopher whose genius has earned him the epithet "the Jewish Plato." His *Fons Vitae* was instrumental in the twelfth and thirteenth centuries in the development of medieval scholasticism. He was also an accomplished poet in both Hebrew and Arabic. Evident in his religious poetry is considerable Jewish learning (the Talmud and the Midrash), while his secular poetry evinces a thorough absorption of Arab culture. He wrote with such facility in Latin and Arabic that it was not discovered that he was a Jew until 1846.[3]

Another major literary figure was Ibn-Ḥazm (994–1064), a theologian who, in Játiba in eastern Spain in the early 1020s, composed a work on comparative religion and, around 1022, an epistolary treatise on platonic and courtly love, *Ṭawq al-Ḥammāma (The Dove's Neck-Ring,* subtitled *On Love and Lovers).* The latter, written many decades before the first troubadour lyrics of Provence, could almost have served, as several scholars have pointed out, as a textbook for them in theories of love. The courtly-love philosophy and formulae described in the *Ṭawq al-Ḥammāma* were not new, but rather represented a clear exposition of ideas already current in Arab Spain. The poet Ibn-Zaydūn (1003–70) was famous for his love poems to the princess Wallāda —herself a poet—which express and dramatize many aspects of the courtly love of Ibn-Ḥazm's treatise.

A strophic form peculiar to Andalusia and very rare in other Arab countries, the *muwashshaḥ,* which had been in existence for well over a century, gave rise during the *mulūk al-ṭawā'if* to the *zajal,* the strophe which provided structural models for trouba-

[3] Israel Zangwill, trans., *Selected Religious Poems of Solomon Ibn Gabirol* (Philadelphia, 1923), pp. xxxii–xli. For other Jewish poets who were heavily influenced by Arabic poetry and philosophy, see David Goldstein, trans., *Hebrew Poems from Spain* (New York, 1966), an anthology in translation of Hebrew poets in Spain from the tenth to the thirteenth centuries. There is also reason to suspect a large Jewish contribution to medieval European thought and folklore in addition to the Arab one through Spain.

dour lyrics. The eleventh century was a golden age for poetic experimentation and invention in Spain; while the new strophes continued to flourish, poetry after this century consisted more or less of imitation and refinement of existing models.

The Moorish Period

The lack of political unity among the Arabs from 1030 to 1090 helped facilitate the Christian reconquest of Spain which nevertheless proceeded at a rather slow pace, partly because of a similar lack of unity among the Christians themselves. The Moorish period saw the major part of the *reconquista* and the acceleration en masse of the translation of Arabic documents into Latin which had begun in the preceding period. To the Moorish period belong the great Spanish-Arab philosophers Ibn-Bājjah and Ibn-Rushd; another philosopher not as well known in the west, Ibn-Ṭufayl; and the philosopher-mystic Ibn-ᶜArabī. The first two were to have a profound effect on Latin scholastic philosophy in the thirteenth century when European philosophers became involved in the reconciliation of science and Aristotelianism with Christianity.

Several developments in southern France, while not Spanish history per se, were closely related to events and matters in Spain in the twelfth century. It was during this period that the monastery of Cluny reached the height of its power and influence in France and Spain; a sudden flowering of lyric poetry appeared in Provence, soon to be followed by rapid blossoming of written vernacular literature in France and other countries of Western Europe; and the Albigensians became a thorn in the side of Catholicism.

The Almorávid period (1090–1146). Under the *Almorávides,* Ibn-Bājjah (Latin *Avempace,* 1070–1138) wrote commentaries on Plato and Aristotle which, along with the works of these philosophers, were translated into Latin and studied throughout Western Europe. He influenced the thought of both Ibn-Rushd and Thomas Aquinas. Perhaps less well known is the fact that he also wrote on music, as did Ibn-Rushd and most of the Persian and Arab philosophers, who considered it as important a branch of the quadrivium as geometry, arithmetic, and astronomy.[4] His *Tadbīr al-Mutawaḥḥid, Rule for One Who Wants to Live as a Hermit,* written in protest against the materialism and corruption in society of his day, was translated into Latin as *Regimine Solitarii* (and also into Hebrew) and merits mentioning in that while it was not concerned specifically with science or philosophy, it still reached the Latin world.

Pedro Alfonso (1062–1135), a Jew of Aragon baptized in 1106, was responsible for the dissemination of both science and folklore from Spain into England and other countries of Western Europe. He was renowned for his work in astronomy, his *Dialogi cum Judeo* (a Christian apology), and his *Disciplina Clericalis* (a collection of tales and legends purporting to serve as *exempla*).[5] The latter part of his life he spent in England, where he was physician to Henry I and where he composed the *Disciplina,* which enjoyed a wide popularity in the Latin world with many of its tales being borrowed by both ecclesiastics and other writers and with its influence being detectable in such works as *Don Quixote* and the *Decameron.*

Other Spanish literature of the period included the poetry of Ibn-Quzmān (fl. early twelfth century) and the *Poema de Mío Cid,* composed around 1140. The strophes of Ibn-Quzmān illustrate a late, well-developed form of the *zajal.* His poems are thus often compared with those of the Provençal troubadours. The *Cid,* the great Spanish epic, marks the beginning of Castilian literature and is replete with Arabic cultural and social influences.

A philosopher who bridged the *Almorávid* and *Almóhad* periods was Ibn-Ṭufayl (1110–85), also, like Pedro Alfonso, a physician. His *Ḥayy Ibn-Yaqdhān* (*Alive, Son of Alert*) is an allegory of a man who grew up on a desert island without human guidance or companionship. Set on the island as an infant, he was nursed by a gazelle at whose death the inquisitive boy dissected her. His anatomical findings are described in a striking passage,

4 Henry George Farmer, *A History of Arabian Music* (London, 1967), pp. 222–25.

5 Charles Homer Haskins, *Studies in the History of Medieval Science,* 2nd ed. (New York, 1960), pp. 118–19.

all the more unusual in that dissection was a virtually unheard-of practice in Western Europe in the twelfth century. The boy, who naturally has had to learn self-sufficiency as he grows to manhood, also acquires on his own a complete philosophical system which includes a doctrine of God and the attainment of mystical ecstasy. When Asāl, a philosopher schooled in traditional institutions, comes to the island and finds Ḥayy, a discussion between the two men reveals that Ḥayy's knowledge of the sciences, his philosophy, and his religion are identical with and in some respects superior to those of Asāl acquired through formal education.

Ibn-Ṭufayl's work was not to exert its influence outside of the Islamic sphere until five centuries later, when the manuscript, discovered in Morocco, was brought to England and translated into Latin by Edward Pocock in 1671. It was translated from Latin to English by the Quaker George Keith in 1674 and again by the Anglo-Catholic George Ashwell in 1686. Another translation direct from Arabic to English entitled *The Improvement of Human Reason* was made in 1708 by Simon Ockley. The piece had a particular appeal to the Quakers, who saw in it a confirmation of their doctrine of inner light, the ability to perceive and apprehend divine truths from intuition. Because the work was still in vogue in the early eighteenth century, it has been suggested that the story of a young man surviving and prospering on a desert island inspired Daniel Defoe's *Robinson Crusoe*, written between 1718 and 1723.[6]

The Almóhad period (1127–1248). During the rule of the *Almóhades*, the Spanish Arab philosophers Ibn-Rushd and Ibn-ᶜArabī flourished. Ibn-Rushd (Latin *Averroes*, 1126–98), of Cordoban origin, was the first systematizer of Aristotle and was instrumental in presenting the works of the Greek philosopher in a form which facilitated their transmission and absorption into the Latin world. He edited a complete critical text of Aristotle's works, provided an abridged text with an introduction for students, and composed a lengthy and thorough commentary on the works. His name was to become so intimately connected with that

[6] Antonio Pastor, *The Idea of Robinson Crusoe* (Watford, England, 1930). The data on Latin and English translations are from Pastor.

of Aristotle that later Latin writers frequently quoted from Ibn-Rushd rather than from the Greek himself.

Another work of Ibn-Rushd's was his *Tahāfut al-Tahāfut*, the *Rebuttal of the Rebuttal*,[7] a reply to Ghazzālī's (died in 1111) *Tahāfut al-Falāsifa, Rebuttal of the Philosophers.* Ghazzālī, of the East, was a voluminous writer, and in this work he set out to destroy all of the major philosophical systems; later he became one of the great mystics of Islam. The mystic writings of Ghazzālī were known in Spain, where they exerted influence on the Spanish mystic Ibn-ᶜArabī (1164–1240) of Murcia, whose *al-Futūḥāt al-Makkiyya* (*Meccan Revelations*) contains visions of the afterworld which may have influenced later Latin, French, and English visions in the same vein, as well as Dante's *Commedia.*

Also important during this period was Ibn-Saᶜīd who compiled an anthology of poetry in 1243 entitled *The Pennants,* which, with the anthology *The Unique Necklace* of three centuries earlier, helped document the thematic development of early Spanish-Arabic poetry. Ibn-Saᶜīd's anthology is extant.[8]

The reconquista. The reconquest of Spain by the Christians can be said to have begun in the eleventh century, prior to which most of the battles waged on the peninsula, including those in which Charlemagne took part and those enumerated in the *Cid,* consisted of Muslims and Christians uniting in personal political causes against other groups of both Muslims and Christians. It was not completed until the fall of Granada in 1492. As a direct result of the *reconquista,* the Latin world discovered and began translating the wealth of manuscripts found in the conquered cities, especially in Toledo, but also in Murcia and Seville. Significant in the early period of the *reconquista* was the fall of Toledo in 1085 to Alfonso VI after which time it became a capital for the translation of manuscripts from Arabic to Latin and be-

7 The word *Tahāfut* appears in most history texts as *incoherence,* which is not quite an exact translation. Watt, *History of Islamic Spain,* 140, calls it the *inconsistency.* I have followed the suggestion of Thomas B. Irving in using the term *rebuttal.*

8 García Gómez edited the Arabic edition in 1942. For an English translation with commentary, see Arthur J. Arberry, trans., *Moorish Poetry: A Translation of "The Pennants," an Anthology Compiled in 1243 by the Andalusian Ibn-Saᶜīd* (Cambridge, England, 1953).

came as well a famous center of learning for scholars from Italy, the Holy Roman Empire, France, and England. The reconquest and translation continued concurrently. In 1212, with the Battle of the Navas de Tolosa, Almóhad power was decisively broken in Spain; in 1236 and 1248, Cordoba and Seville, respectively, were taken by Ferdinand III, father of Alfonso X. By the middle of the thirteenth century, Islamic rule in Spain was confined to the area surrounding Granada in the south, where it continued for another two and a half centuries.

The translations. The massive translation projects in Spain and Sicily in the twelfth century had had their earlier counterpart from the middle of the eighth century to the middle of the ninth in Baghdad, where, under al-Maʾmūn, in 830, a *Bayt al-Ḥikma* ("House of Wisdom") was instituted, similar to that later established at Toledo.[9] In the earlier period Greek learning, preserved in the Byzantine Empire, was translated into Arabic. The use of dragomen or intermediaries, often Nestorian Christians, in the eighth and ninth centuries to translate the Greek into Syriac, the spoken language, from which it was then transcribed in Arabic, was paralleled in Spain. There the dragomen were frequently Jews who translated from Arabic to Romance, the spoken language, from which it was transcribed in Latin. From the time of the discovery of Greek learning in the eighth century in the East to the rediscovery of it in the West, however, that learning had been advanced and expanded enormously in philosophy, in medicine, and in all areas of the quadrivium, and the list of known translators and works translated in Spain is correspondingly quite long.[10]

[9] For a fuller discussion of the earlier translations, see Hitti, *History of the Arabs*, pp. 310 ff.; Nicholson, *Literary History of the Arabs*, pp. 358 ff.; and De Lacy O'Leary, *Arabic Thought and Its Place in History*, rev. ed. (New York, 1939), pp. 105–22.

[10] The best-known authorities in the field, with regard to scientific works, are Sarton and Haskins, and, with regard to magic, alchemy, and astrology, Thorndike. See C. H. Haskins, *Studies in the History of Medieval Science*; George Sarton, *Introduction to the History of Science*, 3 vols. (Washington, 1927–48); Lynn Thorndike and Pearl Kibre, *A Catalogue of Incipits of Mediaeval Scientific Writings in Latin*, rev. ed. (Cambridge, Mass., 1963); and Lynn Thorndike, *A History of Magic and Experimental Science*, 4 vols. (New York, 1923). Thorndike, in his *History of Magic*, shows that a vast amount of material in astrology, magic, and alchemy was

One of the translators, Robert of Ketton[11] (fl. ca. 1110–60), was an Englishman who worked in northern Spain between 1141 and 1147 and who was appointed archdeacon of Pamplona in Navarre in 1143. His chief interests were alchemy and algebra, in which fields he translated various works. In 1143, Robert, along with Hermann of Carinthia (also called Hermann of Dalmatia), was commissioned by Peter the Venerable, Abbot of Cluny, to render the *Qurʾān* from Arabic into Latin. This was the first translation of the *Qurʾān* into a European language. Its having been done by an Englishman in the employment of a French abbot emphasizes the truly international character of the translation efforts; illustrates the fact that translation was not confined solely to works of secular provenance; and suggests one route through which Islamic, specifically Qurʾānic, stories and themes might have traveled as far north as England.

That the writings of the mystic Ghazzālī (Latin *Algazel*) were known in Spain has already been pointed out. He was also made partially accessible to the Christian world when a number of his works were translated into Latin some time before 1150 by Domingo Gundisalvo, the archdeacon of Segovia. Ghazzālī may have indirectly influenced Christian vision-literature of the twelfth through the fourteenth centuries through Ibn-ʿArabī and other mystics of Spain who were familiar with his works.

Among the translators of astronomy and astrology was John of Seville (also called Johannis Hispalensis), a converted Jew who worked at Seville and Toledo. Astronomers whose works were translated by John of Seville are mentioned not only in later Latin works but also in the writings of poets; al-Farghānī, for example, is cited by Dante, among others.

By the end of the thirteenth century, the program of translation was practically completed. Throughout the twelfth century

---

brought into Western Europe along with the more scientific matter. Thomas B. Irving provides a convenient outline of the major translators and focuses attention on the many close links between the translators and the rest of Western Europe in his article, "How Arab Learning Reached Western Europe," *Islamic Literature*, 16 (August, 1970), 453–62.

[11] Also called Robert of Ketene, Robert of Chester, Robertas Retinensis, Robert of Reading, etc., due to confusion of his name in various manuscripts. See Sarton, *History of Science*, II, 167–68.

and into the thirteenth, Western Europe was faced with the necessity for intellectual expansion to cope with the new science and philosophy, which were of sufficient magnitude for the period to be named "the Twelfth-Century Renaissance." A sudden growth of European universities in the twelfth century from the former cathedral schools at Salerno, Bologne, Paris, and Montpelier was the result.[12] The new learning gave to the great scholastic philosophers of the thirteenth century, Albertus Magnus and Thomas Aquinas, the task of reconciling Aristotelianism and scientific experimentation and discoveries with Christian theology. But the ancient Greek contributions which made the period a true renaissance for Europe tell only part of the story. The other part is represented in the contributions over the centuries of the Persian, Arab, and Jewish scholars, scientists and translators. Their impact was such that if the Arabic and Hebrew elements are not included with the Latin in a study of medieval thought, the result can only be incomplete and erroneous.[13]

The Monastery at Cluny. Founded in 910 in France, Cluny had become by the twelfth century the "capital of a monastic empire."[14] It is important to the literature of Spain for two reasons, the translation of the *Qurʾān* and the fostering of pilgrimages to the shrine of Santiago de Compostela in Galicia.

Peter the Venerable became abbot of Cluny in 1122 and, in 1143, employed Robert of Ketton and Hermann of Carinthia to translate the *Qurʾān* and other Islamic works. Among the items included in MS 1162, in twelfth-century script, of the Bibliothèque de l'Arsenal in Paris, are the *Qurʾān* translated by Robert, a collection of Islamic traditions translated by Robert, and the *Liber generationis Mahomet et nutritia eius* translated by Hermann. Hermann identifies his Arabic original for the *Liber*; it contains the doctrine of prophetic light emanating from Adam to

[12] Charles Homer Haskins, *The Renaissance of the Twelfth Century* (Cambridge, Mass., 1927); and James Westfall Thompson and Edgar Nathaniel Johnson, *An Introduction to Medieval Europe, 300–1500*, rev. ed. (New York, 1965), Chap. 23. See also Charles Homer Haskins, *The Rise of Universities* (New York, 1923), pp. 7–8.

[13] Sarton, *History of Science*, II, 3.

[14] James Kritzeck, *Peter the Venerable and Islam* (Princeton, 1964), p. 3. In the information on Peter the Venerable and the translations commissioned by him, I follow Kritzeck, pp. 3, 27–36, 75–80, 125–51.

Muḥammad. But Robert omitted the chain of authorities in his translation of the traditions, for which there are many possible Arabic sources.

Peter's purpose in commissioning a translation of the *Qur'ān* was to compose a rebuttal to it, his *Liber contra sectam sive Haeresim Saracenorum*, of 1143. Later he wrote the *Summa totius Haeresis Saracenorum* for Bernard of Clairvaux. Included in the *Summa* was material from the *Qur'ān* and from some of the other Islamic works he had had translated. The *Summa* is full of errors and contains slanted legendary material such as the statement that Muḥammad was epileptic. Nevertheless, Peter's works are of interest in that the Saracens are regarded in them as Christian heretics rather than pagans, a view shared by other ecclesiastics and later writers; further, they were possibly partly responsible for the spread of derogatory legends about Islam in medieval Europe.

Cluniac patronage and sponsorship of pilgrimages to the shrine of Saint James at Compostela helped make it a very important object of pilgrimage for all of Christendom. Originally, according to legend, the apostle James had come west to Christianize Spain and was buried there. A similar legend later grew up around Joseph of Arimathea, who supposedly came to Christianize Britain and was buried at Glastonbury Abbey. At some point early in the history of the Spanish legend, James the Apostle at Compostela was confused with James, brother of Jesus.[15] The shrine brought large numbers of French and other pilgrims into Spain, providing an additional contact between Spain and countries of the north.

The troubadours. Beginning in the late eleventh century and continuing through the twelfth, the troubadour poets of southern France came into prominence. Their works were characterized by two non-Germanic traditions: end rime and romantic (often courtly) love, traditions which were already well developed in Arab Spain.

15 Mentioned in Matthew 13:55. See Américo Castro, *The Structure of Spanish History*, trans. Edmund L. King (Princeton, 1954), pp. 130–70, for a complete discussion of the legend. Gerald Brenan, *The Literature of the Spanish People*, p. 37, points out the Cluniac role in sponsoring pilgrimages to the shrine.

The troubadours seem to have had many connections with Spain. They were, in conjunction with their profession, travelers, and were usually included with the trains and courts of nobles in their moves among various countries. There were numerous movements of troubadours to and from Castile and Aragon, and there were many political-marital ties between the nobles of Poitiers, Toulouse, and Burgundy and those of Aragon, Castile, and Catalonia.[16] Provence itself was periodically attached to Aragon until its annexation by France following the Albigensian Crusade when a number of the troubadours fled to Spain.

Perhaps the most interesting connections of the troubadours with Spain were linguistic ones. The language in which they composed their lyrics, Provençal, was closely allied to Catalan, the language of eastern Spain at that time.[17] Even more significant is the derivation of the words *troubadour* and *trobar* from the much older Arabic *ṭarraba,* "to sing, entertain, or arouse emotion."[18]

The Spanish language. A Spanish critic, in discussing the Arabic theory of origin for Provençal troubadour poetry, makes the observation that the resistance of many scholars to accepting the influence of the Andalusian strophes upon the primitive troubadour lyrics is founded on an insupportable prejudice, a mistaken belief that there was no intellectual communication between the Christian and Islamic spheres.[19] The extent to which there *was* communication between the Islamic and Christian Spaniards is perhaps best evinced by the Spanish language itself.

There were four languages in use in Islamic Spain: Classical Arabic, used by men of letters; Colloquial Arabic, used in administration and government; Ecclesiastical Latin, used by the Church; and Romance, used by laymen. Until the thirteenth century, Romance itself was divided into four distinct dialects: Castilian of central Spain, Catalan of the east, Galician of the north-

16 These are detailed by Robert S. Briffault, *The Troubadours,* pp. 57–72.

17 Ernest Mérimée, *A History of Spanish Literature,* trans. S. Griswold Morley (New York, 1930), p. 10.

18 J. B. Trend, "Spain and Portugal," in *The Legacy of Islam,* ed. Arnold and Guillaume, p. 17. Others have noticed this too.

19 Ramón Menéndez Pidal, *Poesía arabe y poesía europea,* pp. 39–40.

west, and Portuguese of the west. Castilian, from which modern Spanish evolved, did not dominate until the thirteenth and fourteenth centuries.[20]

Spanish Christians were influenced by the Arabic language and poetry from an early date, as is illustrated by the complaint in *Indiculus luminosus* by the Christian writer Alvar in 854:

> Our Christian young men, with their elegant airs and fluent speech, are showy in their dress and carriage, and are famed for the learning of the gentiles; intoxicated with Arab eloquence, they greedily handle, eagerly devour and zealously discuss the books of the Chaldeans (i.e., Muhammedans), and make them known by praising them with every flourish of rhetoric, knowing nothing of the beauty of the Church's literature, and looking down with contempt on the dreams of the Church that flow forth from Paradise; alas! the Christians are so ignorant of their own law, the Latins pay so little attention to their own language, that in the whole Christian flock there is hardly one man in a thousand who can write a letter to inquire after a friend's health intelligibly, while you may find a countless rabble of all kinds of them who can learnedly roll out the grandiloquent periods of the Chaldean tongue. They can even make poems, every line ending with the same letter [syllable], which display high flights of beauty and more skill in handling metre than the gentiles themselves possess.[21]

Intercourse between the Christians (including the clergy) and Muslims of Spain was so extensive that in 936 it was felt to be necessary to hold a council at Toledo to discuss means of reducing and preventing such intercourse lest it contaminate the Christian faith.[22]

From the beginning of the ninth century, native Christians of Spain who imitated the Arab way of life were called *Mozarabs* (from the Arabic *Mustaʿrib,* "one who adopts the Arabic language and customs"). In addition, a type of bastard literature,

[20] Trend, "Spain and Portugal," p. 7; and Mérimée, *History of Spanish Literature,* pp. 1–11. For a full discussion of the evolution of the Spanish language, see William J. Entwhistle, *The Spanish Language* (London, 1936).

[21] Quoted by Thomas Walker Arnold, *The Preaching of Islam: A History of the Propagation of the Muslim Faith,* 3rd ed. (Lahore, Pakistan, 1965), pp. 139–40.

[22] *Ibid.*, p. 141.

aljamiado (from the Arabic *al-aᶜjamīyah,* "foreign, outlandish tongue"), arose in which a Romance dialect was written with Arabic script. It is represented largely by a group of manuscripts discovered in the early twentieth century under the floor of an old house in Aragon, where they had been hidden from the Inquisition.[23] A good example of *aljamiado* literature is the *Poema de Yúçuf* (ca. 1299–1335), whose verse form was French, whose language was the Romance dialect of Aragon, but which was written in Arabic characters. The story is derived from the *Qurʾān* and other Islamic sources.[24]

As a natural consequence of the mingling of the two cultures, there is a large number of Arabic-derived words in modern Spanish. A glossary of Spanish and Portuguese words derived from Arabic lists some 650 items representing all levels of life; another shows that influences on the Spanish vocabulary are detectable not only in philosophy, medicine, and astronomy, but also in words for flora, in colors, in building, in official titles, in business, in crafts, and in other areas. Further, there are many Spanish expressions and proverbs drawn from the *Qurʾān.*[25]

In addition to the large number of Arabic words which penetrated into the Spanish language, certain terms were imported into Europe during the translation period. Since there were no Latin equivalents for technical terms in chemistry, mathematics, and astronomy, the Arabic terms were frequently merely Latinized. During this same period, which was also that of the Provençal troubadours, Eastern musical instruments were brought into France and England through Spain, along with their Arabic names, for example, the lute (Arabic *al-ᶜūd*), the guitar (Arabic

23 Hitti, *History of the Arabs,* p. 556, *n.* 1. Hitti points out that these manuscripts were edited and published by Ribera and Asín Palacios under the title *Manuscritos arabes y aljamiados de la Biblioteca de la Junta* (Madrid, 1912), and discussed by A. R. Nykl in *A Compendium of Aljamiado Literature* (Paris, 1928).

24 Trend, "Spain and Portugal," pp. 37–38. See also George Ticknor, *History of Spanish Literature* (Boston, 1872), III (Appendix H), 528–29.

25 Reinhart Dozy and W. H. Engelmann, *Glossaire des mots espagnols et portugais dérivés de l'arabe,* 2nd ed. (Amsterdam, 1915); A. Mekinassi, *Léxico de las palabras Españolas de origen Arabe* (Tétuan, 1963), p. xi; and Castro, *Structure of Spanish History,* pp. 96–102.

qītāra, from Greek *kithara*), and Chaucer's "rebek" (Arabic *rabāb*).[26]

By the end of the Moorish period, Europe's contact with Arab Spain had been extensive. The Latin translations included Islamic as well as scientific and philosophical works; and between Spain and France there was, in addition to scholarly endeavors and political connections, further personal contact through the shrine at Compostela and through the troubadours. Within Spain itself a fusion of Christian and Islamic culture is illustrated by the content of Arabic words in the Spanish language and by *aljamiado* literature, the Romance dialect written in Arabic script.

The Granada Period (1230–1492)

Martyrs. Two of the Christian martyrs of Spain, Raymond Martín and Raymond Lull, knew Arabic and showed the influence of Arab thought in their writings. The Dominican Raymond Martín (ca. 1238–86) of Catalonia knew Hebrew as well as Arabic, and in his writings on the afterlife, Islamic influence is apparent. Raymond Lull (ca. 1233–1315) wrote in both Arabic and Catalan; among his books written in Catalan are the *Book of the Lover and the Beloved,* the *Liber de Gentili* (on mysticism and the afterlife), and the *Book on the Order of Chivalry.* Arabic influences are detectable in the first two of these. Both Lull and Martín seem to have been influenced by Islamic eschatology,[27] and at least one of Lull's books reached England. His *Book on the Order of Chivalry* is extant in Catalan, Old-French, Middle-English, and Scottish manuscripts.

Poets and Tellers of Tales. To the Granada Period belong Juan Ruiz, Don Juan Manuel, and Lisān al-Dīn Ibn-al-Khaṭīb, a priest, a prince, and a minister of state, respectively. Juan Ruiz, Archpriest of Hita (born ca. 1280), incorporates Arabic themes.

26 Trend, "Spain and Portugal," p. 16. The examples and derivations are cited from Trend's article.

27 Miguel Asín Palacios, *Islam and the Divine Comedy,* trans. Harold Sunderland (London, 1926), pp. 139–40 (originally published in 1919 under the title *La Escatología Musulmana en la Divina Commedia*).

verse forms, and expressions in his *Libro de Buen Amor,* which consists of a series of risqué adventures interspersed with *zajals,* narrated by a picaresque hero for whom there are many Persian and Arabic prototypes. Similarly, in *El Conde Lucanor,* a collection of tales for the instruction of a nobleman's son by Don Juan Manuel (1282–1347), are to be found Arabic influences in the language, in the form, and in many of the individual tales incorporated in the work. Some of *Lucanor*'s tales recur in the later European *Gesta Romanorum.* Lisān al-Dīn Ibn-al-Khaṭīb (1313–74), a minister of Granada, is also known to have composed *maqāmas* or tales interspersed with poetry, but he is primarily significant as an anthologizer of earlier Spanish *muwashshaḥs* and *zajals* in the Hebrew, Arabic, and Romance languages.

Alfonso X of Castile.[28] Alfonso X (ruled 1252–84), because of his work in astronomy, his poetry, the translations he commissioned, his direction of legal treatises and historical chronicles, and his patronage of other writers, is referred to by historians as "Alfonso el Sabio," or Alfonso the Scholar. The works he sponsored, including translations, were written in Castilian rather than Latin, and a large number of them have survived. In the translations he commissioned, Alfonso deliberately eliminated the second member of the translation team, as he wanted to foment a national vernacular.

Among the translations commissioned by Alfonso were a treatise on chess, the *Kalīlah wa Dimnah,* and the *Libro de los engaños e asayamientos de las mujeres (Book of the Wiles and Devices of Women).* Chess, which came from India to Persia to Spain, apparently was introduced into Europe through Spain, since the earliest references to chess in Europe are found in Spain (1008–17).[29] Alfonso's translation was the first systematic treatment of it in a West European language. *Kalīlah wa Dimnah* was the Arabic version of the Middle-Persian *Bidpai Fables* (ulti-

[28] The information on Alfonso and his works, except where noted, is from Evelyn S. Procter, *Alfonso X of Castile: Patron of Literature and Learning* (Oxford, 1951), pp. 4–27. See also John Esten Keller, *Alfonso X, el Sabio,* Twayne's World Authors Series, No. 12 (New York, 1967).

[29] Trend, "Spain and Portugal," pp. 32–33.

mately the Buddhist *Panchatantra*, in Sanskrit), known in Western Europe through the *Directorium Humanae Vitae*. The *Libro de los engaños* was known in Europe in the form of *The Seven Sages of Rome*.

Two of the works for which Alfonso was responsible are known to have found their way to France and England. The first of these was the *Alfonsine Tables* (also known as the *Tables Toletanes*), on the movements of the planets. The tables were recast in Paris in the early fourteenth century and are found in unpublished English manuscripts of the fourteenth and fifteenth centuries. They were based on the work of Khwarīzmi, Bitrūji, and Majrīṭī. The second work was the *Livre de Leschiele Mahomet*, describing Muḥammad's visit to the otherworld and visions of heaven and hell; it is extant only in an Old-French version. According to the prologue,[30] the work was put into Castilian from Arabic under Alfonso X, and into French from Castilian in 1264. The manuscript, given by Laud, is in the Bodleian Library. How it got to England seems to be a mystery like that of the appearance of *The Vercelli Book* of Old-English writings in Italy. It might be mentioned, however, that Alfonso's half-sister Eleanor was married to Edward I of England in 1254.

Alfonso's own work, his *Cantigas de Santa María*, a collection of over four hundred poems, survives in four manuscripts with the music. The verse form of the *Cantigas* is modeled directly after an early form of Spanish-Arabic poetry. The *Cantigas*, unlike the works done under Alfonso, are written in the Galician dialect.

Conclusion

The Arab culture of medieval Spain was integrated in large part into the Christian culture within the country; portions of it also reached Europe, in literary fields as well as in science and philosophy. There can be no question about the Arabic language and literature having influenced Spanish Christians from the

[30] The prologue is reproduced by Evelyn S. Procter in "The Scientific Works of the Court of Alfonso of Castile: The King and His Collaborators," *Modern Language Review*, 40 (1945), 22–23.

ninth century on. Its reflection can be seen in the Spanish language and early literature.

Many of the connections between medieval Spain and Europe involving political ties, trade, art, and architecture have been omitted. Yet enough connections have been sketched in—those evident from the pilgrimages to Compostela, the troubadours of Provence and Aragon, the translation and dissemination of scientific and philosophical works, and known cases of direct transmission of literature of a religious and belletristic nature—to suggest that Spanish history and literature in the medieval period have relevance to the history and literature of other Western European countries.

Arabic poetry in Spain was cultivated and anthologized as early as the tenth century. Love, romantic and platonic, was a major theme. Both the lyric forms and love themes found in the works of the troubadours of Provence were developed in the tenth and eleventh centuries in Spain, long before the first troubadour lyrics were written.

Mysticism and eschatological visions were, like poetry, popular in Arab Spain from a very early date. Documents on *Ṣūfī* mysticism from the East were brought to Spain in the ninth century, and dream-visions of the afterlife appeared in the works of both a major mystic whose works were known in Spain and the Spanish mystic Ibn-ᶜArabī. One such vision has been found translated into Old French from Castilian and, in turn, from Arabic. Other Islamic materials, including the *Qurʾān,* were not only known but translated into Latin in the first half of the twelfth century. Considering the popularity visions of the afterlife enjoyed in Europe from the twelfth century through the fifteenth, and since many of the European visions contain obviously Oriental motifs and ideas, there could well have been some connection between the Christian and the Islamic visionary traditions through Spain.

The immense popularity of collections of tales and fables in Latin and European vernacular languages and the spread of certain oriental tales in Europe by works such as the *Disciplina Clericalis* also invite a closer look at similar tales and collections of older provenance in Spain. While a number of tales were no doubt brought back from the East by returning crusaders, others can be shown to have reached Europe through such works as the *Disciplina*.

Finally, the fact that Spanish-Arab culture, both scientific and literary, could and did penetrate as far north as England is specifically illustrated by the appearance in England of Raymond Lull's *Book on the Order of Chivalry*, the *Alfonsine Tables*, and the *Livre de Leschiele Mahomet*. Further connections between Spain and England are indicated by the immigration of Pedro Alfonso to England, where he composed the *Disciplina Clericalis* which contains many tales of Arab origin, and by the travel of Englishmen such as Robert of Ketton, the first to render the *Qurʾān* into Latin, to Spain to participate in the translation of Arabic manuscripts. The appearance then of Arabic and Islamic motifs in later Old-French and Middle-English literature should not be dismissed as an impossibility. The historians of the medieval period have shown that their appearance would accord with the events of history. Indeed, a *lack* of such motifs would be strange!

CHAPTER III

LYRIC POETRY

PART I—EUROPEAN

Spanish-Arabic Poetry

Forms. There were in Arab Spain two traditions of Arabic poetry. One was formal classical Arabic poetry, the tradition of the monorime odes with conventional themes and tropes, descended from the pre-Islamic *muᶜallaqat* ("suspended poems," hung in the *kaᶜaba* at Mecca), the oldest of which was composed by Imruᶜu ᵓl-Qays (d. 540).[1] The second was a popular tradition, consisting of poetry written not in classical literary (highly inflected) Arabic, but rather in the spoken Arabic of Spain. The latter type of poetry was, like the *Arabian Nights*, looked down upon and considered unworthy to be called literature by the Arabs. The condescension which was shown to the popular Andalusian poetry by the Arab classicists and purists is comparable to the attitude of American poets and scholars towards the poems of Edgar A. Guest, extremely popular among hoi polloi, but never recognized (nor should he be) by the literati. It was the popular or vulgar Andalusian poetry, not classical Arabic tradition, whose forms provided models for troubadour poetry and, in turn, for the poetry of France, England, Germany, and Italy.

Popular Arabic poetry developed two forms which were unique to Andalusia. These were the *muwashshaḥ*, dating from around 900, and its offspring the *zajal*, dating from some time before 1100. They were short poems, usually of five to nine strophes of varying but relatively short line-lengths. The major difference between them was that the *muwashshaḥ* was in literary Arabic

[1] Reynold A. Nicholson, *A Literary History of the Arabs*, pp. 101–104.

(except for the concluding lines) and on traditional themes, while the *zajal* was in vulgar or spoken Arabic and on light themes. In the *muwashshaḥ* a theme stanza at the beginning, a type of epigraph called the *markaz* ("center") was usually its controlling feature, and in the *zajal* emphasis was on the concluding lines, which produced a shock effect,[2] like the punchline in a modern English limerick. The final lines in both the *muwashshaḥ* and the *zajal* were ordinarily put in the mouth of a speaker other than the poet and consisted of words of women, of youth, or of drunken persons. Often inanimate objects were introduced, and the speaker might be a personification of a city, Fame, War, etc.[3] In most of the poems, however, the speaker of the concluding lines would be a woman, and the language, unlike that of the preceding strophes, would be vulgar Arabic in the *muwashshaḥ* or the Romance dialect in the *zajal*, all written in Arabic characters.

The typical *muwashshaḥ* structure is: *AA* bbbAA cccAA. In stanza form, it would look like this:

> *AA*–*markaz* ("statement" or "center"); the epigraph or prelude which sets the theme.

The *bayt* or stanza, in two parts:

> bbb–*ghuṣan* ("branch"), Spanish *mudanza*; that section of the stanza in which the rimes vary among stanzas.
>
> AA–*simṭ* ("thread"), Spanish *vuelta*; the concluding lines of each stanza which use the rimes of the *markaz*.
>
> (*A*) (*A*)–*kharja* ("refrain"), Spanish *estribillo*. This may or may not occur.

When the *kharja* is found, its rimes are those of the *markaz*, and it often consists of a repetition of the lines of the *markaz* after each stanza. Many variations of the basic *muwashshaḥ* were possible, for example, *ABAB* cdcdcdABAB, efefefABAB.[4]

2 Gerald Brenan, *The Literature of the Spanish People*, pp. 27, 468, 470.

3 S. M. Stern, *Les Chansons mozarabes* (Oxford, 1964), pp. xv–xvi.

4 The structure and variations of the *muwashshaḥ* and *zajal* forms are from Stern, *Les Chansons mozarabes*, pp. xiii–xv. I have not followed Stern's referring to the concluding lines (punch lines) as the *kharja* which in other usage means *refrain*. There is considerable confusion among Hispanists with regard to the correct Arabic

The *zajal* was somewhat simpler: *AA* bbbA cccA, with a typical variation being *AB* cccB dddB. Its chief structural deviation from the *muwashshaḥ* was in the *bayt* (stanza) which reproduced only half of the rimes of the prelude or *markaz*, bbbA, in comparison with the *muwashshaḥ* bbbAA. The basic *zajal* stanza, consisting of the *ghuṣan* and *simṭ* without the prelude (bbbA cccA) called the *murabbaᶜ* (cf. *rubāᶜī*, "quatrain," plural *rubāᶜyāt*) reappears among the Provençal troubadour lyrics.

Development of the forms.[5] Beginning with the *muwashshaḥ* in the ninth century and the *zajal* in the tenth, the *Almorávid* and *Almóhad* periods (1090–1248) saw the greatest flourishing of the two forms which continued to be popular through the Granadine period (to 1492). They are peculiar to Andalusian poetry and very rare—in fact, almost nonexistent—in Eastern Arabic and Persian verse.[6] The earliest extant *muwashshaḥ* dates from the early eleventh century, although the form is known to have been used around 900. Several texts have survived from the eleventh century, and many of the surviving poems are written in Hebrew, using the Romance dialect in Hebrew script in the concluding lines.

The fact that the forms existed earlier than the eleventh century is attested to by several historians. Ibn-Bassām (d. 1146), for example, tells of the blind poet Muqaddam or al-Qabrī (of Cabra, to the south of Cordoba) having composed *zajals* in the ninth and tenth centuries, and describes them as having short lines and us-

terms for parts of the poems. The labels here, due to lack of standardization in their use by various scholars, represent my own attempt to make order from chaos. See, for example, Eleanor L. Turnbull, ed., *Ten Centuries of Spanish Poetry* (New York, 1955), pp. 2–5. My analysis is fairly close to that of Ramón Menéndez Pidal in *Poesía arabe y poesía europea* (p. 17), and W. Montgomery Watt in *A History of Islamic Spain* (p. 119).

5 The developmental history of the form is taken from A. R. Nykl, *Hispano-Arabic Poetry and Its Relations with the Old Provençal Troubadours*, pp. 339, 357; Stern, *Les Chansons mozarabes*, pp. xvi–xix; Brenan, *Literature of the Spanish People*, p. 26; and Robert S. Briffault, *The Troubadours*, p. 46. An old but good German study on the form is Martin Hartmann, *Das arabische Strophengedicht: I. das Muwashshaḥ*, Semitische Studien (Weimar, 1897). See also Selīm al-Ḥalū, *al-Muwashshaḥat al-Āndalusīa* (Beirut, 1960), which not only discusses the origin and evolution of the form but also reproduces various old and modern melodies which may be descended from the original melodies which accompanied *muwashshaḥs*.

6 Edward G. Browne, *A Literary History of Persia*, II (New York, 1906), 23.

ing the ʿ*ajamī* (foreign) or Romance idiom; a twelfth-century Egyptian writer, Ibn-Sanaʾ al-Mulk, composed a treatise on the *muwashshaḥ* in which, in discussing the form of the unusual poetry of Andalusia, he pointed out that the conclusion was in vulgar Arabic and sometimes in Romance. Evidently then, by the twelfth century, the forms were not only fully developed from earlier beginnings but also relatively widely known. The attitude of the Arab classicists towards the popular poetry can be seen in the remarks of the *Almóhades*' historian ʿAbd-al-Walid al-Marrākushī, who praises the *zajals* of the physician Ibn-Zuhr, Latin *Abenzoar* (b. 1114), and says that he would like to quote one, but cannot, since his book is "for scholars."[7]

Ibn-Quzmān. One of the most famous writers of *muwashshaḥs* and *zajals* was Ibn-Quzmān of Cordoba (ca. 1070–1160),[8] contemporary with the earliest troubadour. Because Ibn-Quzmān's *diwān* (collected works) of 140 *zajals* has survived, his poems have been used as bases for detailed comparison with the troubadour lyrics to show the indebtedness of the troubadours to Andalusian poets. Ibn-Quzmān's *zajals* are in vulgar Arabic, with some using Romance words, and fall into seven categories: love poems, spring songs, drinking songs, satires, colloquies in slang, moral pieces, and licentious or Goliardic pieces. Many of them are addressed to men as are many of the troubadour works. Love in Ibn-Quzmān is extramarital, as it is in troubadour courtly-love lyrics on the unattainable lady love.

The major similarities in form which have been found between his works and those of the troubadours are:

1. The rime is that of many troubadour lyrics.

[7] Ibn-Zuhr's poems are discussesd by Arthur J. Arberry, *Arabic Poetry: A Primer for Students* (Cambridge, England, 1965), pp. 21–22; and by Nykl, *Hispano-Arabic Poetry*, pp. 248–51.

[8] Information on Ibn-Quzmān is taken from Brenan, *Literature of the Spanish People*, pp. 28–30; Briffault, *The Troubadours*, pp. 47–48; and Nykl, *Hispano-Arabic Poetry*, pp. 271–74. For a more detailed study of Ibn-Quzmān, see Emilio García Gómez, *Todo Ben Quzmān*, 3 vols. (Madrid, 1972). Vols. I and II include the *zajals* in transcription, translations, and notes. Vol. III includes a discussion of the metrics and the Romance expressions of the *zajals*. There is a supplementary bibliography in each section. See also S. M. Stern, "Studies on Ibn-Quzmān," *Al-Andalus*, 16 (1951), 379–425.

2. The majority of the *zajals* are of five to seven strophes in length, similar to the oldest lays of the troubadours.

3. The *zajals* employ a *kharja* or refrain of from one to four lines like the troubadour *tornada.*

And in regard to content, the following characteristics of Ibn-Quzmān's lyrics have been pointed out as also characteristic of the Provençal lyrics:

1. There is much reference to the *lauzengier* or backbiter.
2. A fictitious name or *senhal* is used as the masculine form of address for a lady, the Provençal *midons.*
3. Being bewitched by a look, complaining of the lady's tyranny, cruelty, and disdain, and suffering from weeping, insomnia, emaciation, and weakness are commonplaces.
4. A confidante or go-between is employed.
5. It is the lover's duty to submit to the wishes of his beloved.
6. The love poems contain a spring atmosphere and much sensuous imagery.

Most of the courtly-love themes and behavior of the lover in Ibn-Quzmān's *zajals* had been dealt with in some detail at least three quarters of a century earlier in Ibn-Ḥazm's treatise on love.

Later discoveries. In 1949, a manuscript was discovered in Morocco which had been compiled by Ibn-Bushra at the end of the fourteenth century and which contains *muwashshaḥs* in Hebrew script, with the concluding lines also written in Hebrew letters but in the Romance dialect. Soon afterwards, a manuscript of similar poems in Arabic script, also containing portions in the Romance dialect but in Arabic script, was discovered at the Zaytūna Mosque in Tunis.[9] It had been compiled by the Granadine minister of state Lisān al-Dīn Ibn-al-Khaṭīb (1313–74), himself a poet and a writer of *maqāmas* (coffee-house picaresque tales interspersed with poems). The manuscripts, like other Hebrew and Arabic manuscripts, were removed to North Africa by Jews and Arabs fleeing the Spanish Christian *conquistadores.*

The Hebrew poems discovered in Morocco are patterned closely after the Arabic ones. Emphasis in both falls on the conclud-

9 Stern, *Les Chansons mozarabes,* pp. xxiv, 51. See also Stern, "ᶜĀshiqayn Iᶜtanaqā: An Arabic Muwashshaḥ and Its Hebrew Imitations," *Al-Andalus,* 28 (1963), 155–70.

ing lines, with the poem leading up to them. The conclusions are, for the most part, spoken by a girl, who is not the speaker of the other strophes. A few of them, where the author's name is given, date from the early eleventh century. The manuscripts should be of inestimable value to linguists as the earliest extant examples of the Romance or Mozarabic dialect spoken in Islamic Spain. Unfortunately, only portions of the poems (the concluding lines in Romance) have been printed. Not all of these have been deciphered because of the lack of vowels in ordinary Arabic and Hebrew scripts which, in effect, omit all short-vowel sounds, and which, where the language represented (such as Old-Spanish Romance) is not known, cause considerable difficulty in reconstructing it. Printing the entire poems would have helped in deciphering the Romance lines which could then be studied within the contexts of the poems. This is an area in which a great deal of linguistic research and metrical analysis remains to be done.[10]

Spanish adaptations. Two Spanish Christians, Alfonso X in his *Cantigas de Santa María* and Juan Ruiz, the archpriest of Hita, in his *Libro de Buen Amor,* copy the *zajal* forms as found in Ibn-Quzmān very closely. The *Cantigas* are almost entirely in the *muwashshaḥ* and *zajal* forms. Manuscripts of the poems, which are in the Galician dialect, contain musical notations; and in one of the manuscripts there is a miniature depicting side by side two *jongleurs,* one a Moor and one a Christian,[11] visual proof of the association of Christian and Islamic entertainers. Alfonso's poems represent early Spanish adaptation of the popular and

[10] Some articles of interest are S. M. Stern, "Miscelánea internácional sobre las jarchas mozárabes," *Al-Andalus,* 18 (1953), 133–48; Emilio García Gómez, "Veinticuatro Jarchas romances en muwashshaḥas arabes," *Al-Andalus,* 17 (1952), 57–127; and J. M. Solá-Solé, "Nuevas Kharjas mozárabes," *Kentucky Romance Quarterly,* 17 (1970), 29–46. Some fairly recent book-length studies are Emilio García Gómez, *Las jarchas romances de la serie árabe en su marco* (Madrid, 1965); and Mīshel ᶜAsi, ed., *Ājmal al-Muwashshaḥat* (Beirut, 1968). ᶜAsi's book is a general anthology of *muwashshaḥs,* of all dates, including some written by Lisān al-Dīn, Ibn-Sanaᵓ al-Mulk, and others mentioned in Chapter II above. Especially interesting is the collection of Lisān al-Dīn's *muwashshaḥs* (a fourteenth-century minister of Granada) in Lisān al-Dīn Ibn-al-Khaṭīb, *Jaish al-Taushiḥ,* ed. Ḥilal Najī and Muḥammad Maḍhūr (Tunis, 1967).

[11] The miniature is reproduced by Menéndez Pidal, *Poesía arabe y poesía europea,* p. 75.

secular type of strophe of Andalusia to Christian religious use. One of them, number LX, is a comparison and contrast between Eve and Mary, beginning with the *markaz* which is repeated as the *kharja* at the end of each strophe:

> Between Mary and Eve
> is a vast difference.[12]

The contrasting of Eve and Mary, a favorite topic for early medieval Christian lyrics, is found not infrequently in Middle-English lyrics, although not in the *zajal* form as such. Later Castilian folk songs, the *villancico* (now usually a Christmas carol) and the *estribote* (a poem using an *estribillo* for its refrain) are descendants of the *zajal*, and the popular *copla* sung in the streets of Seville today is descended from it.[13]

Themes in The Pennants. Ibn-Saʿīd's anthology *The Pennants* of 1243, although not a collection of *zajals* or folk tradition, contains several poems of an early date on themes which were to become popular later in Old-French and Middle-English poetry. In addition to the Arabic commonplace themes on the beauties of nature, the happiness of love, and the praise of generous patrons, for example, are a love poem on the marguerite of the early eleventh century and a poem on chess as a game of fortune, written in the mid-eleventh century. Chess was brought into Europe through Arab Spain, and the marguerite, like chess, was to become a favorite poetic theme in thirteenth- and fourteenth-century France and England, once lyric poetry had been developed in these countries.

One other poem of *The Pennants* is of interest as it involves the mysterious Khaḍir ("Green One"). In al-Asamm's "The Unripe Orange," of the twelfth century, the last stanza reads, in Arberry's translation:

[12] Alfonso X, *Cantiga* LX, in *Antología de Alfonso X, el Sabio*, ed. Antonio G. Solalinde (Buenos Aires, 1940), p. 25.

[13] Brenan, *Literature of the Spanish People*, p. x. For examples of continuation of the *zajal* tradition in the popular and modern poetry of Spain, see Damaso Alonso y Jose M. Blecua, eds., *Antología de la poesía española: Poesía de tipo tradicional* (Madrid, 1956); and Margit Frenk Alatorre, ed., *Lírica hispánia de tipo popular*, Colección Nuestros Clásicos, 31 (Mexico City, 1966).

Moses, God's apostle, lit
Here a flame, yet brightly seen;
Khadhir of the mystic green
There his hand laid over it.[14]

This is the Khaḍir of the *Ṣūfīs* (Islamic mystics) who will be encountered in subsequent chapters, seen in this poem in relation to Moses with whom he is associated in the *Qurʾān* and in his possibly far more ancient role as a vegetation figure. The ripe part of the orange is represented by the flame of Moses, a guiding light, and the green, unripe part by the influence of Khaḍir, who causes the earth to turn green with buds and sprouts wherever he touches it. Such a conceit or comparison is characteristic of Arabic poetry. It entails a recognition of Khaḍir as a vegetation figure and of the episode in the *Qurʾān* in which Khaḍir serves as a guide for Moses, as green precedes the orange.

Themes in The Dove's Neck-Ring. Ibn-Ḥazm's *Ṭawq al-Ḥammāma,* written around 1022 in the form of a long essay (*risāla,* or "epistle"), reflects ancient Arabic traditions both in its format and in the attitude reflected towards romantic love. Its format is made up of an alternation of prose and verse, found as early as the seventh century in Arabic and represented later by the Persian and Arabic *Thousand and One Nights,* the Spanish *Libro de Buen Amor,* and the French *Aucassin et Nicolette.*[15] The ideal of platonic love, although it begins with physical love and then ascends to the platonic or spiritual level in Ibn-Ḥazm, the principle of submission of the lover to the beloved, and the extolling of chastity have a long history in Arabic poetry. Ibn-Ḥazm mentions and quotes from Ibn-Daʾūd (868–909) of Baghdad and from Plato in stressing the spiritual aspects of love.[16] Love is seen as a desire for reunion by two souls separated from each other and from the "all-encompassing Spirit" at creation. It often begins

14 Al-Asamm, "The Unripe Orange," in *Moorish Poetry: A Translation of "The Pennants," an Anthology Compiled in 1243 by the Andalusian Ibn-Saʿīd,* trans. Arthur J. Arberry, p. 55. Poems on the marguerite and chess are on pages 77 and 174, respectively.

15 Américo Castro, *Structure of Spanish History,* pp. 435–36.

16 A. R. Nykl, trans., *A Book Containing the Risāla Known as The Dove's Neck-Ring about Love and Lovers,* by ʿAlī Ibn-Aḥmad Ibn-Ḥazm, pp. lxi–lxii.

with an attraction to external beauty—if true beauty is found inside, love may result; if not, love does not go beyond the form and is thus mere passion.

Beginning with an explanation of the necessity for disguising names, Ibn-Ḥazm then discusses love as an incurable but desirable disease, the symptoms of which include confusion, inability to eat, drink, or talk, moodiness, and a desire for solitude. The lover grows thin, sighs, sobs, weeps, and is unable to sleep. But he is also ennobled by his love and must be willing to perform any service for the beloved. One can fall in love through a dream, from description, at first sight, and from long intercourse as friends, the last being the preferable means. There are sections on the need for a friend to confide in, on messages, on the use of a go-between, preferably an old woman, on the need for secrecy, and on the use of a *senhal* or false name. The lover is enjoined to be faithful and constant in his service and to beware of slanderers and backbiters. Physical love is sanctioned, but continence is urged. Illicit love, in which either the lady or the lover is married, is roundly condemned by Ibn-Ḥazm, and this is the major difference between the love extolled in *The Dove's Neck-Ring* and that of Ibn-Quzmān's *zajals* and the troubadour lyrics. In Ibn-Quzmān and in the troubadours, the lady is married.

The poems of Ibn-Zaydūn (1003–71) of Cordoba to his beloved Wallāda, a lady of higher station, are early examples of courtly-love lyrics and laments. Ibn-Zaydūn frequently writes nostalgically of the time he and his lady love have spent together, the moments when, in a garden, they enjoyed pure love. Now, emaciated, despairing of seeing her again, he wishes for death as the only solace.[17] In tone and in specific motifs and circumstances, Ibn-Zaydūn's poems illustrate the precepts outlined in Ibn-Ḥazm's treatise.[18]

17 Ibn-Zaydūn's poems are discussed by Arberry in *Arabic Poetry: A Primer*, pp. 114–16.

18 For a thorough discussion and analysis of troubadour lyrics, see Alfred Jeanroy, *La Poésie lyrique des troubadours*, 2 vols. (Paris, 1934). For a discussion of similarities between works of the troubadours and those of the Arab poets of Spain, see Briffault, *The Troubadours*; Nykl, *Hispano-Arabic Poetry*; and Nykl's translation of *The Dove's Neck-Ring*. Of interest also is Emilio García Gómez, "Un precedente y una consecuencia del 'Collar de la Paloma,'" *Al-Andalus*, 16 (1951), 309–30.

The Provençal Troubadours

Music. The troubadours apparently took the name *troubadour* and the word for their songs, *trobar,* from the Arabic *Ṭarraba,* "to sing, entertain, or evoke emotion," as has already been mentioned. They did not hesitate, either, to refer to the music of their songs and to their instruments as Saracen, a carryover of which can perhaps be seen much later in the English Morris (Moorish) dances.[19] Very little study has been done on the music of the troubadours because not much of it has survived. Only 264 melodies have been preserved, mostly of the later troubadours, as compared to over two thousand from the *trouvères* of northern France. Although the music has not been compared with that of Arab Spain, several musical instruments, along with their Arabic names, are known to have been introduced into Europe through Spain; among these are the lute, the guitar, the rebec, and the *qānūn* (Spanish *caño* and *mediocaño,* French *canon* and *micanon,* and German *Kanon* and *Metzkanon*).[20] And who, if not the troubadours, would have brought musical instruments from Spain to France and Germany? Possibly a study of the troubadour music which has survived in comparison with certain folk music of Spain and of Algeria, Tunisia, and Morocco, where Spanish Arabs fled during the *reconquista* and the Inquisition, could reveal why the troubadours referred to their music as Saracen.

Types of poems. Of the seven major types of troubadour poetry,[21] two, the *canzon* (love song) and the *alba* (dawn song), have close models in Arabic. The *canzon,* consisting of six- to eight-line strophes ending with a short *tornado* or appeal, is perhaps best represented by Bernart de Ventadorn (fl. 1150–80), who visited England around 1154; by Jaufré Rudel (ca. 1150), with his distant unseen lady; Arnaut Daniel (fl. 1180–1210), whom Dante placed in Purgatory for his erotic scatology; and in the late

19 Briffault, *The Troubadours,* pp. 74–76.

20 Théodore Gérold, *La Musique au moyen âge* (Paris, 1932), pp. 107, 113, 377–87. The figures given are Gérold's.

21 See W. T. H. Jackson, *Medieval Literature: A History and a Guide,* pp. 109–10. Except as otherwise noted, the general observations in this paragraph are from Jackson.

twelfth century, by Giraut de Bornelh and Peire Vidal. The *alba* or dawn song found in most of the troubadours' works is patterned directly after the *murabbaᶜ* (bbbA) stanza of the *zajal*.[22] Marcabru (ca. 1150) and Bertran de Born were known for their *sirventès*, political or moral pieces which were often satire. Other types of troubadour poems included the *pastorelle* (a pastoral poem), the *joc partit* (a discussion or dialogue on love), the *tenson* (debate), and the *planh* (lament).

Styles. Three styles of composition were recognized among the troubadours, the *trobar plan* (in comparatively plain style), *trobar ric* (in an ornate and highly metaphoric style), and the *trobar clus* (in language so ornate as to be obscure to the uninitiated). Known for use of the *trobar ric* was Peire d'Auverne (fl. 1138–80) and for use of the *trobar clus* Marcabru (ca. 1150) and Rimbaut d'Orange (fl. 1150–73).[23] Denis de Rougemont views the *trobar clus* style as a vehicle to disguise Albigensian thought.

Form. The *murabbaᶜ* stanza of the *zajal* has a major schematic similarity to troubadour lyric stanzaic structure. Of the eleven surviving songs of Guilhem IX of Aquitaine (1071–1127), for example, the three composed before he went to the Crusades in 1101–2 are of a nontroubadour type, while of the remaining eight, six follow the *zajal* model and two differ only in variations on the form. The form appears most often among the early troubadours (Guilhem of Aquitaine, Marcabru, and Cercamon), and although it is also to be found among the later troubadour songs, it tends to occur then with more variations.[24] The aaaBcccB form is, in turn, later prominent in the early Middle-English tail-rime romances, drama, and lyrics.

The troubadours and Arthurian matter. Troubadours frequently cited the various characters of Arthurian romance. Curiously, of all the major figures, including Arthur, Gawain, and Perceval, Tristan was the most frequently cited by both troubadours and *trouvères*, but in consonance with this, the story of Tristan and Isolt contains certain Arab-Persian elements mixed

22 Briffault, *The Troubadours*, p. 36, and Jackson, *Medieval Literature*, p. 108.
23 Jackson, *Medieval Literature*, pp. 109–10.
24 Briffault, *The Troubadours*, pp. 43–58.

in with its originally Celtic story, a topic to be treated in a later chapter. There is evidence that the troubadours were expected to be familiar with Arthurian figures and stories.[25] The ideals and concepts of courtly love as found in troubadour lyrics are generally believed to have been incorporated in Arthurian romance as a result of troubadour influence. Courtly love, along with otherworld material, became an integral part of the romance tradition.

The troubadours and courtly love. Most of the scholars and critics who discuss troubadour indebtedness to Arabic poetic forms also suggest that they found their models for courtly love in Arabic Spain. Romantic love, both chaste and earthy, as found among the troubadours' addresses to an unnamed highborn lady, closely resembles that found in Ibn-Ḥazm's *Dove's Neck-Ring*. In addition, the suffering and self-sacrifice of the lover in troubadour lyrics are of the type found earlier in both Ibn-Ḥazm and *Ṣūfī* religious poetry.[26] Another reason for suspecting Spanish-Arabic influence in the concept of courtly love is that romantic love is not native to Christian, Celtic, or Germanic tradition. If the ideas on love as found in Ibn-Ḥazm and other Arab writers influenced the troubadours and European tradition, it may be that the crystallization of love into an extramarital phenomenon with a code of artificial behavioral precepts—as exemplified in the debates on love in Languedoc castles and in the "cases" tried in Marie de Champagne's court—was a result of the contact and conflict of romantic love with Christianity. Chronologically, there is none of the set courtly manner in Guilhem IX, the first known troubadour; *fin amor* is first differentiated from gross love in Marcabru. And later, in Bernart de Ventadorn, the courtly manner is found fully developed.[27] That the troubadour love poetry of Provence was brought to a full stop with the Albigensian Crusade of 1209–13 perhaps further emphasizes its non-Christian aspect. Following the Crusade, the rhetoric of courtly love was

25 See Rita Lejeune, "The Troubadours," in *Arthurian Literature in the Middle Ages*, ed. Roger Sherman Loomis (Oxford, 1959), pp. 393–99.

26 Briffault, *The Troubadours*, p. 98.

27 *Ibid.*, pp. 80–83.

transferred to religious lyrics, particularly those in honor of Mary, by the Franciscans and others.

C. S. Lewis. C. S. Lewis, in accounting for courtly love, traces the separation of desire from virtue to the pre-Christian Roman world in which the Aristotelian concept of a truly virtuous man as one who was so from natural desire was exchanged for the idea that man had to fight with himself and conquer desire in order to be virtuous. With the establishment of an irreconcilable conflict between desire and virtue, man had to resort to allegory for rhetoric with which to describe and discuss his inner battle, and hence metaphors of warfare came to be applied to desire and love. This concept and its rhetoric were absorbed by Christianity and continued through the Middle Ages, when love between man and woman—including marital love—was considered a sin, an evil desire to be conquered and overcome, by many of the ecclesiastical writers. The appearance of courtly love in Provence in the late eleventh century is then attributed by Lewis to serious interpretation of Ovid's *Ars Amatoria* which was meant by Ovid to be a joke.[28] But if courtly love had resulted from a misreading of Ovid, would it not have begun among another group than the troubadours, since neither the troubadours nor their noble patrons knew Latin? More likely Ovid's work served merely to reinforce the realization among the clerics, when they discovered the themes of the troubadours' songs and the later romances, that neither courtly love nor romantic love was compatible with medieval Christianity.

Denis de Rougemont. Rougemont connects courtly love in Provence to the Albigensians of Languedoc.[29] The Albigensian sect (also called the *Cathari*, "the pure") was a major concern to Roman Catholicism in the eleventh and twelfth centuries. The heresy was widespread in France in the eleventh century, a fact substantiated by the many decrees forbidding the practice of it.

28 C. S. Lewis, *The Allegory of Love* (New York, 1958), pp. 5–8. (Originally published in 1936.)

29 Denis de Rougemont, *Love in the Western World*, rev. ed., trans. Montgomery Belgion (New York, 1956); and the same author's sequel, *Love Declared*, trans. Richard Howard (Boston, 1963).

By the twelfth century, it was confined to Provence and lower Languedoc, where it thrived among both the nobility and the masses. The Albigensians were denounced by the Church as worse heretics than the Saracens; the Cistercian Saint Bernard and Saint Dominic and other Dominicans made large-scale efforts to convert them to orthodoxy. But the heresy seems to have been too deeply rooted for either persuasion or threats to affect it, and in 1208, Innocent III called a crusade against the Albigensians. Led by Simon de Montfort—a name which has been associated with villainy ever since—the crusade lasted from 1209 to 1213 and was characterized by wholesale massacre and plunder of Agen, Marseilles, Montauban, Montpellier, Narbonne, and Toulouse, the cities where the sect was most prominent.

Albigensianism seems to have drawn largely from Manichaean dualism for its basic belief in a conflict between light and dark, good and evil, the spirit and the flesh. Jesus was all light and neither born of woman nor crucified. To reproduce earthly life was evil and therefore chastity was enjoined; to destroy earthly life was also evil and therefore no animal food was to be eaten. The Albigensians rejected, in addition to the virgin birth, baptism, miracles, saint worship, purgatory, and the leadership of Rome.

Along with its affinities with Manichaeism, Albigensianism also had affinities with ascetic Sufism, which was, in turn, close to Arianism. Spain had been a stronghold of Arianism after it was defeated elsewhere in Europe, and Catholic persecution of Arianism in Spain in the eighth century had led many Spanish Visigoths to assist the more tolerant Muslim invaders in their conquest of Spain. The Arian belief was actually closer to Islam than to Roman Catholicism.[30] Whatever its ultimate derivation, the Albigensian heresy did not continue to exist and grow in a vacuum. Provence and Languedoc were exposed to Islamic Sufism from Spain as well as to the earlier Arianism and Manichaeism.

[30] "Albigenses" and "Arianism" in *Encyclopedia of Religion and Ethics*, ed. James Hastings (New York, 1951), I, 277–87, 775–86. The Albigensian Heresy and Crusade are also discussed very briefly in James Westfall Thompson and Edgar Nathanial Johnson, *An Introduction to Medieval Europe, 300–1500*, pp. 499–501.

Thus, both geographically and chronologically, there apparently was some connection between the troubadours and the Cathars of southern France.

Rougemont, noticing the similarities between Albigensian beliefs and Manichaeism and *Ṣūfī* mysticism, considers the troubadour love lyrics, especially those of the *trobar clus,* to be Albigensian songs clothed in love rhetoric (characteristic of Sufism) to disguise their true nature. He finds coincidences between the Albigensians and the troubadours in their view of marriage, their rhetoric, their geographical locations, and their dates. He notes that both the Albigensians and the troubadours scoffed at marriage; that both praised chastity, the troubadours doing so with the rhetoric of the *Ṣūfī* mystics; that the centers of the heresy were the castles of Orleans, Poitou, Aquitaine, and lower Languedoc, specifically Agen, Marseilles, Montauban, Montpellier, Narbonne, and Toulouse, where the troubadours flourished; and that the massacre of the heretics during the Albigensian Crusade put an end to the troubadours as well as to the Cathars.

It is possible that, with their close connections with Spain, the troubadours were influenced by *Ṣūfī* religious love poetry, and possibly the enforcement of Cathar beliefs was provided by Sufism. But to equate the troubadours absolutely with the Albigensians would require more substantiation than Rougemont provides, since the troubadours composed other types of songs in addition to the *canzon* or love song. Even the love songs were at times earthy and referred to physical love (sometimes scatologically) as well as to chaste love. Rougemont's thesis points up the need for further comparative research on the *Ṣūfīs* and Albigensians and their relationships to the Provençal troubadours.

A. J. Denomy. Denomy proposes that courtly love arose not from popular Arabic poetic tradition or from Albigensianism or Sufism, but from the Arab philosophers Ibn-Sīnā, al-Fārābī, and Ibn-Rushd, whose works were translated into Latin in the twelfth century. He finds a parallel between Ibn-Rushd's problem of reason versus revelation and the "double truth" of Andreas Capellanus' *De Amore* in which the first two books, containing model speeches for lovers and judgments given in Marie de Champagne's courts of love, advocate courtly love, while the third book is a retraction. Thus, "What Andreas teaches to be true according to nature and reason, he teaches to be false according to grace and divine authority."[31] Andreas' work reflects the conflict of courtly love with Christianity, however, and not the philosophical speculations of Ibn-Sīnā and Ibn-Rushd in reconciling scientific truths with revealed or religious truths. Further, the troubadours themselves could not very well be expected to be familiar with formal philosophical works translated from Arabic into Latin at the time they were composing their songs.[32] The need to reconcile scientific with revealed truths among the Arab philosophers had little to do with romantic love, which was never considered to conflict with religious dogma unless it was adulterous or otherwise illicit or scandalous, while both romantic love and extramarital courtly love conflicted in essence with the monastic medieval Christian view of woman. Denomy's theory, like that of C. S. Lewis, subsumes a familiarity on the part of the Provençal troubadours with learned and philosophical authors and their works and overlooks the fact that the troubadours were composing their lyrics in a popular, not learned, tradition. We would not expect the popular guitar-picking "rock" singers of the 1960s and 1970s to be familiar with the types of works Ph.D. candidates read and study in working for an advanced degree.

Twelfth- and Thirteenth-Century Latin Lyrics

The Goliards. The secular Latin poetry of the Goliards, who were contemporary with the troubadours, shows no trace of courtly love.[33] It does, however, show a debt to troubadour and *trouvère* forms in its frequent repetition of a word in the last line

[31] Alexander J. Denomy, *The Heresy of Courtly Love* (Gloucester, Mass., 1965), p. 39.

[32] Theodore Silverstein, "Andreas, Plato, and the Arabs: Remarks on Some Recent Accounts of Courtly Love," *Modern Philology*, 47 (1949), 117–26.

[33] See George F. Whicher, trans., *The Goliard Poets: Medieval Latin Songs and Satires* (N.P., 1949); and Helen Waddell, *The Wandering Scholars*, rev. ed. (London, 1947).

of a stanza in the first line of the next for unity, a device often employed in the *chansons de geste* of the *trouvères,* but sparingly used by the troubadours who were more likely to rime the first line of a stanza with the last line of the preceding one. Although the favorite Goliardic meter appeared in monorimed quatrains, there were exceptions among their verses. The thirteenth-century "Sequence for a Drunkard's Mass," to cite one instance, follows the *murabba*ᶜ aaaBcccB pattern, the same as that found in the Provençal dawn song and in late-twelfth-century Latin sequences.[34]

The Franciscans. Religious songs, carols, and canticles patterned after the aaaBcccB form became very popular in the latter part of the thirteenth century, with Latin tercets in church carols appearing about a century after the troubadours. The Franciscans are believed to have played an important part in transforming the profane songs of the troubadours into songs on Christian themes.[35] In taking over the courtly-love rhetoric of the troubadours for songs to the Virgin, they may also have borrowed some of the forms from the troubadours, in particular, the *murabba*ᶜ rime. In Spain, Alfonso X had used such profane forms as the *murabba*ᶜ in his *Cantigas de Santa María* in the mid-thirteenth century.

PART II—MIDDLE ENGLISH

Middle-English Lyrics

The influence of Provençal lyrics on French and on English lyrics is well documented and needs little discussion here. It is also well known that with the marriage of Eleanor of Guienne (Aquitaine) to Henry II, many of the Provençal troubadours came to the English court where they had many connections with

34 F. Brittain, *The Medieval Latin and Romance Lyric to A.D. 1300* (Cambridge, England, 1937), pp. 22, 118, 138–40.

35 Briffault, *The Troubadours,* pp. 40–41; Edmund K. Chambers and F. Sidgwick, eds., *Early English Lyrics: Amorous, Divine, Moral, and Trivial* (London, 1921), pp. 272 ff.

English politics.[36] The effects of French culture on England following the Norman Conquest were pervasive; French was the language of the court, of the law, and of commerce, and was the fashionable language up to the mid-fourteenth century. By the time English as a language was cultivated as fashionable, there had been a heavy infusion of French into the Anglo-Saxon of before the conquest. A broad parallel can be seen in the effect of the Arabic language in Spain.

Provençal and French influence are quite apparent in the Middle-English lyrics. Love and lyric poetry were not characteristic of the Anglo-Saxon temper, and when lyrics did begin to appear in England, there were for some time far more religious than love lyrics. The earliest surviving Middle-English lyrics date only from the thirteenth century, while most of them are from the fourteenth and fifteenth centuries, especially the carols.[37]

To cite a few examples of direct borrowing from Provençal types and forms in the English lyrics, the *canzon* or love song with five- to seven-line stanzas with a *tornado* is seen in "Alysoun," and the *tenson* in debates between "The Owl and the Nightingale," "Mary and the Cross," and "The Body and the Soul." Provençal stanza-linking devices, repetition of a word or of the rime of the last line of a stanza in the first line of the next, are also present. Among the many rime schemes imported from Provence are aBaBBcBc, aaBccBddBeeB, and aaaBcccB. The first of these was used by several troubadours and is found in one of the Middle English poems, *"Quia amore langueo"*; the form aaBccBddB, first elaborated by Marcabru, is found in many of the lyrics and was frequently used in the tail-rime romances; and the Provençal aaaBcccB, the Andalusian *murabba*ᶜ, was very popular among the

36 Claude Colleer Abbott, *Early Mediaeval French Lyrics* (London, 1932), pp. xxv–xxvii; John Edwin Wells, *A Manual of the Writings in Middle English, 1050–1400* (New Haven, 1916), p. 485; and H. J. Chaytor, *The Troubadours and England* (Cambridge, England, 1923). Chaytor divides his attention between the troubadours' connections with English politics and their influences on English lyrics.

37 John Speirs, *Medieval English Poetry: The Non-Chaucerian Tradition* (London, 1957), pp. 45, 50. See also Chambers and Sidgwick eds., *Early English Lyrics*, pp. 272–82; and Carleton F. Brown, ed., *Religious Lyrics of the XIVth Century*, 2nd ed. (Oxford, 1952).

early lyric writers in England.[38] The *aube* or dawn song, frequently written in the *murabba*^{c} rime by the troubadours and more common in French and German than in Middle English, is found in Chaucer's *Troilus* (III, ll. 1427–42) converted to rime royal.[39]

The importance of the *murabba*^{c} form of rime in early English lyrics can be seen in the 102 lyrics in the Chambers and Sidgwick anthology, of which forty-four are *murabba*^{c}*s*.[40] The form appeared in love lyrics, sometimes including courtly-love motifs, in light and humorous lyrics and in religious ones where again courtly-love motifs appear. "Blow Northern Wind," in a Harley manuscript of the fourteenth century, uses the *murabba*^{c} to address Love; the poet describes his beloved's appearance, her personality, and his love for her, and in the last stanza, the speaker becomes pale, weak, and unable to sleep.[41] Of the group of lyrics listed by Chambers and Sidgwick as "trivial," several are based on the *murabba*^{c} and even begin with an epigraph-type couplet similar to the *markaz* of the Andalusian *zajal*. Among these are CXVII, a warning not to take old wives; CXIX, a complaint of the evils of married life; and CXXIV, on the evils of women, with the rime aaaBaB, a rime also found in a Harley manuscript poem on the five joys of Mary.[42]

Early English Drama

The metrics of early English drama provide an interesting picture of the later adaptation of Provençal poetic forms and devices to medieval mystery plays of the Chester, York, and Wakefield cycles. The meter of the Chester plays, considered the oldest English cycle extant, differs from that of the later cycles in its

[38] Chaytor, *The Troubadours and England*, pp. 102–106, 124–28, and Appendix I.

[39] F. N. Robinson, ed., *The Works of Geoffrey Chaucer*, 2nd ed. (Boston, 1961), p. 826. All later citations of Chaucer are from this edition.

[40] Briffault, *The Troubadours*, p. 238, *n.* 40. He cites "Blow Northern Wind" and "Alysoun" as examples in the same note.

[41] Lyric 29 in *One Hundred Middle English Lyrics*, ed. Robert D. Stevick (New York, 1964), pp. 43–46; also reproduced in *English Lyrics of the XIIIth Century*, ed. Carleton F. Brown (Oxford, 1932), pp. 148–50.

[42] See Lyric 33 in Stevick, ed., *One Hundred Middle English Lyrics*, pp. 52–54.

uniformity. The meter's pattern is aaaBcccB, with the a- and c-lines containing four stresses and the B-lines containing three. Again the *murabba*ᶜ form is clearly discernible. It is a form of *rime couée* or tail-rime meter used in earlier romances and more suitable for lyrics and romance narratives than for dramatic dialogue.[43]

The York cycle, later in date than the Chester cycle, contains more variety in its stanza forms. Some twelve plays of the York cycle use a cross-rime stanza aBaBaBaBcDcD (the first eight lines being four-stress and the last four or *cauda* being three-stress), a modification of one of the troubadour forms. This stanza, like the earlier *Gospel of Nicodemus,* apparently influenced the poet of the Middle-English *Pearl.* The Provençal device of linking a stanza's beginning with the end of the preceding stanza is also found in the York plays and in the *Pearl.* In such York plays as the Condemnation, the lines of the *cauda* are separated from the preceding verses of the stanza by a one-stress line known as a "bob," a device used later by the *Pearl*-poet in *Sir Gawain and the Green Knight.*[44]

Other adaptations of tail-rime stanzas, Provençal patterns, and the *murabba*ᶜ form are evident in the Wakefield cycle and in the twelve long plays of the *Ludus Coventrae* group. The five plays of the Wakefield Master, for example, with the pattern aBaBaBaB (two-stress), C (one-stress), dddC (two-stress) represent variations and combinations of several already known patterns.

Conclusion

Neither rime nor romantic and courtly love was native to the Germanic temper of medieval Europe, and the lyric poetry of France and England probably owes its initial inspiration in rime, strophic structure, types, and love motifs to the troubadours of Provence who, in turn, seem to have been influenced by the popular tradition in Andalusian poetry. Romantic love, long a

43 Edmund K. Chambers, "Medieval Drama," in *English Literature at the Close of the Middle Ages* (Oxford, 1945), p. 25.

44 *Ibid.*, pp. 29–31. For Chambers' analysis of the Wakefield Master's meter, see p. 37.

characteristic of Arabic poetry, is found in Arab Spain over a century before the first troubadours flourished, already developed to the extent that it could have served as a blueprint for courtly love for the poets of Provence. Through the Provençal poets, courtly love was further developed and spread into northern France and into England where it is found in lyric poetry, both secular and religious, and in the romances. Courtly love, which conflicted with medieval Christian ideals, both as love and as adultery, was, following the Albigensian Crusade, appropriated to religious lyrics, with its rhetoric reappearing in later English religious and secular lyrics. Other themes, such as the marguerite and chess as a game of fortune, are found in Andalusian poetry many decades before they appeared in Old-French and Middle-English literature.

The strophic structure, rime schemes, and major types of the poems of troubadour composition also had strikingly close parallels with earlier Andalusian popular poetry, which had developed along lines not characteristic of Arabic poetry of the East but peculiar to Spain. A large number of the rime schemes and types of songs popularized by the troubadours are, in turn, identifiable in later Middle-English lyrics, romances, and drama.

Troubadour connections and movements between Spain and Provence and between Provence and England have been well documented by historians and scholars of the eleventh and twelfth centuries, suggesting that the Pyrenees presented no more of a physical or political barrier in the spread of lyric poetry than did the English Channel. Aragon and Provence were in fact one cultural area. That the Provençal poets may have received their inspiration both for lyric poetry and for courtly love from Andalusia has been sufficiently substantiated to date to indicate that an Hispano-Arabic theory of origin for European lyric poetry and for courtly love is an hypothesis which cannot be lightly dismissed. Both lyric forms and poetic themes can be traced chronologically and geographically from Andalusia to Provence to England. This being so, we should expect to find other related literary influences which filtered north at the same time.

CHAPTER IV

Visions of the Afterlife

PART I—GENERAL SURVEY

Celtic and Oriental Elements

In Christian Latin and very early vernacular literature, some visions of the rewards and punishments after death were in existence in England and on the Continent, but beginning with the twelfth century, such works greatly multiplied. The vision as a device was later adapted to allegory and love themes as in the *Roman de la Rose* and teaching instruments as in *Piers Ploughman.*[1] Concern here is with the vision in its earlier form, that is, as a vision of the otherworld or the afterlife.

The major medieval concepts of the otherworld have been classified into two broad categories, Eastern or Oriental and Celtic.[2] Distinctly Celtic are the journey or voyage (as opposed to the Eastern ascension in a dream, coma, or other type of vision) to the otherworld, which may be misty lands under the waves, island paradises—both usually in the West—or underground palaces in fairy mounds. Celtic also is the appearance of a fairy mistress who, with a golden or silver branch, lures the mortal hero away to her land, as in the *Voyage of Bran.* The silver branch or bough is a token for admission to the Celtic otherworld. The branch—sometimes a silver apple—brought to the king or his son before he

[1] Good translations of these works are Guillaume de Lorris and Jean de Meun, *The Romance of the Rose,* trans. Harry W. Robbins, ed. Charles W. Dunn (New York, 1962); and William Langland, *Piers Ploughman,* trans. J. F. Goodridge (Baltimore, 1959).

[2] Howard Rollin Patch, "Some Elements in Mediaeval Descriptions of the Otherworld," *PMLA,* n.s., 26 (1918), 601–43; and Patch, *The Other World According to Descriptions in Medieval Literature* (Cambridge, Mass., 1950). My discussion of Celtic and Oriental elements follows Patch.

mates with the queen of Elysium relates to the king's life; if he loses it, he loses his life. When the hero wishes to return to the real world, he is permitted to do so, but cautioned not to set foot on dry land or he will immediately turn to dust—for what has seemed to him to be a few months or years turns out to have been centuries.[3]

Distinctly Oriental motifs include an ascent to heaven, the location of the earthly paradise in the East (as opposed to the Celtic West) on a holy mountain, and a water barrier spanned by a bridge. The setting of the earthly paradise on a mountain is in sharp contrast to the Celtic otherworld on an island or inside a hill. The Oriental river is usually a roaring, ugly, often fiery torrent which a knight must cross by means of a bridge, *al-sirāṭ*, also referred to as the "soul bridge" over which souls must pass after death and which extends over hell to the earthly paradise. It is "finer than a hair and sharper than the edge of a sword or razor"; the righteous find it wide enough to cross, while for sinners it is impossible. The soul bridge is pre-Islamic, having been taken over in Islamic (but not Qurʾānic) tradition from an earlier Persian and originally Hindu concept, and is generally thought to have come to Europe through Islamic tradition.[4] The river and the bridge are obviously not in any way related to Celtic journeys to lands under the waves or beyond the mist or to island paradises.[5] These classifications were based on Irish voyages and Irish and European visions of the otherworld. Such classification of the otherworld traditions in vision literature also has application to the medieval romances, which contain a great amount of material drawn from otherworld voyage and vision traditions. Much of the otherworld detail in Arthurian romance, for example, was absorbed from Oriental as well as Celtic sources.[6]

3 For a fuller discussion, see Eleanor Hull, "The Silver Bough in Irish Legend," *Folk-Lore*, 12 (1901), 431–45; and Arthur Bernard Cook, "The European Sky-God," *Folk-Lore*, 17 (1906), 141–73.

4 See Géza Róheim, *Animism, Magic, and the Divine King* (London, 1930), pp. 39–40.

5 Patch, "Mediaeval Descriptions of the Otherworld," p. 634.

6 Patch, *The Other World*, p. 230; and "Mediaeval Descriptions of the Otherworld," p. 642. The data on visions in the European tradition which follows is, except where otherwise noted, from Patch, *The Other World*, pp. 101, 104–105, 107, 110–11, 124–25.

The European Tradition

Early Latin visions. The visions of *Furseus* and *Drihthelm,* ascribed to the seventh century, are recorded in Bede's *Ecclesiastical History.* Lofty mountains appear in *Drihthelm* and again in the *Vision of the Monk of Wenlok*[7] of the early eighth century, but the mountains are not locations for the earthly paradise. A form of the Oriental *sirāṭ* or soul bridge has been noted in *Wenlok,* where it occurs as a piece of timber over a boiling, flaming river. Mountains appear again in the *Vision of Wettin* (early ninth century) and in the *Vision of the Monk of Evesham* (ca. 1200), the latter following *Drihthelm* fairly closely, and the former containing the fiery stream of *Wenlok.* Thus, while these visions contain Oriental motifs, the motifs are not markedly Islamic.

Later Latin and vernacular visions. In the later visions, most of which predate Dante's *Commedia,* the *sirāṭ* and the river come to resemble those in Islamic visions. Further, the suiting of the punishments of hell to the sin to be expiated or to the part of the body with which it was committed and the placement of the earthly paradise on a mountain, elements not characteristic of the earlier visions, become prominent. In the *Vision of Adamnán,* for example, punishments are devised according to the sin committed. Further, the classifications of punishments in *Thurcil, Alberic, Saint Patrick's Purgatory,* and *Tundale* appear to be of Islamic derivation.[8]

The Irish *Vision of Adamnán,* which first appears in the eleventh-century *Book of the Dun Cow,* is a precursor of Dante in that the punishments in Adamnán's hell fit the crimes.[9] It includes an enormous bridge over hell, which is wide or narrow according to the virtue of the traveler, typical of an Islamic description of the bridge. Admittedly *Adamnán* is early, but not too early for its author to have had some contact with the Eastern

[7] *Drihthelm* and *Wenlok* are discussed in Ernest J. Becker, *A Contribution to the Comparative Study of the Medieval Visions of Heaven and Hell, with Special Reference to the Middle-English Versions* (Baltimore, 1899), pp. 13, 95.

[8] Miguel Asín Palacios, *Islam and the Divine Comedy,* pp. 186–93.

[9] Myles Dillon, *Early Irish Literature* (Chicago, 1948), p. 137, points this out.

ideas contained in it, ideas which, as several critics have shown, could not be derived from Celtic tradition.

In two Continental visions of the thirteenth century, the river and bridge are noticeably Islamic in their details. The Spanish *Vida de Santo Domingo de Silas* of Gonzalo de Berceo contains a terrible roaring river with a slippery bridge of glass; and the "Vision of the Third Robber" in the *Fioretti* of Saint Francis contains a bridge which is frail, slippery, and narrow, over a river of beasts, monsters, and stench. Another Continental vision is that of *Alberic,* written in Italy in the late twelfth or thirteenth century. In *Alberic,* the visionary is an eight-year-old child whose guides are Peter and two angels; he sleeps for nine days and has a vision in which he is shown the torments of hell followed by the rewards of paradise. The bridge over hell in this vision, like the *sirāṭ,* becomes wide or narrow according to the traveler. There are several similarities between *Alberic* and the *Divina Commedia,* including the placing of the earthly paradise on a high plain near heaven.

The development of Oriental motifs in Continental visions is paralleled in those visions written in England.[10] In the Latin *Vision of Thurcil* (ca. 1206), the dreamer is a husbandman whose soul leaves his body and is guided by Saint Julian through hell and paradise. There is a bridge of nails and spikes (a unique description of the bridge) to the Mount of Joy, atop which is the earthly paradise with its fountain, fruits, and the Tree of Life beneath which Adam sits. The use of three judges and a pair of scales to weigh souls in this vision has been noticed as a survival of Egyptian Judgment.[11]

There were three visions of hell and paradise in Middle English prior to 1400. One of these, the *Vision of Saint Paul,* was originally known in Greek in the fourth century and appeared in Latin in the sixth century. It enjoyed a wide popularity in Eng-

[10] Details and outlines of the English visions are taken from John Edwin Wells, *A Manual of the Writings in Middle English, 1050–1400,* pp. 332–36; from W. L. Renwick and Harold Orton, eds., *The Beginnings of English Literature to Skelton 1509,* 3rd ed., rev. (London, 1966), pp. 365–76; and from Becker, *Medieval Visions of Heaven and Hell,* pp. 18, 74–78, 82.

[11] Becker, *Medieval Visions of Heaven and Hell,* p. 16.

land and Europe, with six versions extant in Middle English and five in French. It was the earliest Christian vision to use the *sirāṭ*. Another, *Saint Patrick's Purgatory*, dating perhaps from the twelfth century (the earliest Middle-English manuscripts are late thirteenth century), exists in Latin and French versions as well as Middle English. The hero Owayn Miles enters the underworld through a cavern, typical of Celtic journeys to the otherworld. Over an Oriental type of torrent of burning sulphur is a narrow, slippery bridge which broadens with every step across it stretching from purgatory to the earthly paradise. The bridge is identical with the Islamic *sirāṭ* in detail and in position, and, actually, only the setting in *Saint Patrick's Purgatory* is Irish.[12] This vision was, incidentally, known to Froissart and Marie de France.[13]

The *Vision of Tundale* was evidently one of the most popular of the medieval visions, judging from the number of extant manuscripts of it. The prologue gives its date of composition as 1149 and its author as an Irish monk, but the English edition dates from no earlier than 1400, with several fifteenth-century manuscripts. Editions of it are found in many languages; between the twelfth and fifteenth centuries are to be found some fifty-four Latin texts. Tundale, a rich, wicked Irishman, is struck unconscious at a meal. He has a vision of hell and its torments and repents; he then has to take a cow across a bridge a hand's-breadth wide, over the stinking abyss of hell to the earthly paradise. Much of *Tundale*'s imagery in hell and paradise belongs to a common stock of such imagery found in Christian and Islamic visions, but it is very graphically developed in *Tundale*. Asín Palacios, in his discussion of this vision, suggests its pre-Latin origin:

> The author of the Latin version, an Irish monk, states that he composed it from a text written in a barbarous tongue. Was this an Arabic text? The great number of Moslem features, several of them very striking, would seem to suggest it.[14]

It is an intriguing possibility. Reference to a barbarous or heathen tongue usually did mean Arabic.

12 *Ibid.*, p. 93; Dillon, *Early Irish Literature*, p. 133.
13 Patch, *The Other World*, p. 114.
14 Asín Palacios, *Islam and the Divine Comedy*, p. 186.

In two other major medieval eschatological works, the *Commedia* of Dante and the fourteenth-century Middle-English vision *Pearl,* with the introduction of a lost beloved female as a guide through paradise, appears a tradition which the Islamic *Ṣūfīs* had developed from the ninth century. The female guide as conceived by the Islamic mystics and as found in *Pearl* and Dante's *Paradiso* in no way resembles the Celtic fairy mistress who lures mortal heroes into a never-never land, but rather fills the role played in other Christian visions by various saints and angels in guiding and instructing the dreamer. Indeed,

> To arrange, as the climax of a journey to the regions beyond the grave, the meeting of the pilgrim with his lost Beloved is a poetic conceit that will in vain be sought for in any of the Christian precursors of the *Divine Comedy*.[15]

The Islamic Tradition

The Qurʾān and Ḥadīths. The first translation of the *Qurʾān,* along with other materials, into Latin by Robert of Ketton was mentioned in an earlier chapter. Robert's work was apparently known to others besides Peter the Venerable who commissioned it; his *Qurʾān* had an annotator, and the Irish Franciscan pilgrim Simon Simeon quoted from Robert's translation.[16] The preface to it is reproduced in Migne's *Patrologiae.* It is unfortunate that Robert did not identify, or rather, omitted in his preface the source of the traditions which he also translated.

The *Ḥadīths,* "news" or traditions, related to the *Qurʾān* had an approximate parallel in Christianity in the writings of the earliest Christians. They can be defined as sayings of the Prophet Muḥammad, which were memorized and quoted from one person to another during his lifetime and then recorded in later centuries.[17] The verification of the authenticity of these sayings be-

[15] *Ibid.*, p. 128.

[16] Norman Daniel, *Islam and the West: The Making of an Image* (Edinburgh, 1962), pp. 153, 171. For the preface to Robert of Ketton's work, see Jacques Paul Migne, ed., *Patrologiae Cursus Completus, Series Latina,* CLXXXIX (Paris, 1890), Col. 659.

[17] Najib Ullah, *Islamic Literature: An Introductory History with Selections* (New York, 1963), p. 27.

came a science. One of the most famous collectors of *Ḥadīths* was Bukhārī (810–70), whose collection of traditions is entitled *al-Ṣaḥiḥ, The Genuine*. Bukhārī also wrote one of the best-known commentaries on the *Qur'ān*. His work was known in Spain; a second translation of the *Qur'ān* into Latin was done in the late twelfth century by Mark of Toledo, a church deacon, who quotes from Bukhārī (as "Bohari") on the *Qur'ān*.[18]

Sufism. The presence of the *Qur'ān* and *Ḥadīths* in Spain and the contacts of medieval Europe with Spain would not perhaps of themselves be sufficient to account for the development of Islamic motifs in European vision literature from the twelfth through the fifteenth centuries. Such development suggests in several respects contact with Sufism, Islamic mysticism.

The term *Ṣūfī* is derived from the word for wool, *Ṣūf*; *Ṣūfīs* were ascetics clad in wool, just as the name for the Capuchin monks was derived from the hood (*cappuccio*) they wore.[19] Sufism was, along with other aspects of Islam. widespread in Spain. The mysticism of any major monotheistic religion, as the mystics in general renounce the world to seek union with the Deity, tends to resemble that of another, no matter how different the separate dogmas of the two religions may be. And it may be that it was through the *Ṣūfī* mysticism of Spain that Christianity and Islam found their closest affinities in the Middle Ages.

The four principal foreign sources of Sufism are Christianity, Neo-Platonism, Gnosticism, and Indian asceticism and religious philosophy; the *Ṣūfī* brotherhood had gradually developed, by the tenth century, into a monastic system and a school for saints.[20] Among the goals of Sufism are isolation from the material world and union with the godhead. Members of the brotherhood are expected to travel and have an obligation to teach others their experiences. Their beliefs and teachings, correlated with Arabic and Persian astronomy, astrology, and other sciences, are found

[18] Daniel, *Islam and the West*, pp. 28–29.

[19] Reynold A. Nicholson, *A Literary History of the Arabs*, p. 228.

[20] *Ibid.*, pp. 393 ff.; see also "Ikhwān al-Ṣafā," in *The Encyclopedia of Islam*, ed. M. Th. Houtsma, T. W. Arnold, and others, II (London, 1927), 459–60. (A new edition of *The Encyclopedia of Islam* is now in process and some volumes have been published.)

in the fifty-two *Epistles*, which Maslamah of Madrid brought into Spain from the East before 1006. Ghazzālī was instrumental in gaining the acceptance of Sufism by orthodoxy, and Ibn-ᶜArabī, who studied under Ghazzālī in his travels in the East, is considered, along with Ghazzālī, one of the greatest of the *Ṣūfī* mystics. Ibn-Masarra (883–931), the first of the Spanish-Arab scholars to go east to study, had introduced Sufism into Spain, along with Neo-Platonism and asceticism, and influenced later Spanish-Arab philosophers such as Ibn-Ḥazm and Ibn-ᶜArabī.[21]

Sufism has relevance to Western literature in six respects: (1) the development of a pre-Islamic figure known as al-Khaḍir, "the Green One," into a representative of the Divinity; (2) the elaboration of the legend of the ascension of Muḥammad with its similarities to later Christian works, including those of Dante; (3) the placement of the earthly paradise on a mountain; (4) the detailing of an astronomical paradise and corresponding structuring of hell and its punishments; (5) the use of mystical, erotic poetry to describe allegorically the experience of union with God; and (6) the use of a woman as the beloved representing God and as a guide and instructor along the path to union with God.

Khaḍir. "The Green One," al-Khaḍir, incorporated into Islam from ancient Persian legends, has been identified with Elijah, Saint George, Osiris, a sea demon, a patron saint of mariners, and a figure from primitive vegetation myths.[22] Found in the *Qur'ān* as an unnamed guide and instructor of Moses (where he is identified by Bukhārī as Khaḍir), in Arabic poetry in Spain (as was seen in the preceding chapter), in legends of Alexander the Great, in the *Arabian Nights*, and though not named, possibly in the *Gesta Romanorum*, he is one of the most widely known figures in Islam. He was also very important among the *Ṣūfī* visionaries. To

21 See Miguel Cruz Hernández, *Historia de la filosofía española: Filosofía hispano-musulmana* (Madrid, 1957), pp. 221–38; and Miguel Asín Palacios, "Abenmasarra y su escuela," *Discurso de recepción* (Madrid, 1914).

22 "Khaḍir," *Encyclopedia of Religion and Ethics*, VII, 693–95; "al-Khaḍir," *The Encyclopedia of Islam*, II, 861–65; and "al-Khaḍir," *Shorter Encyclopedia of Islam*, ed. H. A. R. Gibb and J. H. Kramers (Leiden, 1965), pp. 232–35. Shaheer Nazi, "The Identification of al-Khidr," *The Muslim Digest*, 21 (November, 1970), 99–100, mentions his confusion with Saint George but sheds no new light (and very little old light) on the subject of Khaḍir's origins.

the *Ṣūfīs*, to be regarded as a disciple of Khaḍir involved having Khaḍir as an unearthly spiritual guide symbolized by receiving a mantle from him and having a personal and immediate bond with the Creator. Khaḍir was an invisible, spiritual master to those destined to achieve a direct relationship with God.[23] Ibn-ᶜArabī, in Book I of his *al-Futūḥāt al-Makkiyya* (*Meccan Revelations*), relates two instances of contact with Khaḍir, the first instance occurring in his youth when he met a stranger in Seville. He did not realize until later that the man he had met was Khaḍir, who often appears as a mysterious stranger. The second instance related in the *Futūḥāt* took place in 1204, in a garden in Mosul, where Ibn-ᶜArabī was invested with the mantle of Khaḍir by a friend who had, in turn, received it from Khaḍir himself. He relates another meeting with Khaḍir as a mysterious stranger in his *Rūh al-Quds*.[24]

The ascension. The story of the ascension of Muḥammad developed from the first verse of *Sura* 17 of the *Qurʾān*, referring to Muḥammad's dream in which he was carried to the Dome of the Rock in Jerusalem from Mecca, by Būrāgh under the guidance of the archangel Gabriel. A group of legends, for which the *Ṣūfīs* were largely responsible, grew up around the passage. Three cycles of the legend have been distinguished. Cycle 1, dating from the ninth century, is the *isrā* or journey to Jerusalem which developed from six *Ḥadīths* on Muḥammad's journey in the *Qurʾān*. Cycle 2 is older than the ninth century and is mentioned by Bukhārī, among others. This is the *miᶜrāj* or ascension of Muḥammad in which he is guided by Gabriel to the heavens where he is shown views of paradise and hell. Cycle 3 is a combination of the first two. The *Ṣūfīs* took up the *miᶜrāj* idea to generalize on the soul's ascent to God, and the *miᶜrāj* is found in Ghazzālī and Ibn-ᶜArabī.[25]

The *Livre de Leschiele Mahomet*, which was translated from

23 Henry Corbin, *Creative Imagination in the Ṣufism of Ibn-ᶜArabī*, trans. Ralph Manheim (Princeton, 1969), pp. 54–55. The two instances which follow appear on pp. 63–64 in Corbin.

24 See Ibn-ᶜArabī, *Sufis of Andalusia: The Rūh al-Quds and al-Durrat al-Fākhirah*, trans. R. W. J. Austin (London, 1971).

25 Asín Palacios, *Islam and the Divine Comedy*, pp. 4–18, 45.

Arabic into Castilian and thence into Old French in 1264, is of the third cycle. Its prologue mentions the Arabic *miʿrāj* as *"halmacreig."* In this vision, Muḥammad is awakened from sleep by Gabriel and taken to Jerusalem where he ascends by a ladder through the astronomically structured heavens. Gabriel, his guide and instructor, leaves him at the highest heaven. This episode is repeated twice, with a description of the earthly paradise atop the holy mountain between. Then, before returning to Mecca, Muḥammad is shown hell, with its divisions of torments, the weighing of souls, and the bridge *al-sirāṭ* over hell. The story of Muḥammad's ascension was well known in Spain, and Christians as well as Muslims were familiar with it. Archbishop Rodrigo Jiménez de Rada of Toledo, in that portion of his *Historia Arabum* dealing with the life of Muḥammad, gives a short version of the third cycle of the legend, and San Pedro Pascual, Bishop of Jaén, while in captivity in Granada, 1298–1300, used the vision, drawn from Islamic sources, in his refutation of Islam.[26]

The earthly paradise. The placement of the earthly paradise atop a mountain in the East, as it appears in later Christian visions, had been made popular through the *Ṣūfī Epistles.* (It was one of the Christian motifs taken over and elaborated by Islam.) It is described in one of the *Epistles* as a garden with lush, sensuous imagery.[27] Similar descriptions are to be found in the ascension legends (including the *Livre de Leschiele Mahomet,* in Ibn-ʿArabī's *Futūḥāt,* in Dante's *Commedia,* and in the Middle-English *Pearl.*

In Islam as in Christianity, the earthly paradise was sometimes confused with the heavenly one. The idea of two heavens, described in detail in the *Futūḥāt* and found also in Ghazzālī and Ibn-Rushd, involves a material and an ideal paradise. In the *Futūḥāt,* "There are two heavens—the one sensible; and the other, ideal. In the one, both the animal spirits and the rational souls enjoy bliss; in the other, the rational souls alone. The latter paradise is the heaven of knowledge and intuition." Ibn-ʿArabī

26 Evelyn S. Procter, *Alfonso X of Castile,* pp. 17–20.

27 A more complete description appears in Asín Palacios, *Islam and the Divine Comedy,* p. 123.

goes on to explain: "God has depicted paradise in accordance with the different degrees of man's understanding." The same idea on the double nature of paradise is repeated by Raymond Lull in *Liber de Gentili* and Raymond Martín in *Explanatio Simboli*, with the latter even quoting from Ghazzālī.[28]

The astronomical paradise. The astronomical heavens of paradise seem to have been related to the *Ṣūfī* mystical treatment of astronomy and astrology in the *Epistles*. Characteristic of Islamic ascension legends, such as the *Livre de Leschiele Mahomet* and that in the *Futūḥāt*, was a structuring of the seven heavens astronomically and a corresponding structuring of hell in which punishments are devised at each level appropriate to the sin or to the part of the body responsible for a particular sin. The parallels in geography, imagery, and structure, between the paradise and hell in Ibn-ᶜArabī's *Futūḥāt* and those of Dante's *Commedia* of a century later, are too close to be attributed to mere coincidence. Dante is known to have been familiar with various astronomical works translated into Latin in Spain and Sicily in the eleventh and twelfth centuries. It is not unlikely, with such works as the *Livre de Leschiele Mahomet* also available, that he could have come into contact, at least indirectly, with some of the Islamic mystical treatments of the afterlife.

Erotic poetry. Love poetry was an important means of expressing Sufism. Such poetry, as used by eleventh-century Spanish poets, was characterized by erotic and bacchic terminology with allegorical meanings.[29] It employed many of the concepts later associated with the courtly-love rhetoric of the troubadours from whom it seems to have been appropriated in the religious poetry of the Franciscans and others. Ibn-ᶜArabī was one of many Arab writers known for such mystical poetry. He too had his Beatrice, in this case named Niḍām ᶜAin al-Shams whom he had met in Mecca, and he too, like Dante, found it necessary to compose a commentary on his mystical odes in order to convince critics of

28 *Ibid.*, pp. 138–40. The information and translation from the *Futūḥāt* are Asín Palacios'.

29 See Arthur J. Arberry, *Sufism: An Account of the Mystics of Islam* (London, 1950), pp. 61–63; and Robert S. Briffault, *The Troubadours*, pp. 26; 228, *n.* 5.

their true meaning as religious allegory rather than sensuous love poems.[30]

The beloved as guide. Closely related to the love poetry of the *Ṣūfīs* was their use in vision literature of a female guide, sometimes a lost beloved, as a promised bride in the life to come and as an instructor and a means of holy inspiration. In Christian religious literature of the Middle Ages, the woman symbolized the sinful and the forbidden. But in the Arabic religious literature, woman was an incentive for purity and godliness.[31] The latter was the case with Ibn-ᶜArabī's Niḍām and later with Dante's Beatrice and the *Pearl*-poet's Pearl. The heavenly bride was a prominent feature in Islamic visions of the afterlife.

The *Ṣūfī* maiden as guide and adviser to a pilgrim in the other world developed from a relatively minor passage in the *Qurʾān*, that referring to Muḥammad's *isrā* (nocturnal journey) and the *miᶜrāj* (ascension) to the spheres of the afterlife. The Qurʾānic passage reads: "Glory to Him Who carried His servant by night from the Sacred Mosque to the Remote Mosque [from the mosque at Mecca to that of the Dome of the Rock at Jerusalem], whose precincts We blessed, that We might show him of Our signs."[32] It was from this very short verse and its related *Ḥadīths* that the three cycles or groups of legends of the *isrā* and *miᶜrāj* of Muḥammad were developed. The heavenly maiden as a guide first appears in eighth-century commentaries on the verse, and by the tenth century she had become quite prominent in *Ṣūfī* visions of the afterlife. There is a long list of Islamic mystics of the ninth century through the eleventh century who, in visions, see a heavenly maiden who promises the visionary she is to be his bride in paradise, and her dowry is that he renounce the world and earthly loves and keep his soul unspotted.[33] In Ghazzālī's *al-*

[30] Reynold A. Nicholson, "Mysticism," in *The Legacy of Islam*, ed. Arnold and Guillaume, p. 227. See also R. W. J. Austin's discussion in *Sufis of Andalusia*, pp. 36–43.

[31] Américo Castro, *The Structure of Spanish History*, p. 345.

[32] Maulānā Muḥammad ᶜAlī, trans. and ed., *The Holy Qurʾān: Arabic Text, Translation, and Commentary*, rev. ed. (Lahore, Pakistan, 1951), Pt. 4, *Sura* 17, v. 1. All citations to the *Qurʾān* are to this edition.

[33] Asín Palacios cites these in *Islam and the Divine Comedy*, pp. 60, 131–32.

Durra al-Fākhira, The Precious Pearl, an eschatological treatise on death. Judgment Day, and rewards and punishments to be meted out, the heavenly maiden appears to the virtuous dead man in the tomb as the personification of his good deeds to be his companion until Judgment Day.[34] The Islamic bride is no merely sensuous "houri," a common misconception, and she is quite different from the Celtic fairy mistress who lures the hero to the otherworld as her lover. The meeting of Beatrice and Dante, her chastising him for his sins, and her furnishing solutions to questions of theology were all foreign and unprecedented in medieval Christianity, but they had earlier parallels in the Islamic tradition.[35] These three elements also reappear in the Middle-English *Pearl.*

Conclusion

From an early date the *Ṣūfīs* were active in medieval Spain. The *Epistles,* the compendium of the beliefs of the brotherhood, had been brought into Spain in the tenth century; the works of Ghazzālī were known and partially translated in Spain; and one of the greatest of the Islamic mystics, Ibn-ᶜArabī, was a Spaniard. The *Ṣūfīs* were instrumental in developing from a single verse in the *Qurʾān* a group of legends concerning the ascension of Muḥammad to paradise where he is shown views of both the paradise and the hell of the afterlife. Characteristic of *Ṣūfī* visions was the *sirāṭ,* soul bridge, extending over the abyss or river of hell to the earthly paradise which was situated atop a holy, inaccessible mountain in the East; the astronomical division of the heavens of paradise with a similar layering of hell; and the establishment of tortures of hell appropriate to the sins committed. Another recurring motif in *Ṣūfī* visions was the use of a promised bride as an incentive to a pure life on earth and as an instructor in theology and in the will of God.

The Christian visions of the afterlife which proliferated from

34 Abū-Ḥāmid al-Ghazzālī, *al-Durra al-Fākhira, La Perle précieuse,* trans. Lucien Gautier (Geneva, 1878). Both the Arabic original and the French translation are included in Gautier's edition. This is an interesting work which should be translated into English.

35 Asín Palacios, *Islam and the Divine Comedy,* pp. 129–30.

around the twelfth century reflect earlier, more primitive Oriental motifs involving the bridge, mountains, and river, but in visions of the twelfth through the fifteenth centuries, the forms become more and more Islamic in detail. In addition, in Dante and in the *Pearl*-poet, is to be found a female heavenly beloved as guide and instructor, a personage who has absolutely no Christian predecessors but who has a long and full history among Islamic *Ṣūfī* visionaries and poets.

In Spain during the translation period, many works of a religious as well as of a scientific and philosophical nature were translated into Latin. In addition to the *Qur'ān*, twice translated into Latin in the twelfth century, were other treatises on Islam, with the legend of the ascension of Muḥammad having been translated into Castilian and Old French in the thirteenth century. Several Spanish-Christian writers, even martyrs, quoted from Islamic and *Ṣūfī* works, including versions of the ascension. There is a good possibility, then, that the marked Islamic development of Oriental motifs in Christian visions of the afterlife and the appearance of new, definitely Islamic ones, in visions and in the works of later Christian poets could have been a result of European contact with Arabic lore in Spain and Sicily concurrent with, and as a result of, the translation of Eastern learning into Latin in the twelfth century.

Let us see now how a recognition of possibly Arabic and Islamic motifs in the Middle-English *Pearl* affects an explication of the poem. It is a work which has not hitherto been associated, even remotely, with Spanish-Arabic materials.

PART II—THE MIDDLE-ENGLISH *PEARL*

Background

In a unique manuscript (Cotton Nero A.X) dating from around 1400, in the Northwest-Midland dialect, occur the four poems *Pearl, Purity* (or *Cleanness*), *Patience*, and *Sir Gawain and the Green Knight*, all written in the same scribal hand and generally considered to date from the third quarter of the fourteenth century and to have been the works of one author whose identity is not known. Another poem, *Saint Erkenwald,* which appears in Harley Manuscript 1150, in late-fifteenth-century script, was at one time attributed to the same poet, but Larry Benson has convincingly dismissed it from among the *Pearl*-poet's works.[36] There are no titles to the poems in the Cotton manuscript which includes twelve somewhat crude illustrations, four for *Pearl,* two each for *Purity* and *Patience,* and four for *Sir Gawain and the Green Knight. Sir Gawain* was first edited for the Early English Text Society in 1864 by Richard Morris, who also edited the first edition of the other three poems; and a facsimile of the manuscript was prepared by Sir Israel Gollancz in 1923.[37] The facsimile is becoming of increasing value since portions of the original manuscript have, since its discovery, become almost illegible.

Although there is a complete lack of clues to identify the author of the four poems, various speculations have been made as to his identity based on internal and external evidence of *Pearl* and *Sir Gawain.* Among suggestions for his identity are "Huchown of the Awle Ryale" mentioned by Wyntoun in his chronicle of 1390; Ralph Strode, a name which seems to apply to three men, a logician at Oxford, a poet at Merton College around 1360, and a Sergeant of London (d. 1387); and Hugh de Mascy, a pearl fancier at the court of Edward III who gave two thousand pearls to his daughter Margaret at her marriage to the Earl of Pembroke and whose granddaughter died in infancy.[38] Each of these proposed identifications is based on *Pearl;* needless to say, none of them completely satisfies the conditions of the poem. They are

[36] See Larry D. Benson, "The Authorship of *St. Erkenwald,*" *Journal of English and Germanic Philology,* 14 (1965), 393–405.

[37] *Early English Alliterative Poems,* ed. Richard Morris, *Early English Text Society,* 1 (1864); *Sir Gawayne and the Green Knight: An Alliterative Romance-Poem,* ed. Richard Morris, *Early English Text Society,* 4 (1864); and *Pearl, Cleanness, Patience and Sir Gawain,* ed. Israel Gollancz, *Early English Text Society,* 162, (1931). There is also a 1971 reprint of this facsimile. For a good general study of all four poems which is not as basic as that of Margaret Williams (note 38 below), see Charles Moorman, *The Pearl-Poet,* Twayne's English Authors Series, No. 64 (New York, 1968).

[38] Margaret Williams, trans., *The Pearl-Poet: His Complete Works* (New York, 1970), pp. 11–13.

highly speculative, and without further evidence they are not worthy of serious consideration.

Several attempts have also been made to find a clue to the poet's identity by linking him with the green knight in *Sir Gawain* as a living person. Among these proposals are two Englishmen and two Frenchmen. One of the Englishmen was Ralph Holmes, surnamed the "Green Squire," a follower of the Black Prince mentioned in Froissart's chronicle as having been slain along with Pedro I of Spain in 1369. The other was a West-Midlands man, Simon Newton, also known as "Scudifer Viridis," who was in Avignon from 1365 to 1366. The two Frenchmen were Amadeus VI, Count of Savoy, called "il conte verde," who dressed in green for tournaments, and Enguerrant, Sire de Coucy.[39] Such attempts are even more speculative than those based on *Pearl*. It is not likely that a poet in the fourteenth century would have given attributes such as green skin and red eyes to a man who represented his patron or a noble he sought to impress favorably or to compliment. It would be more profitable and more in keeping with the tone and descriptive content of *Sir Gawain* to look for the green knight among legendary and fantastic figures in medieval folklore. The poet of the four poems will probably never be known, unless additional evidence outside of the poems which links him with them is uncovered.

It has been established with little doubt, however, that the poems were probably written by the same author, through the many thematic and philological links among them.[40] All four poems belong to the alliterative tradition. *Purity* and *Patience* are made up of unrimed alliterative lines, apparently in quatrains, judging from scribal marks appearing in the margin every

39 *Ibid.*, p. 52; S. R. T. O. D'Ardenne, "The Green Count and *Sir Gawain and the Green Knight*," *Review of English Studies*, n.s., 10 (1959), 113–14; J. R. L. Highfield, "The Green Squire," *Medium Ævum*, 22 (1953), 18–23; and Henry Lyttleton Savage, *The Gawain-Poet: Studies in His Personality and Background* (Chapel Hill, 1956), pp. 102 ff.

40 The links among the poems are summarized by Hartley Bateson, ed., *Patience: A West-Midland Poem of the Fourteenth Century* (Manchester, England, 1912). See also J. J. Anderson, ed., *Patience* (Manchester, England, 1972); and Robert J. Menner, ed., *Purity: A Middle English Poem, Yale Studies in English*, 61 (1970).

four lines which are still visible in the facsimile edition. *Pearl,* with its elaborate stanzaic structure and rime scheme, presents a complete fusion of the English alliterative tradition with French (including Provençal) prosody, and *Sir Gawain* superimposes the end-rimed short line upon alliterative verses at the end of each strophe. With the latter two works, especially with *Pearl,* the poet displays a remarkable ability to work within both traditions. His works are usually grouped with others of the so-called "alliterative revival" (more accurately, "survival") of the fourteenth century, represented by such alliterative works as the *Wars of Alexander, William of Palerne, Joseph of Arimathie,* and by the later *Winner and Waster, Parliament of the Three Ages,* and *Awntyrs of Arthure.* These poems, as well as the works of the *Pearl*-poet and others, represent not so much an attempt to return to a native English prosody as, rather, an attempt on the part of the poets of the North and North-Midlands to assert a native tradition that had not completely died out in spite of the importation of end rime and the appearance of French and Provençal forms in English verse. Even Chaucer's works illustrate the survival of the alliterative tradition. When, in the "Parson's Prologue," the Parson remarks,

> But trusteth wel, I am a Southren man.
> I kan nat geeste 'rum, ram, ruf,' by lettre (ll. 42–43),

he is referring to the alliterative tradition which was more prominent in the northern districts. And yet in *The Canterbury Tales,* written by that "Southren man," many alliterative lines can be cited with three alliterating consonants, and a few with four, particularly in the "Knight's Tale." In fact, there are sufficient alliterative (although syllabic and rimed) lines in Chaucer's works to suggest that while he may not have desired to work within that tradition, he was apparently thoroughly familiar with it.

The dialect of the *Pearl*-poet, that of the Northwest Midlands, lent itself more readily to alliteration than did the London English of Chaucer's day, from which modern English descended. There has been a suggestion that the poet may have chosen "such an obscure dialect" for his works because he had been influenced by Dante who defended the writing of poetry in the native speech in his *Convivio*.[41] "Obscure" is an unfortunate word, since the dialect in which these poems were written was no doubt current at the time of their composition. It is almost certain that *Sir Gawain*, for example, was designed for recitation, which would of course have been useless if the language had been obscure to its audience.

Even though the *Pearl*-poet was working within native English poetic tradition, however, his poems display knowledge or familiarity with a large quantity and great variety of materials. Among the works which the author apparently knew, as evidenced from his writings, are the Vulgate Bible; the *Roman de la Rose*; alliterative romances; Dante's *Commedia, Vita Nuova*, and *Convivio*; Boccaccio's "Olympia"; Chaucer's *Book of the Duchess* and *Legend of Good Women*; the French version of *Mandeville's Travels; Cursor Mundi*; Andreas Capellanus' *De Arte Honesti Amandi*; lapidaries; legends of the Jews; Bishop Bradwardine's *De Causa Dei Contra Pelagium*; Albertus Magnus' *De Laudibus Beatae Mariae*; Chrétien de Troyes' *Le Livre de Caradoc; Perlesvaus*; and other French romances, including the Arthurian Vulgate Cycle of grail romances.[42] And the list above is not complete. Apparently then, while his works are not characterized by the mercantile, middle-class attitudes in Chaucer's *Canterbury Tales* or by London speech, he was familiar with many of the works also known to Chaucer, Gower, and to other contemporaries of his, and he shared the broad medieval heritage of the more cosmopolitan poets of the fourteenth century.

The author of the *Pearl* and *Sir Gawain and the Green Knight* has thus, with the vast variety of materials which he brings together, provided posterity with two of the most enigmatic poems in the Middle-English period, and, in fact, judging from the

41 G. H. Gerould, "The Gawain-Poet and Dante: A Conjecture," *PMLA*, 51 (1936), 31–36.

42 These are listed, with others, by Margaret Williams, trans., *The Pearl-Poet*, pp. 14–15. Coolidge Otis Chapman, in "The Musical Training of the *Pearl* Poet," *PMLA*, 46 (1931), 177–81, suggests that the poet was educated in a chorister's school.

voluminous critical commentary which both works have elicited, perhaps in the entire English language. With regard to *Pearl,* problems arise as to whether it is elegiacal or allegorical, whether it is a dream vision of a beloved maiden or an eschatological treatise, and whether its theology is orthodox Catholic or Pelagian. The exact symbolic significance of the *Pearl* is also a matter for difference of opinion since the pearl was a traditional Christian symbol for purity, life, the soul, heavenly saints, heavenly grace, good works of the soul, Christ, and Mary. The poet in the *Pearl* has assembled a myriad of motifs in the structure and eschatology of the poem from a number of unrelated sources, and, as a result, no single allegorical interpretation of the *Pearl* has proven entirely satisfactory.

Prosody—Alliteration and Rime

The verses of *Pearl* contain four lifts or stresses, and the number of unaccented syllables varies as it does in older, purely alliterative poetry. Thus, in spite of being rimed in the French tradition, the lines are not syllabic French verse. The number of alliterating consonants also varies. Sometimes all four of the lifts alliterate; sometimes only two or three of them do; and in some lines, none do.

The stanzas themselves are rimed in the pattern aBaBaBaBBcBc, a pattern also found in the York mystery plays. Some twelve plays of the York cycle, not the earliest of the cycles, use the rime scheme aBaBaBaBBcBc, but it differs from the *Pearl* in that the first eight lines are four-stress while the final four are three-stress. The earliest version of this scheme and the one closest to that in *Pearl,* in that all of its lines are four-stress, is found in the Middle-English *Gospel of Nicodemus* (ca. 1300–25), extant in several manuscripts, which served as a source for the Northern playwrights.[43] The pattern is further identifiable as an elaboration of the Provençal rime scheme aBaBBcBc.

The poem contains 101 stanzas organized into groups of five,

[43] See Edmund K. Chambers, "Medieval Drama," in *English Literature at the Close of the Middle Ages*, pp. 29–30. The York cycle and its relationship to the *Pearl* are discussed by Chambers on pp. 31–32.

except for the fifteenth group which contains six stanzas. The *c* rime within each group of five stanzas is the same; for example, *yot* and *spot* in the first stanza, *clot* and *spotte* in the second, and so forth.

In addition to a rime scheme which appears to have been adapted earlier from a Provençal one and the use of a linking rime within the stanza groups, the *Pearl* also employs the stanza-linking device of repeating a word in the last line of one stanza in the first line of the next, a device which had been employed by the troubadours and *trouvères*. Linking rime, in turn, derives from the *simṭ* (thread) of the Andalusian *muwashshaḥ* and *zajal*. Concatenation or the linking up of the beginning of a stanza with the end of the preceding one is also found in the York cycle of plays, whose relationship to the *Pearl* in this respect is suggested by E. K. Chambers. Linking appears in *Pearl* both within each group of five stanzas and among each group. For example, the word *spot* appears in the last line of stanzas two through six. In the last line of stanza six occurs the word *adubmente*, which is repeated in the first and last lines of the succeeding group of stanzas. Such links served a functional as well as an ornamental purpose in facilitating recital from memory.

Even with the addition of end rime and stanza links, however, the lines remain basically alliterative. *Pearl* thus presents an admixture of traditions, the native English alliterative line with French and Provençal end rime and stanza linking.

Genre—Elegy or Allegory

Structurally the *Pearl* is not an elegy, although its theme is elegiac. That the poet is mourning a lost girl, probably a daughter, in the first four stanzas seems hardly questionable, especially in such lines as:

> To þenke hir color so clad in clot
> O moul þou marreȝ a myry iuele
> My priuy perle wythouten spotte. (ll. 22–24)[44]

[44] All citations to the poem are to *The Pearl*, ed. Sara deFord and others (New York, 1967).

Later, she says of the stream which separates her from the narrator, "to passe þys water fre/þat may no ioyful jueler" (ll. 299–300), because it is the traditional symbol of death, the stream through which she has already passed and through which the narrator cannot yet pass to be with her in the otherworld.

Some critics have argued, however, that the poem is not elegiac but purely allegorical—they reject the interpretation that anyone is being mourned. Schofield, for example, insists that the child is an allegorical representative of purity or chastity, and that she did not exist as a real person; hence the poem is not an elegy. He cites in support of his view "her absolute lack of tenderness in her treatment of her father, her coldly stern rebukes, her never-changing austerity."[45] But her rebukes and austerity relate to the tradition of Dante and Beatrice, and to a lesser extent, to that of Boccaccio and Olympia. Beatrice's chastising of Dante could hardly be seen as proof that she never existed as a person. In the appendix of his paper, Schofield calls attention to the fact that a parallel exists between the *Pearl* and Boccaccio's eclogue "Olympia," an elegy on his five-year-old daughter Violante, a parallel which tends to disprove his thesis. The Pearl in the poem is obviously a representative of purity, but that does not, in turn, cancel out the elegiac theme.

R. M. Garrett rejects the elegiac theme for an allegory of the Eucharist, in which the poet is gazing at the elevated Host in the hands of a priest, and Sister M. Madeleva rejects it for an allegory of the poet's loss of touch with God and consequently reads the poem as a study in spiritual dryness. She sees the grave plot as a typical monastery garden and argues further that a two-year-old (the age of Pearl at her death) cannot be in the procession of the Holy Innocents, an argument which Elizabeth Hart disproves by pointing out a similar situation in Chaucer's "Prioress' Tale" in which a seven-year-old boy joins the procession. Further, as Sister

[45] William Henry Schofield, "The Nature and Fabric of *The Pearl*," *PMLA*, 19 (1904), 201. See also Schofield's article "Symbolism, Allegory and Autobiography in *The Pearl*," *PMLA*, 24 (1909), 585–675. His allegorical reading of the *Pearl* as maidenhood is rejected by Charles G. Osgood, ed., *The Pearl: A Middle English Poem*, Belles Lettres Series (Boston, 1906), xxxiv; and by G. C. Coulton, "In Defence of the Pearl," *Modern Language Review*, 2 (1907), 39.

Mary Hillman points out, since one of the meanings of the pearl is the soul, grief over its loss would seem to be unchristian, but Sister Hillman still believes that the pearl of the poem represents the soul, and Marie Hamilton supports her thesis.[46] Another critic, Walter K. Greene, sees the discussion between the narrator-dreamer and the maiden as a mere literary device for introducing spiritual teachings.[47] Greene's point is a valid one, since the discussion is certainly a well-known literary device, with a history which goes back to the troubadour *tenson,* but the appearance of a beautiful maiden who chastises the dreamer and teaches him was not European and consequently cannot be traced to French or English literary tradition.

John Conley finds the theme of the poem to be "the sovereign theme of the Christian tradition, as of life itself: the nature of happiness, and specifically false and true happiness."[48] An elegiac reading of the poem is also rejected by such critics as D. W. Robertson, Jr., who apply patristic exegesis to it. Robertson applies all four levels of scriptural exegesis, finding the Pearl literally a gem, allegorically a maiden in the heavenly procession, tropologically the soul, and anagogically the life of innocence.[49] While such approaches may offer some insight into the poem and are within the context of thought of the medieval period, inherent in them is a basic fallacy, in that the tendency to overlay all late medieval literary works with heavy Christian symbolism is a modern one, a point emphasized by Morton Bloomfield, who

46 Sister M. Madeleva, *Pearl: A Study in Spiritual Dryness* (New York, 1925), pp. 22, 208; Elizabeth Hart, "The Heaven of Virgins," *Modern Language Notes,* 42 (1927), 113–16; Sister Mary Vincent Hillman, "Some Debatable Words in *Pearl* and Its Theme," *Modern Language Notes,* 60 (1945), 242–43; Marie Padgett Hamilton, "The Meaning of the Middle English *Pearl,*" in *Sir Gawain and Pearl: Critical Essays,* ed. Robert J. Blanch (Bloomington, 1966), pp. 38–39; and René Wellek, "The *Pearl:* An Interpretation of the Middle English Poem," in *Sir Gawain and Pearl,* p. 17. Wellek provides a convenient summary of the highlights of criticism on *Pearl* up to 1965, including arguments as to whether or not the poet was an ecclesiastic, which are not discussed here.

47 Walter Kirkland Greene, "*The Pearl*—A New Interpretation," *PMLA,* 40 (1925), 814–27.

48 John Conley, "*Pearl* and a Lost Tradition," *Journal of English and Germanic Philology,* 54 (1955), 341.

49 D. W. Robertson, Jr., "The Pearl as a Symbol," *Modern Language Notes,* 65 (1950), 160.

objects, justifiably, to modern patristic exegesis of nontheological works of the medieval period. As Gollancz had shown earlier, "The Pearl of the Gospel was a favorite allegorical theme with medieval theologians, but rarely with the poets."[50] And the *Pearl* is neither a formal theological treatise nor a homily.

None of the allegorical interpretations suggested above is completely satisfactory because, in the first place, they reject the elegiac theme so succinctly stated in the poem; in the second place, each allegorical reading requires a rejection of those facets of the poem which conflict with it. To interpret the Pearl as maidenhood, the Eucharist, the grace of God, or a purely literary device of abstract personification for didactic purposes, each mutually exclusive, requires distorting some passages and ignoring others.

Critical views against allegorical readings include those of A. C. Spearing and Stanton Hoffman.[51] The latter argues for a reading of the poem as an elegy with its major emphasis on the consolation of promised resurrection, the opposite extreme of those critics who see the poem as an allegory with no elegiac meaning.

In his 1921 edition of *Pearl,* Sir Israel Gollancz also reproduces Boccaccio's Latin eclogue "Olympia" of 1361, the elegy on his daughter Violante, along with certain letters by Boccaccio explicating the eclogue's personal references. When Boccaccio (as Sylvius) beholds Olympia, he is surprised that she has grown to maturity in so brief a time, as she appears to him like a bride. She states that the Virgin clothed her and she shows him her comrades. When he wishes to join her in her new life, she chides him. The Pearl similarly appears royally berobed by the Virgin and full grown, at which the narrator exclaims,

> Þou lyfed not two ȝer in oure þede
> Þou cowþes neuer God nauþer plese ne pray
> Ne neuer nawþer Pater ne Crede
> & quen mad on þe fyrst day! (ll. 483–86)

[50] Morton W. Bloomfield, "Symbolism in Medieval Literature," *Modern Philology,* 56 (1958), 73–81; Israel Gollancz, ed., *Pearl* (London, 1921), pp. xv–xvi.

[51] A. C. Spearing, "Symbolic and Dramatic Development in *Pearl,*" in *Sir Gawain and Pearl,* ed. Blanch, pp. 98–118; and Stanton de Voren Hoffman, "The *Pearl*: Notes for an Interpretation," *Modern Philology,* 58 (1960), 73–80.

Like Olympia, she is part of a procession, and, as in "Olympia," when the poet attempts to join his maid, he is chided for it and fails. Such similarities, in addition to statements within the *Pearl* itself, would seem to present a strong case for the *Pearl*'s being a personal elegy, whatever else it may represent.

Clark Northrup pointed out early in this century that the poem's framework—that of a vision with a debate within it—does not preclude its being based on personal experience. And Charles Moorman has shown that the narrator in the vision is as important as the maiden; they are separated by a stream, the emphasis in the poem is on the difference between them, and therefore both roles are vital ones to the poem.[52] The *Pearl* simply does not lend itself to a restrictive explication as either an elegy or an allegory. It is both and more. As René Wellek aptly summarizes it: "The poem is a vision of the other world, in which the poet is administering consolation to himself for a personal loss. Inside of this vision we have a debate between the dreaming poet and the girl. In addition, the whole is permeated by the allegory of the Pearl."[53]

Structure—Dream Vision or Eschatological Treatise

Much of the disagreement as to what the pearl symbolizes, and hence what the poem means, seems to grow out of the disparagement between form or genre and theme in the work when these are considered in the light of related medieval Christian and profane traditions. The poem is elegiac, but makes use of few of the traditional elegiac conventions and has none of the characteristics of the classical or pastoral elegy. Its genre is the medieval dream vision, a form not usually associated with elegy except in Chaucer's *Book of the Duchess,* which also combines the love vision and the elegy. The *Pearl* shares basic structural elements with Machaut's *Le Dit de l'Alerion,* but Machaut's *Dit,* like the great majority of similar dream visions, is concerned with love,

52 Clark S. Northrup, "Recent Studies of *The Pearl,*" *Modern Language Notes,* 22 (1907), 21–22; Charles Moorman, "The Role of the Narrator in *Pearl,*" *Modern Philology,* 53 (1955), 73–81.

53 Wellek, "*Pearl*: An Interpretation," p. 24.

specifically, courtly love, and with hunting, while the *Pearl's* themes are elegiac and eschatological and thus far removed from those of a typical dream vision.[54] It is, of course, related to the earlier tradition of eschatological visions such as those English, French, and Latin visions cited in Part I above, but it is also elegiac, which these visions are not. Further, it uses a maiden as guide and instructor in the afterlife, which the other visions do not do.

Like the *Book of the Duchess*, the *Pearl* is an elegy within a dream vision, and, like the *Book of the Duchess*, it contains remnants of the love complaint characteristic of the love-vision form. The narrator in Chaucer's *Book* begins with a fifty-odd-line complaint of sleeplessness and melancholy, with typical courtly-love–complaint imagery and rhetorical devices, vestigial remnants of which can also be noted in the first five stanzas of the *Pearl*, in spite of the fact that the Pearl was to the dreamer "nerre þen aunte or nece" (l. 233) and that she had "lyfed not two ȝer in oure þede" (l. 483), in such lines as the narrator's statement "I dewyne fordolked of luf daungere" (l. 11). Yet, unlike the *Book of the Duchess*, the *Pearl* presents a vision of the otherworld, and unlike anything in Christian literature prior to the *Divina Commedia*, the poet is led and instructed in the otherworld by a former beloved maiden. Thus the *Pearl* is a work which is structurally unique in Middle-English literature.

The *Pearl* opens with the narrator lamenting the loss of his Pearl in the first two stanzas, describing the "erbere" where he lost her (her grave) in the next two, and falling asleep in the fifth stanza. The poet's description of the "erbere" is worth noting:

> Þat spot of spyseȝ [mo]t nedeȝ sprede
> Þer such rycheȝ to rot is runne
> Blomeȝ blayke & blwe & rede
> Þer schyneȝ ful schyr agayn þe sunne
> Flor & fryte may not be fede
> Þer hit doun drof in moldeȝ dunne
> For vch gresse mot grow of grayneȝ dede

54 C. A. Luttrell, "*Pearl*: Symbolism in a Garden Setting," in *Sir Gawain and Pearl*, ed. Blanch, pp. 77–80, points out similarities and differences between the *Dit* and the *Pearl*.

No whete were elleʒ to woneʒ wonne
Of goud vch goude is ay bygonne
So semly a sede moʒt fayly not
Þat spryg ande spyceʒ vp ne sponne
Of þat precios perle wythouten spotte.

To þat spot þat I in speche expoun
I entred in þat erber grene
In Auguste in a hyʒ seysoun
Quen corne is coruen wyth crokeʒ kene
On huyle þer perle hit trendeled doun
Schadowed þis worteʒ ful schyre & schene
Gilofre gyngure & gromylyoun
& pyonys powdered ay bytwene
Ʒif hit watʒ semly on to sene
A fayr reflayr ʒet fro hit flot. (ll. 25–46)

The cycle of grass growing from grains which have fallen and
died and of fruit, flowers, and herbs growing on the spot where
the Pearl was buried is a miniature, vegetative version of the
larger, spiritual cycle with which the poem is concerned, that of
the new life gained by death and rebirth or the entry of the Pearl
into paradise. Eternity is suggested by the lines "Flor & fryte may
not be fede" and "So semly a sede moʒt fayly not," and with its
profusion of flowers, herbs, and grasses, the plot is a veritable
Eden, an earthly garden. But, even with its suggestion of eternal
vegetation, it is difficult to relate the *erbere* to the traditional
terrestrial paradise, because after the poet falls asleep he describes
such a terrestrial paradise quite separate from the garden where
his Pearl lies buried. The type of setting, with the exception of
the grave, provided for the poet before going to sleep seems to be
related to the traditional garden settings in the opening portions
of most love visions, settings with which it was conventional to
begin such visions.

Marie Hamilton has stated, however, that the first garden in
the poem, the *erbere*, could also signify, in addition to Eden,
Christ's resurrection and the Church and the terrestrial paradise
and future Church, since scholastic writers such as Saint Bernard
and Gregory the Great associated the garden with the resurrection, while Cyprian, Isidore of Seville, Bede, Rabanus Maurus,

and Saint Bonaventure traditionally associated the terrestrial paradise with the future Church. Miss Hamilton equates the grave plot with the paradise at the summit of Dante's purgatory: "The Terrestrial Paradise, where the pearl had 'trendeled doun,' was traditionally placed on a hill or mountain. Consequently it would seem logical to a medieval man for the restored Eden of the Church to have the same setting, and the more so since hill and mountain were recognized symbols of Christ and the Church." She concludes that the grave or hill then "stands for the *montem magnum et altum* of Apocalypse XXXI.10." Further substantiation for this, according to Miss Hamilton, is the fact that all of the plants named are medicinal, in token of the healing functions of the Church and of the Virgin. The setting of the poem in August suggests to her the Feast of the Assumption, "for the festival commemorates the restoration through Mary of what mankind forfeited through Eve."[55] True, these suggestions can be inferred from the imagery of the first garden, but it is hard to imagine the beautiful little plot producing such a heavy crop of theological symbolism. The suggestions of an earthly paradise are much more succinct in the garden described *after* the poet falls asleep, in which, for example, to suggest the *montem magnum et altum* there are crystal cliffs rather than a small grave mound. Whereas the imagery in the first garden is one of living nature (flowers, herbs, seeds, etc.), the garden which the poet sees after he falls asleep is characterized by precious metals and stones as well as by trees, herbs, spices, fruits, and birds.

The *Pearl*-poet has thus apparently retained the separate identity of his garden setting for the dream and the later terrestrial paradise, just as the latter is separated from the heavenly paradise or New Jerusalem by the river which the poet cannot cross. He is physically present in the *erbere*, but when he appears in the second garden, he does so in spirit only:

[55] Hamilton, "The Meaning of the Middle English *Pearl*," pp. 46–51; 248, *n.* 40. The inclusion of "gyngure" (l. 43), a spice not native to England, is curious, in spite of the spice's "healing powers." It is one of the delights of the Qurʾānic paradise: "And they are made to drink therein a cup tempered with ginger" (*Qurʾān*, Pt. 29, *Sura* 76, v. 17).

Fro spot my spyryt þer sprang in space
My body on balke þer bod in sweuen
My goste is gon in Godeȝ grace
In auenture þer meruayles meuen
I ne wyste in þis worlde quere þat hit wace. (ll. 61–65)

He describes its splendors by the use of hyperboles and superlatives, to which he did not resort in the first garden.

The second garden is described at great length. There are "klyffeȝ," "a foreste," and "rych rokkeȝ" (ll. 66–68). Four stanzas are then devoted to a description of the scene which includes "crystal klyffeȝ" and "holte wodeȝ,"

Of bolleȝ as blwe as ble of ynde
As bornyst syluer þe lef onslydeȝ
Þat þike con trylle on vch a tynde
Quen glem of glodeȝ agaynȝ hem glydeȝ
Wyth schymeryng schene ful schrylle þat schynde. (ll. 76–80)

The gravel on the ground was "precious perleȝ of Oryente" (l. 82). There were "frech flauoreȝ of fryteȝ" (l. 86) and "Fowleȝ þer flowen in fryth in fere" (l. 88) who

. . . songen wyth a swete asent
So gracios gle couþe no mon gete
As here & se her adubbement. (ll. 93–95)

The poet continues:

Þe fyrre in þe fryth þe fei[r]er con ryse
Þe playn þe plontteȝ be spyse þe pereȝ
& raweȝ & randeȝ & rych reuereȝ
As fyldor fyn her b[o]nkes brent. (ll. 103–106)

There were "bonkeȝ bene of beryl bryȝt" (l. 110) and the stones on the bottom were "emerad" and "saffer" (l. 118). The high cliffs of this paradise and the stream separating it from the heavenly one in which Pearl appears relate it to Oriental concepts of paradise. In this garden, as in the precious stone imagery used so expansively in the description of the New Jerusalem, the poet appears to have had extensive recourse to medieval lapidaries, although exactly which one or ones has not been determined, as the lapidaries each tended to differ both in the stones included and in the symbolic significance attached to each stone. There were countless lapidaries available in medieval Europe following the twelfth-century translation projects in Spain.

The following is a brief summary of the remainder of the poem: When the narrator sees the Pearl maiden, he remarks, "I hope þat gostly watȝ þat porpose" (l. 185), and there follows a long description of her pearl-ornamented attire. Pearl, after remonstrating with him for grieving over his loss of her on earth and for thinking he cannot attain her, explains that the young and innocent are received in paradise on a par with those who lived to complete a long life of good works, illustrating her thesis with the parable of the vineyard from Matthew. She then urges him to renounce worldly things and purchase the pearl of price (again a parable from Matthew), and discusses events of the Old and New Jerusalem from the Apocalypse. The narrator is permitted a glimpse of the city, toward which she leads him from the opposite bank of the stream. He sees the procession of virgins with the Lamb and, on catching sight of his Pearl again, attempts to plunge into the stream and awakes from his dream.

The descriptions and ideas incorporated in the paradise and the meeting of the Pearl maiden seem to be drawn from a medley of sources, some Christian and some Islamic, and some which seem to be a fusion of the two. Particularly important is the poet's separation of the terrestrial paradise from the heavenly one as Dante separates the paradise at the top of the mount of purgatory from heaven, a separation which was not always maintained either in medieval Christian or in Islamic eschatology. In fact, the separation between Christian and Islamic paradises is not always clear. In a thirteenth-century Christian poem, *Le Vergier du paradis*, of Jubinal, for example, is to be found a mixture of the Qurʾānic terrestrial garden-paradise with all its sensuous delights and the celestial Jerusalem of Revelation.[56]

The silver-and-crystal imagery of the *Pearl*-poet was common in medieval descriptions of the earthly paradise which is inferior to the heavenly paradise, as crystal and silver are inferior to

[56] Asín Palacios, *Islam and the Divine Comedy*, p. 200.

gold.[57] Such imagery is, incidentally, to be found in the Qurʾānic paradise, but there it is not used in descriptions of nature as in the *Pearl* and other medieval Christian works.[58] Characteristic of both the Islamic paradise and the Christian terrestrial paradise are the trees with extensive shade, water gushing, breezes blowing, birds singing, fruit, meat, and wine. We need not be concerned with these effects in the *Pearl*, except to note that they are clearly not a part of the New Jerusalem or heavenly paradise, which the narrator gazes upon from across the stream. The terrestrial paradise in the *Pearl* in many respects resembles that on Dante's mount of purgatory which also mixes Christian and Islamic sensuous paradisical imagery.

Although the terrestrial paradise of Islam is a sensuous one, it is by no means the only one in Islamic eschatology. The idea of two heavens, one material and one ideal, as expounded by Ghazzālī, Ibn-Rushd, and Ibn-ᶜArabī, was elaborated by Ibn-ᶜArabī in his *al-Futūḥāt al-Makkiyya,* along with an explanation of the sensuous paradise of the *Qurʾān* having been provided because God had depicted paradise in terms of human understanding. Two Christian Spaniards well versed in Islam, Raymond Lull (in *Liber de Gentili*) and Raymond Martín (in *Explanatio Simboli*) echoed the Islamic philosophers and mystics, as Asín Palacios points out: "Far from falling into the common error of attributing to all Moslems the belief in a voluptuous paradise, they repeat almost literally what those thinkers had affirmed; and Raymond Martín even quotes passages from Algazel [Ghazzālī], full of the loftiest metaphysical thought, in which this prince of Moslem mystics pictures the sublime delights of the Beatific Vision."[59]

Other elements shared by Christian and Islamic eschatological writings and found in the *Pearl* include the procession with attendant music and rejoicing and the decking of the participants in the procession with pearls. A whole cycle of legends of festivals and processions in paradise, replete with music and dancing and

57 Robert J. Blanch, "Precious Metal and Gem Symbolism in *Pearl*," in *Sir Gawain and Pearl*, p. 87.

58 For instance, there are "vessels of silver and goblets of glass" (*Qurʾān*, Pt. 29, *Sura* 76, v. 15).

59 Asín Palacios, *Islam and the Divine Comedy*, pp. 139–40.

resembling the revelry of a feudal lord's court, had grown up in both Christianity and Islam. Pearl imagery was so widely used in scholastic theological treatises that it needs no discussion here. The pearl was also a favorite image of Islamic mystics and theologians. Ghazzālī entitled his popular eschatological treatise *al-Durra al Fākhira, The Precious Pearl,* and Ibn-ᶜArabī used the same title for a book of biographical sketches of saints and holy men. A perhaps lesser-known parallel between the *Pearl* and the *Qur'ān* can be seen in the use of pearls in the descriptions of the maidens and youths of paradise. The Middle-English Pearl is lavishly bedecked with pearls, and she herself is represented as a spotless pearl, as are the other 143,999 virgins and children of the procession. In comparison, the youths and maidens of the Islamic paradise are described as "hidden pearls" and "scattered pearls."[60]

The one element in the *Pearl* most foreign to Christian eschatology is, perhaps surprisingly, the appearance of the Pearl herself. The meeting of a pilgrim or dreamer with his lost beloved in paradise is not to be found in any Christian writings prior to the *Divina Commedia.* The earthly and heavenly paradises alone or the appearance of a maiden alone would not be remarkable, but the use of the two together, with the maiden functioning as guide, adviser, and teacher regarding the otherworld in Dante and in the *Pearl*-poet is remarkable. Such a combination was common in Islamic lore, which probably indirectly influenced Dante's masterpiece. Such a maiden is of *Ṣūfī,* and not of Celtic fairy-mistress, ancestry. She does not lure the dreamer to come with her as her lover, as the Celtic mistress does, but rather instructs and corrects him and urges him to renounce earthly desires in order to be with her in paradise after his death. In Christian otherworld visions up to the fourteenth century, she appears only in the *Divina Commedia* and in the *Pearl.* (Some aspects of her are apparent in Boccaccio's "Olympia," but she is not as distinctly Islamic there as in the other two works.)

Many close parallels between Dante's *Commedia* and the works of Ibn-ᶜArabī and other Islamic writers have been shown

60 *Qur'ān,* Pt. 27, *Sura* 52, v. 24, and *Sura* 56, vv. 22–23.

in detail by Asín Palacios, and several corresponding parallels between the *commedia* and the *Pearl* have been noticed by Patricia Kean.[61] When Dante reaches the earthly paradise atop the mount of purgatory, he is led by a maiden named Matilda, who walks along the opposite bank of a stream until they reach the procession of maidens and elders where he meets Beatrice, just as the *Pearl*-narrator in his terrestrial paradise is led by the Pearl from across the stream until they reach the celestial city and the procession of virgins and the Lamb. The *Pearl*-poet, unlike Dante, however, cannot cross the stream. When Dante meets Beatrice, it is a reunion of the poet with a lost beloved. This is also the case with the *Pearl*-poet, whose maiden, like Boccaccio's Olympia, appears as a young bride even though she died in infancy. Beatrice reproaches Dante for not having been faithful and then furnishes solutions to Dante's questions on theology. Similarly, the Pearl chastises the narrator for bemoaning his loss of her and instructs him in problems of a theological nature, including that of a two-year-old child being received in grace along with the elders. The narrator's role in *Pearl* is one of bewailing his loss, desiring to regain it, becoming impatient with things he does not understand, and wishing to join the Pearl, which in this case would be tantamount to suicide if he had succeeded. The narrator, in his impatience, has certain affinities with Jonah in *Patience*, and the poem has many affinities with *Purity* in the Pearl's exhortations to lead a clean life free from sin. The vision of Pearl and the New Jerusalem (and the terrestrial paradise) thus have a two-fold function: To console the poet over his loss by letting him see the beauty and glory to which his Pearl has ascended and to promise him that, through faith, observance of the Church teachings, and leading a pure life, he too can look forward to being a resident of the New Jerusalem for all eternity.

Without the elegiac portions of *Pearl*, the parallels to Islamic visions in which a dreamer is inspired by an angelic maiden are as close and as unusual as the parallels between Dante's Beatrice and the Islamic maiden. It is this tradition, not native to Chris-

[61] Patricia M. Kean provides an excellent comparison of the *Pearl* and Dante's *Divina Commedia* in *The Pearl: An Interpretation* (New York, 1967), pp. 120–30.

tianity, to which the *Pearl,* along with Beatrice and Matilda, seems to belong. But whether the *Pearl*-poet drew directly from Dante or Boccaccio for his female guide or somehow had access to the pre-Dantean Islamic legends and writings which existed in Spain, southern France, Sicily, and other parts of southern Europe is a moot question. It may be, however, that it was the poet's integration of the earlier *Ṣūfī* tradition of the heavenly maiden-guide through the afterlife with the later courtly-love dream-vision form well-known to medieval Christian Europe, a form to which were also added elements from the elegy and the debate or *tenson* of the troubadours, which has led to so much critical confusion as to the meaning of the poem in relation to its unique, mixed genre. Granted, in the *Pearl,* as in Dante, the maiden has been thoroughly Christianized, but it is probably at least in part because of her ultimately non-Christian origin that modern patristic exegesis of the poem and her role in it tends to be insufficient and misleading.

By way of contrast to the foregoing observations, the description of the celestial city and the Lamb in *Pearl,* like the two parables from Saint Matthew elucidated by the Pearl maiden, is exclusively Christian, having been drawn directly from the Apocalypse, which is followed fairly closely in the poem.

Theology—Catholic or Heretic

Wellek provides a good outline of the issue of Pelagianism in relation to the *Pearl.*[62] Pelagianism, still a theological issue of the fourteenth century, derived from Pelagius' doctrine that grace could only be obtained through good works, and not through faith alone. Saint Augustine disagreed with Pelagius on the question of salvation of children. According to Saint Augustine, who recognized two kinds of grace or titles to salvation, one type could occur through baptism of children and was freely given by grace (hereditary), and the second type could occur through good works by which man redeems his fall from grace. The two types of grace are *gratia prima,* freely given at baptism,

[62] The information on Pelagianism is taken, with exceptions noted, from Wellek, "*Pearl*: An Interpretation," pp. 25–32.

and *gratia secunda,* proportioned to merits. Infant baptism could thus guarantee salvation if the child died young. Other ecclesiastics such as Saint Bernard of Clairvaux and Pope Clement IV (early fourteenth century) defended baptism of children as being a guarantee of salvation and as being as valid as the type merited through good works. Although the Augustinian view generally prevailed as orthodox, the Church had not taken a final stand on the issue at the time the *Pearl* was written, and the problem of infant salvation was still a current theological controversy.

Carleton Brown attempts to show that the poet was, because of his treatment of the issue in *Pearl,* an ecclesiastic, an opinion which Wellek refutes. Brown points out the denunciation by Thomas Bradwardine, contemporary of the *Pearl*-poet, of Pelagianism in his doctrine that "salvation is bestowed through the free grace of God, instead of being achieved by any merits." He feels that the author of the *Pearl* goes beyond Bradwardine in expanding the doctrine of free grace by including equal rewards for infants and adults, a concept which was, in spite of the parable of the vineyard, heretical, according to Brown. As evidence of such a view's being heresy, Brown cites the fourth-century heretic Jovinian who also used the vineyard parable to argue salvation entirely through grace.[63] But, as Wellek has shown, the theology in the vineyard was entirely orthodox, with the same parable having been used by Saint Augustine, Gregory the Great, and Saint Thomas Aquinas to support the theory of salvation through baptism of infants.

No mention of Pearl's having been baptised is made in the poem, but the inference is there. She could not possibly be in the procession of innocents if she had not been baptized. This is, as D. W. Robertson, Jr., has shown, the point and meaning of the vineyard parable which is discussed at great length in the poem—that because she had evidently been baptized shortly before her death, she was a newcomer to the vineyard who was as valued by the owner as those who had worked full term.[64] The view of the

[63] Carleton F. Brown, "The Author of *The Pearl* Considered in the Light of His Theological Opinions, *PMLA,* 19 (1904), 115–53.

[64] D. W. Robertson, Jr., "The 'Heresy' of *The Pearl,*" *Modern Language Notes,* 65 (1950), 152–55.

issue which then emerges in the poem is not heretical and, in accepting the theory of double salvation, the poet was more in line with than against scholastic theological opinions of the fourteenth century and was thus dramatizing a debate still in vogue in his day.

The pose of the dreamer in the debate with Pearl on infant salvation in which she explicates the parable as an analogy to her being made a queen in heaven is, in part, functionally similar to that of the dreamer questioning the knight in Chaucer's *Book of the Duchess*. One aspect of that function is a questioning innocence, either genuine or assumed, by the narrator, to elicit the answers from the knight and from the Pearl, providing a dialogue which reveals the story rather than having it related through a straight monologue. The *Pearl*-poet goes farther than Chaucer's narrator, however, and in protesting certain points in order for the Pearl to clarify them, sets up a form of debate. If there is any "heresy" to be attributed to the poet in *Pearl*, it would seem to be in his use of a maiden in the vision to expound matters of Christian theology, a maiden who originated, as pointed out above, in Islamic, not Christian, eschatological tradition.

Symbolism—Meanings of the Pearl

The pearl has, perhaps from time immemorial, represented purity of body, or of soul, or both. This is true in a universal sense; that is, the association with purity is to be found in every medieval European culture, whether pagan, Christian, Jewish, or Islamic. Another universal significance attached to the pearl was that of eternal life; as such, it appears as frequently among the Islamic mystics as among the Christian theologians. In addition to its universal meanings, the pearl has several Christian connotations which have become attached to it as a symbol. Most prominent among these connotations are eternal life, the soul, heavenly saints, heavenly grace, good works, Christ, and Mary, meanings which are all incorporated to some degree in the *Pearl*.

Eternal life. The Church Fathers frequently construed the pearl of price in Matthew as a representation of everlasting life or beatitude. Among scholastics who speak of the pearl in this sense are Gregory the Great, Bede, Rabanus Maurus, Walafridus Strabo, Bruno Astensis, and Hugh of Saint Victor.[65] Eternal life, as well as Christ, is inherent in the meaning of the parable explained by Pearl in which the narrator is urged to sell his worldly goods and give up worldly pleasures to purchase the eternal Pearl.

The soul. The pearl was also frequently used to signify the soul redeemed by baptism. Miss Hamilton explains this association:

> The soul, poetically conceived as feminine, time out of mind, was represented in medieval art as a child; and the figure of the maiden soul of man, raised from her fallen state and espoused by Christ, is a commonplace of medieval treatises. . . . Traditionally, too, the soul as spouse (i.e., the soul in a state of grace) was depicted as adorned, like Pearl, with precious stones, sometimes specified as pearls, betokening virtues bestowed upon her by the Celestial Bridegroom.[66]

Typical of scholastics who speak of this usage of the pearl are Saint Bernard and Hugh of Saint Victor. It was a popular usage among theologians, but, as mentioned earlier, rare among poets. Inherent in the Pearl is a suggestion that she represents a baptized soul, but the suggestion is generally overemphasized by critics of the poem to the detriment of other associations with the symbolic pearl.

Heavenly saints. The pearl was identified with the blessed and saints by Rupert of Deutz, Rabanus Maurus, and Saint Bonaventure.[67] Such an association in *Pearl* appears in the procession of the 144,000, in which she takes part.

Heavenly grace. The association of the pearl with grace, more frequent than that of the pearl with saints, is to be found in Gregory the Great, Petrus Chrysologus, and Petrus Capuanus.[68] The Pearl herself illustrates it by being accepted into heaven on the basis of baptism only, and it is necessary for the narrator in the vision to see and understand her acceptance and her new glory to provide a consolation for his elegiac theme.

65 Hamilton, "The Meaning of the Middle English *Pearl*," pp. 41; 245, *n*. 13.

66 *Ibid.*, p. 42. Miss Hamilton also cites Saint Bernard and Hugh of Saint Victor, p. 246, *n*. 22.

67 Wellek, "*Pearl*: An Interpretation," pp. 34–35, points this out.

68 *Ibid.*

Good works. In the writings of the Syrian scholastic Ephraem, the pearl is linked with good works of the soul. Since this is one of the more interesting, but less frequently noticed, of the pearl's connotations, I will quote a selection from Ephraem: "And since I have wandered in thee, pearl, I will gather up my mind, and by having contemplated thee, would become like thee, in that thou art all gathered up into thyself, and as thou in all times art one, one let me become by thee! Pearls have I gathered together that I might make a crown for the Son in the place of stains. . . . Receive my offering. . . . This crown is all spiritual pearls, which instead of gold are set in love, and instead of ouches in faith."[69] To be noted in this passage is the concept of the union pearl which came to be associated with the union of the Holy Trinity. The gathering of spiritual pearls is remarkable since the maiden Pearl, who did not remain on earth long enough to gather pearls, is covered with them in paradise and chides one much older than herself, the narrator, for not having accumulated such pearls by accepting God's decrees and renouncing worldly evils.

Christ. All of the Latin commentators on the pearl of price in Matthew 13:45–46 brought out the idea that the pearl is One and Christ. Examples are Saint Augustine in *Questiones Septemdecim in Matthaum*, Gregory in *Homilia XII*, and Bede in *Matthaei Evancelium Expositio.*[70] Guillaume le Clerc, in his bestiary, adds a comment on the passage from Matthew on the pearl, in which Christ is "vera Margarita, via et veritas et vita nostra."[71] Another treatise on the pearl as Christ which might be mentioned is one which uses bird and birth imagery in connection with Christ as the pearl born of Mary. This is the Ethiopic version of the Greek *Physiologus* on the birth of the pearl:

> But how is the pearl engendered? It is a bird, called *Bergānō*, which arises from the sea toward the east, and opens its mouth and swallows the dew of heaven at the rising of the sun and

69 Ephraem, quoted by Leo Wiener, *Contributions toward a History of Arabico-Gothic Culture*, IV (Philadelphia, 1921), 150. Since Wiener's basic thesis and his etymologies are highly suspect, to say the least, I have used his work only for its translations.

70 *Ibid.*, 157.

71 Guillaume le Clerc, quoted *ibid.*, 146–47.

> moon and stars. And of all of these rays the pearl is made. And *Bergānā* is a bird which has two wings, with which it surrounds the pearl as in a womb. And this resembles our Savior who is born without semen, from the Virgin alone. . . . But you, oh free man, sell all your goods and give it to the poor so that you may acquire the precious pearl, which is Christ.[72]

The association of the Virgin with another fabulous bird is seen when the dreamer asks the Pearl:

> Art þou þe quene of heuenez blwe
> Þat al þys worlde schal do honour
> We leuen on Marye þat grace of grewe
> Þat ber a barne of vyrgynflor
> . . . .
> Now for synglerty o hyr dousour
> We calle hyr fenyx of arraby
> Þat freles fleȝe of hyr fasor. (ll. 423–31)

The phoenix, the unique, never-duplicated member of its kind, gives birth every five hundred years to another unique, never-duplicated member, and thus lends itself beautifully to an analogy with Mary who gives birth to Christ. The association between the phoenix and Mary was well known.

Mary. Mary, as the representative of virginity, was naturally associated with the pearl (in addition to giving birth to Christ as a pearl) with its connotations of purity and maidenhood. Often there was confusion between Mary as a pearl and Christ as a pearl, which is illustrated in a Coptic homily on the virgin and the birth of Christ: "Joseph renounced all worldly possessions to obtain Mary. She is a pearl in the midst of other jewels, in a meadow girt about by the sea, the fish in which live all at peace. When the pearl's time is fulfilled, it joins that other pearl which lies below the water in the shell . . . and together they mount up and illuminate the field and trees."[73] Similarly in the *Pearl*, the maidenhood of Pearl as well as Christ is symbolized.

With associations of the Pearl in the poem with eternal life, the soul, heavenly saints, heavenly grace, good works, Christ, and

[72] Wiener, *Arabico-Gothic Culture*, IV, 143.
[73] W. E. Crum, quoted *ibid.*, 130.

Mary, as well as with the general concept of purity, it would seem that an allegorical reading of the *Pearl* as signifying only one or two of these unnecessarily limits the poem's major symbol. Part of the beauty in such a symbol as the pearl lies in its ambiguity and in the many connotations which can be associated with it, as the poet was no doubt aware. The critical controversies on the significance of the *Pearl* maiden in the poem are due to some extent to attempts to force an allegorical correspondence upon what was evidently intended to be seen as a many-faceted symbol.

Conclusion

The *Pearl* is not allegorical, but rather symbolical; that is, it encompasses a number of coexistent meanings. The pearl image in the poem functions on many levels of Christian meaning and association, and neither the theme nor the structure of the poem insinuates that adoption of any one association to the exclusion of the others would be desirable. Its genre and eschatology are also multifarious. Just as it is structurally and thematically a fusion of widely varying traditions, the *Pearl* also represents, in its prosody, a fusion of two different poetic traditions, the native English alliterative verse and Provençal rime and stanza links. Perhaps the only regular or orthodox aspect of the poem is its theology, and even this revolves around the fourteenth-century Pelagian controversy and is placed within an eschatological framework consisting of an aggregate of ideas and images of the afterlife.

Set in the genre of the medieval dream vision, a form usually associated with courtly love, the *Pearl* combines an elegiac theme with an eschatological treatise in the form of a debate between the dreamer and a maiden, with the latter functioning also as guide, adviser, and critic of the poet in spiritual matters. The appearance of the heavenly maiden in a vision of the afterlife as guide and instructor was an Islamic convention which Dante also employed in his *Commedia* and which, adapted to the dream vision in the medieval courtly-love tradition, further complicates the genre of the poem. The poem's eschatology, geographically and imagistically, represents a fusion of ideas common to both Christianity and Islam, and only that portion of the celestial paradise drawn from the Apocalypse can be said to be endemic only to Christianity. The poem as a vision of the afterlife does not conform to typical medieval English visions and mystical writings.[74] The poet has drawn from traditions both English and European, both Christian and Islamic, and perhaps the real artistry of the *Pearl* is in its being in almost every respect eclectic. This last is a point which we cannot fully appreciate unless we also take cognizance of the non-Christian, non-Celtic, non-Germanic currents which had flowed north into Europe and England long before the fourteenth century. And these are currents with which, in view of the poet's familiarity with the mainstream of the fourteenth-century heritage, he could be expected to have been familiar, as could Dante.

74 See, for example, E. Colledge, *The Mediaeval Mystics of England* (New York, 1961); and *The Cloud of Unknowing and the Book of Privy Counselling*, ed. Phyllis Hodgson, *Early English Text Society*, 218 (1958).

CHAPTER V

Tales and Fables

PART I—EASTERN AND EUROPEAN

The Tale

The tale has been called "the Orient's greatest single contribution to the literature of the West."[1] Tales, both moral and *fabliau* types, like otherworld-vision literature and lyric poetry, suddenly proliferated in Western Europe beginning in the twelfth century. Some of these tales were incorporated in collections, many of which accrued around a frame story and which borrowed heavily from each other; some were disseminated orally by clerics, *jongleurs*, merchants, and returning crusaders. Whether oral or written, the tales contained much Eastern and Semitic material, if the tales themselves were not Arabic or Persian.

The Oriental tales in medieval Europe are recognized by most scholars and students of the Middle Ages. What is surprising is that no one has seriously considered Moorish and Arab Spain as a bridge over which such tales could have reached Western Europe and England. Courtly love was not the only nonacademic subject that would have interested the troubadours, and the tale, like lyric poetry, had a long and illustrious history in Spain. In fact, a comparative survey of some of the major sourcebooks of tales in Latin, Old French, Middle English, Spanish, and Arabic will show that Spain was in the mainstream in the flow of tales in Western Europe.

Exempla. Exempla, like fantastic travel stories and fabulous legends, illustrate the mobility of medieval Europe in the proliferation of more-than-twice-told tales. *Exempla* had been known

[1] John Esten Keller, trans., *The Book of the Wiles of Women* (Chapel Hill, 1956), p. 1.

as teaching vehicles from the early Middle Ages, but they came into prominent usage in sermons in the thirteenth century with two collections of *exempla*. These were the collection of Jacques de Vitry (d. 1240), *Sermones de Tempore et Sanctis*, and that of the Dominican Etienne de Bourbon (d. 1261), *Liber de Donis*, the latter of whom often copied from the former.[2] The Franciscans and the Dominicans were founded in the early thirteenth century, and as the preaching friars were competing with the popular minstrels and *jongleurs*, they disseminated quite a few Eastern tales which they had appropriated for *exempla*, tales used as examples for moral instruction. Later, many of the *exempla* of Jacques and Etienne, along with those from the *Disciplina Clericalis*, replete with stories of Oriental provenance, found their way into the collection of moral tales known as the *Gesta Romanorum*.

Beast Fables. Often considered endemic to Western Europe, the beast fable, one of the most universal types of the tale, received new inspiration from a collection of fables translated into Latin and Old Spanish in the thirteenth century. This was the *Directorium Humanae Vitae* which, in spite of its impressive Latin title, is but a translation of an Eastern collection of beast fables, first rendered in Latin in the second half of the thirteenth century. Originally used in ancient India for moral and social instruction, the beast fable was a natural for the later *exempla* of the preaching friars and other clerics. It was also suitable for teaching rhetoric in the Middle Ages, in which the student would begin a composition exercise with the simple fable or beast story which he then expanded by using the rhetorical devices of amplification. Chaucer's "Nun's Priest's Tale" of the cock and the fox is a marvelous parody of such an exercise.[3]

Fabliaux. The *fabliau*-type tale, of Oriental provenance, in-

2 W. A. Clouston, *Popular Tales and Fictions* (Detroit, 1968), pp. 12–13. (Originally published in 1887 in two vols.)

3 This tale, in fact, pillories almost all of the principles of rhetoric expounded in one of the textbooks of Chaucer's day, Geoffrey de Vinsauf's *Nova Poetria*. See Charles Sears Baldwin, *Medieval Rhetoric and Poetic* (New York, 1928); John Matthews Manly, "Chaucer and the Rhetoricians," in *Chaucer Criticism*, ed. Richard J. Schoeck and Jerome Taylor (Notre Dame, Ind., 1960); and Bernard F. Huppé and D. W. Robertson, Jr., *Fruyt and Chaf* (Princeton, 1963).

spired the later European *fabliaux*, which also became widespread. Such tales were brought into Europe, along with a quantity of moral tales, from the eleventh century on by crusaders returning from the East. The *fabliau* crops up in the early literature of every country of Western Europe, and the funnier and the more risqué the tale, the more frequently it appears. Often the same story, ultimately oriental, will be found with numerous variations and twists to have been told almost everywhere, since the *fabliau* was especially popular among the seamen, the merchants, and the peasants, though certainly not limited to them. Chaucer's *fabliaux*, for example, have analogues in Flemish, German, French, Spanish, Arabic, Italian, and Persian stories.

Maqāmāt. Closely related to the *fabliau* was the picaresque type of tale called the *maqāma*,[4] which was first created in the East by Badīᶜ al-Zamān ("Wonder of the Age") al-Hamadhānī (969–1008), who devised a collection of fifty such tales, called *maqāmāt* (plural of *maqāma*), "assembly." The hero of the collection was Abū-al-Fatḥ, an unscrupulous rascal who lived by his wits, deceiving and defrauding those with whom he dealt. He met often with the narrator and reporter of his adventures, ᶜĪsā Ibn-al-Hishām. Each *maqāma* is a unit, a separate anecdote or adventure of Abū-al-Fatḥ, and is done in a medley of prose and verse, in which the eloquent style becomes more important than the tale itself. Such a collection of *maqāmāt* with one hero and narrator naturally forms its own frame.

The work of al-Hamadhānī inspired that of al-Ḥarīrī of Baṣra (1054–1122), who is known to have been familiar also with the *Bidpai Fables* translated into Arabic in the eighth century. The hero of al-Ḥarīrī's *maqāmāt* of fifty tales is Abū-al-Zayd, who relates his escapades to the narrator Ḥarīth Ibn-Ḥammām. Like his predecessor's, al-Ḥarīrī's tales are mixtures of prose and verse;

[4] The information on the *maqāmāt* of al-Hamadhānī and al-Ḥarīrī is from the following sources: Edward G. Browne, *A Literary History of Persia*, II (New York, 1906), 112–13; Philip K. Hitti, *History of the Arabs*, pp. 403–404; Reynold A. Nicholson, *A Literary History of the Arabs*, pp. 328–30; Gustave E. von Grunebaum, *Medieval Islam: A Study in Cultural Orientation* (Chicago, 1946), pp. 288–89; and W. Montgomery Watt, *A History of Islamic Spain*, p. 125.

but unlike the earlier composer, al-Ḥarīrī insists that his *maqāmāt* have a moral purpose, and his hero repents at the end of his life.

The picaresque tale of early Spanish and Italian literature has close affinities with the *maqāma,* no doubt a consequence of contact with the Eastern and Arabic culture to which these countries were exposed, partly during the translation period but at other times as well. *Maqāmāt* are known to have been composed in Andalusia beginning in the late eleventh century. The Spanish *Libro de Buen Amor* contains in the adventures of the archpriest both the picaresque hero and the combination of verse and prose which characterize the *maqāma. Aucassin et Nicolette* follows the alternate-verse-and-prose format of the *maqāma* and its form has long been recognized as derived from Arab and Persian tales of this type. Its author had apparently either seen or heard such tales in Spain or in the East.

Frame stories. "Thereby hangs a tale"—as collections of the tales began to be formed, beginning with the *Disciplina Clericalis,* the frame tale, which has a long Oriental history, came into use in Western Europe.[5] Moral stories, including fables, were begun in the East, chiefly in India, as means for training princes in practical ethics or "how to get along with the world." The framework served to help one remember the tales and fables before printing was in use. Later, the framing device was adapted to popular marketplace stories, with similar or no ethics. Most of the collections, such as the *Disciplina, The Seven Sages of Rome,* and the *Gesta Romanorum,* appeared first in Latin and were gradually translated into the vernacular languages. By the time of Boccaccio, Chaucer, and Gower, the framing tale had been adapted to European culture and had become, with its attached varied tales, an immensely popular form of literature.

The framing devices, both in their Oriental forms and in their European adaptations, fall into two broad classifications, dramatic and instructive, according to whether the device is one re-

[5] For a discussion of the frame tale in medieval Western Europe, see Robert A. Pratt and Karl Young, "The Literary Framework of the Canterbury Tales," in *Sources and Analogues of Chaucer's Canterbury Tales,* ed. W. F. Bryan and Germaine Dempster (New York, 1958), pp. 1–81.

quiring dramatic interaction of the narrator(s) with other narrators or participants in the tales, or whether it is one in which the narrator functions to instruct a protegé, son, or daughter by means of the tales he relates. Some examples of dramatic frames are: *The Seven Sages of Rome*, with its situation between Joseph and Potiphar's wife; the *Directorium Humanae Vitae*, with its fables told by various animals in different situations; the *Libro de Buen Amor*, with its picaresque autobiographical narrator; the *Arabian Nights*, with Shahrazād's necessity to keep the king's interest whetted from tale to tale; the *Decameron*, with its narrators fleeing the plague; *The Canterbury Tales*, with its complex of interactions among pilgrims telling their tales enroute to the shrine of Saint Thomas à Becket; and the *Confessio Amantis*, with Venus' chaplain relating tales as he hears the confession of a servant of Venus. The *Confessio* could be considered as either a dramatic or an instructive type of frame.

Instructive frames are those of the *Disciplina Clericalis*, with the philosopher relating moral tales to his pupil; *El Conde Lucanor*, with the counselor answering the young nobleman's questions with tales; and *The Knight of La Tour Landry*, with the father instructing his daughters by means of moral tales.

Disciplina Clericalis

A Spanish Jewish physician and scholar, Rabbi Moseh Sephardi, baptized Pedro Alfonso in 1106, had emigrated to England in 1091 where he remained until his death in 1135. Not only did he help introduce Arabic astronomy into England but in addition, between 1106 and 1110, he composed the *Disciplina Clericalis*, a collection of tales in Latin which became so popular that many scholars consider it one of the most important writings of the Middle Ages.

Through the *Disciplina*, thirty-three Oriental stories were diffused to Western Europe. There are at least sixty-three known manuscripts of it, including a Middle-English translation extant in a fifteenth-century Worcester Cathedral manuscript.[6] Its tales

[6] The Middle-English version was edited by William Henry Hulme, "Peter Alphonse's *Disciplina Clericalis*," *Western Reserve University Bulletin*, 22, No. 3

were later used by the *trouvères* of northern France for *fabliaux* and by Odo of Cheriton, Etienne de Bourbon, Nicholas de Bozon, Clemente Sánchez, and Jacques de Vitry for *exempla.* The tales recur in *The Seven Sages of Rome* and the *Gesta Romanorum;* as a sourcebook, the *Disciplina* influenced Boccaccio's *Decameron* and Chaucer's *Canterbury Tales.*

The frame of the *Disciplina* consists of an Arabian philosopher relating tales to instruct his pupil in Christian morals and virtues. Its sources are mostly Arabic and some of its stories are from the Arabic *Kalīlah wa Dimnah,* which Pedro Alfonso could have known when he lived in Spain.[7]

The Seven Sages of Rome

The framing story for *The Seven Sages,*[8] involving a chaste youth and a lustful stepmother, is first found in the Egyptian tale of *Anpu and Bata,* composed around 1200 B.C., and in Genesis in the story of approximately the same date of Joseph and the wife of Potiphar, the Pharaoh's captain of the guard. It recurs in Greek drama in Euripides' *Hippolytus,* in later hellenized Hebrew versions, in the Persian and Arabic *Yūsuf wa Zulaykha,* and in Hindu and far-eastern lore. There is even an Irish analogue in the *Book of Leinster.* It is also found in the unfinished *Aljamiado* (Spanish language written in Arabic script) *Poema de Yuçuf* of Aragon of the fourteenth century, in which the story of Joseph and Potiphar's wife, related in quatrains, is drawn from both the Bible and the *Qurʾān* (*Sura* 12, verses 23–28).

The story lent itself particularly well to use as a framing device. The stepmother, unable to seduce the prince, accuses him of attempted rape and the king condemns him to death. An astrologer

(1919). Hulme finds that thirteen tales in the fifteenth-century "Alphabet of Tales" are from the *Disciplina* (p. 8).

7 Information on the sources and influence of the *Disciplina* is drawn from Keller, trans., *Book of the Wiles of Women,* pp. 4, 52–53; Américo Castro, *The Structure of Spanish History,* pp. 8, 84; and Joseph Bédier, *Les Fabliaux,* p. 133.

8 The history of the story and its various versions is taken from John D. Yohannan, ed., *Joseph and Potiphar's Wife* (New York, 1968); Donald Keene, "The Hippolytus Triangle, East and West," *The Yearbook of Comparative Literature,* No. 11, Supplement (1962), 162–71; and Ernest Mérimée, *A History of Spanish Literature,* p. 46.

warns the prince that he must not speak for seven days or death is certain. Each day for seven days, the prince's counselor (or other sages) relates a tale (or tales) illustrating the perfidy of women and the king relents, until each night the stepmother tells a tale (or tales) to illustrate the perfidy of men or wicked counselors. On the eighth day, the prince himself speaks, tells one or more tales, and the stepmother is punished, sometimes with death.

The original version of the tale as a framing device was probably an Arabic one which came to the West around 1150. There were two branches, Eastern and Western, of the frame and collection of tales, both of which reached Europe.[9] In the Eastern branch, known as the *Book of Sindibād* (not to be confused with Sindbad the sailor), each sage tells two tales, the prince has an instructor (named Sindibād), and the king is named in Greek, Kurus; in Hebrew, Pai Pur, or Kai Pur; and in Old Spanish, Alcos of Judea. In the Western branch, known as *The Seven Sages of Rome*, an offshoot of the Eastern, each sage tells only one story as opposed to two in the Eastern; the prince has seven counselors as opposed to one; and the prince is Florentine, son of the emperor Diocletian.

The individual tales vary from version to version among the branches, with only four stories common to both the Eastern and the Western branches: *Aper* (the story of a boar who chases a shepherd or a monkey up a tree and is outwitted by him), *Senescalus* (the story of a seneschal rescued from a pit, who, unlike animals also rescued, shows ingratitude), *Avis* (the story of a man, his wife, and the tell-tale bird), and *Canis* (the story of the babe saved from a snake by a faithful dog who is then wrongly killed by his master). These four tales, along with others of *The Seven Sages*, reappear in the *Gesta Romanorum* and later works.

Surviving representatives of the Eastern branch include versions in Syriac, Greek, Hebrew, Old Spanish, Persian, and Ar-

9 Information on the Eastern and Western versions is from Keller, *Book of the Wiles of Women*, pp. 1–55; and Killis Campbell, "A Study of the *Seven Sages* with Special Reference to the Middle English Versions," *PMLA*, n. s. 7 (1899), 1–107. The Middle-English version has been edited by Killis Campbell in *The Seven Sages of Rome* (New York, 1907).

abic. The oldest of these is the Syriac *Sindban* of the tenth century. The Greek *Syntipas* dates from the late eleventh century, the Hebrew *Miscle Sindbad* (translated from an Arabic version) from the first half of the thirteenth century, and the Persian *Sindibād Nameh* from 1375. Although several of the Eastern versions indicate an Arabic source in their prologues, the only extant version in Arabic is that of "The Seven Wazīrs" in the *Arabian Nights.* The Old-Spanish version, in Castilian, which was done for Infante Don Fadrique, brother of Alfonso X, in 1253, is called the *Libro de los Engaños e Asayamientos de las Mujeres (Book of the Wiles and Devices of Women).* Its prologue states that it was translated from an Arabic version and it ends with the problematical question of who, the king, the queen, the prince, or the counselor Sindibād (*Çendubete* in Old Spanish), would have been accountable had the prince been executed before his seven days of silence ended. The Arabic tale of the old woman and her weeping bitch, one of the stories of the Old-Spanish version, is also found in the *Disciplina Clericalis,* a good example of how an Arabic story could and did travel from Spain to England.

Surviving representatives of the Western branch are extant in Latin, Old French, and Middle English. The Latin prose *Dolopathos* dates from the last quarter of the twelfth century. The most widely known version of the Western branch was the fourteenth-century Latin *Historia Septem Sapientum Romae,* an English text of which was printed by Wynkyn de Worde. (In the *Historia,* the wicked stepmother is the wife of the king of Castile.) At least two versions in Old-French verse have survived, the *Sept Sages de Rome* of the mid-twelfth century (the earliest extant version) and the late thirteenth-century *Li Romans des Sept Sages,* and a large number of French prose versions are extant. The collection was not as popular in England as on the Continent, and only nine Middle-English manuscripts of it survive, seven of which appear to have been derived from a single source. The earliest English version is found in an Auchinleck manuscript of around 1330.

Directorium Humanae Vitae

The collection of beast fables known in Arabic as *Kalīlah wa Dimnah* and in Latin as *Directorium Humanae Vitae* derives ultimately from India.[10] From a Sanskrit original, *Panchatantra*, "Five Books" (now lost), the fables were translated into Pahlevi (Middle Persian) and into Syriac in the sixth century. The Persian (Pahlevi) moralists expanded the "Five Books" into six by adding as the second chapter "Dimnah's Trial." The Pahlevi version is lost, but a sixth-century version of the *Panchatantra* is extant, as is the Syriac. From Pahlevi, it was translated into Arabic as *Kalīlah wa Dimnah* (the names of the two jackals whose adventures form the frame story). The eighth-century Arabic version has survived, and its preface indicates that it was translated from a Pahlevi version which had come from India. From the Arabic edition, translations were made into Greek in the eleventh century and into Old Spanish and Hebrew in the mid-thirteenth century. The Hebrew was translated into Latin as *Directorium Humanae Vitae* by John of Capua, 1263–78. Later German, Spanish, and Italian editions were, in turn, translated from the *Directorium*. The Old-Spanish version dates from 1251, having been done for the crown prince Alfonso the year before he became Alfonso X.

Another Latin edition, *Kalilae et Dimnae*, done in 1313 by Raymond de Bézier, is based on both the Old-Spanish *Kalīlah* and John of Capua's *Directorium*,[11] thus indicating that the Spanish version was known outside of Spain. It is significant in that the fables of the collection could have been known in Europe only through the Old-Spanish *Kalīlah wa Dimnah* or through John of Capua's *Directorium Humanae Vitae*. Some of the fables in the latter recur in the *Gesta Romanorum*, and one of the

[10] Bédier, in *Les Fabliaux*, has reconstructed, indicating extant and lost versions, the probable routes of transmission. See his chart facing p. 82. For the translation history, see Bédier, *Les Fabliaux*, pp. 137 ff.; Browne, *Literary History of Persia*, II, 353; Keller, *Book of the Wiles of Women*, pp. 2–3; Hitti, *History of the Arabs*, pp. 308 ff.; H. A. R. Gibb, "Literature," in *The Legacy of Islam*, ed. Arnold and Guillaume, p. 196; and H. A. R. Gibb, *Arabic Literature* (London, 1926).

[11] A. Collingwood Lee, *The Decameron: Its Sources and Analogues* (New York, 1966), pp. 192–93, 267. (Originally published in 1909.)

stories from Raymond de Bézier's version is found later in the *Decameron*.

Gesta Romanorum

One of the best-known sourcebooks of the later Middle Ages, the *Gesta Romanorum*, was a collection of tales, each followed by a moral explication or application, compiled in Latin in the late thirteenth or early fourteenth century.[12] A compendium of Eastern fables, Arabic tales, classical stories, and *exempla*, incorporated into European feudal institutions, the *Gesta Romanorum* was no more "Roman" than the Holy Roman Empire. Almost every scholar who has commented on the work has noticed its large quantity of Oriental stories. Indebted to the *Disciplina Clericalis, Kalīlah wa Dimnah, The Seven Sages of Rome*, and the *exempla* of Jacques de Vitry and Etienne de Bourbon, the *Gesta* was itself used by Chaucer, Gower, Lydgate, and Hoccleve. It had considerable influence on English poetry under Richard II and his successors, its popularity continuing through the Renaissance and into the eighteenth century. The earliest extant manuscript in Middle English, containing seventy stories, is in a folio of around 1440 which also includes a version of *The Canterbury Tales*, part of the *Confessio Amantis*, and some of Lydgate's and Hoccleve's works. Wynkyn de Worde printed an edition of it containing forty-three stories some time between 1510 and 1515.

Many of the tales of the *Gesta* were drawn from the *Disciplina* of Pedro Alfonso. Some examples are: the tale of the knight using an old woman's artifice to retrieve money entrusted to a friend for safekeeping; the tale of Folliculus who, thinking his grey-

[12] The tales and information from the *Gesta Romanorum* are from the following sources: *Gesta Romanorum*, trans. Charles Swan, rev. ed. (New York, 1959), pp. xx–xxxii; Sidney Herrtage, ed., *Gesta Romanorum, Early English Text Society*, Extra Series 33 (1879), xvii–xxv; Thomas Warton, *History of English Poetry*, ed. W. C. Hazlitt (London, 1871), I, 238–305; Clouston, *Popular Tales and Fictions*, pp. 12–13; and Sabine Baring-Gould, *Curious Myths of the Middle Ages* (New York, 1967). (Swan's translation of the *Gesta Romanorum* was originally published in 1824 and revised by Wynnard Hooper in 1876; Warton's *History* first appeared a century prior to Hazlitt's edition of it; and Sabine Baring-Gould's work was first published as essays in two series, 1866 and 1868.) The edition referred to for tale numbers is the Swan translation. The identification of tales in the *Gesta* drawn from the *Disciplina Clericalis* is Warton's.

hound has killed his son, slays him and immediately regrets his error; tale number XXVIII, of the old woman and her weeping bitch; CVI, of the three travelers who quarrel over a loaf of bread; CXIX, of the ungrateful seneschal rescued from a pit; CXXII and CXXIII, of a woman covering her husband's eye or holding up a bed sheet while her lover escapes; CLVII, of the consequences of refusing to pay even unjust taxes; CLXXI, of two friends of Baghdad and Egypt willing to die for each other whose love shames a murderer into confession; and CLXXIV, of the ungrateful serpent who bites the man who freed him from a tree to which he had been tied. Not a complete list, these examples are sufficient to illustrate the variety in types of tales found both in the *Disciplina* and in the *Gesta.*

Among the stories mentioned above, that of Folliculus, who does not realize that the blood on his son's crib is from the faithful dog's battle with a snake who threatened his son, is originally from the *Bidpai Fables,* from which *Kalīlah wa Dimnah* was translated. It is found in all versions, Eastern and Western, of *The Seven Sages of Rome.* The tale of the old woman and her weeping dog is a typical Persian *fabliau* in which a young knight falls in love with a beautiful wife (someone else's, of course) who rejects his suit. The old woman then assists him by feeding her dog pepper or mustard so that she will "weep" and visits the young wife. When the latter asks why the dog weeps, the old woman replies that the dog was her sister, who, through sorcery, was changed into a bitch for rejecting the advances of a young man in love with her. The young wife, frightened, relents. The story also occurs in the *Libro de los Engaños,* the Old-Spanish version of the *Seven Sages.* In the tale of the ungrateful seneschal, a peasant rescues various animals (such as a lion, a monkey, and a serpent, which vary among versions) and a seneschal from a pit. The animals show their gratitude by assisting the peasant in various ways until the seneschal, who once freed refuses to acknowledge his debt, is publicly disgraced. The seneschal story is also found in *Kalīlah wa Dimnah,* in all editions of *The Seven Sages,* in the *Arabian Nights,* in the *Decameron,* and in the *Confessio Amantis.*

One of the tales of the *Gesta Romanorum,* LXXX, of the hermit and the angel, is closely related to a similar story in the *Qur'ān*. The following is a brief summary of the tale:

A hermit sees from his cave a shepherd whose sheep are stolen by a robber while he is sleeping. The owner of the sheep slays the shepherd for his loss. Angry over the injustice God has permitted, the hermit decides to return to the world of men. Enroute to a town, he is joined by a messenger from heaven in the form of a man sent to accompany him. Seeking a place to rest for the night, they arrive at the dwelling of a knight who gives them lodging. The next morning, as they leave, the angel slays the knight's infant son in his crib. On their next stop for lodging, their host is exceptionally kind and generous, but when they depart, the angel steals an ornate, valuable cup from him. When the travelers meet a poor pilgrim crossing a bridge, the angel tosses him into the stream to drown. At their third stop, the man from whom they ask lodging offers them only his pigsty. On leaving the next morning, the angel presents their host with the rich cup stolen from their generous host. The hermit, unable any longer to tolerate what appears to be a string of gross injustices, refuses to accompany the angel farther and the angel then explains the reasons for his strange deeds. The shepherd had died for a prior sin he had committed; the knight's only son was slain because since the birth of his son, the knight, formerly devout and generous to the poor, had become stingy and had turned from God to lavish all his love on his son; the cup had caused their generous host to get drunk and thus befoul an otherwise clean life; the pilgrim, had he lived, was destined to commit a mortal sin, which had been prevented by his early death; and finally, the rich cup had been given to their miserly host because he was damned and the only riches he would ever enjoy were those of this world. The moral is the inscrutability of the divine will which man must accept without questioning the wisdom or justice of God.

The story is strikingly similar in several respects to that of the mystic journey of Moses and the divine messenger in *Sura* XVIII, Sections 9 and 10, of the *Qur'ān*.[13] The title of this *Sura* is "The

[13] Both Baring-Gould, *Curious Myths*, and Clouston, *Popular Tales and Fictions*, note the parallels between the Qur'ānic story and that in the *Gesta*, as does Burton. See Richard F. Burton, trans., *The Book of the Thousand Nights and a Night*, 6 vols. (New York, 1934), III, 1899. Later citations to the *Arabian Nights* are to Burton's translation.

Cave," pertaining to the sleepers of Ephesus. The following is a condensation of the Qurʾānic story, for comparison:

> Moses and his servant reach the junction of the two rivers. There they meet one of the Lord's messengers and servants, to whom He had imparted divine knowledge. Moses asks to follow him and learn from him, but the stranger replies that Moses does not have enough patience in matters about which he does not have a comprehensive knowledge. But Moses promises not to question him about anything that happens and the stranger agrees to Moses' traveling with him. After they cross a river, the messenger destroys their boat which had belonged to poverty-stricken people. Next he slays a boy much beloved of his true-believing and righteous parents. Then, in a hostile town, he rebuilds a wall which is crumbling. Finally, at Moses' insistence because he cannot bear the seeming injustices any longer, the messenger explains the significance of his deeds. He had destroyed the boat to prevent a king's seizing it by force and using it against the people. The boy was slain because his parents were believers while he was not, and he would therefore have led them astray and caused their damnation had he lived. The wall belonged to two orphan boys in the city. There was a treasure for them buried beneath it by their father, and the wall had to be rebuilt to prevent the boys' getting the treasure and losing it before they reached maturity.

The general outline of the Qurʾānic episode is followed by the story in the *Gesta*. Moses, like the hermit, is accompanied on a journey by a divine messenger, and like the hermit, he becomes impatient and angry over what appears to be a series of injustices perpetrated by the messenger. When he can keep silence no longer, Moses demands an explanation and the messenger gives one for each incident. The moral is the same, the necessity for man to accept with patience those events which he does not understand, since God's wisdom and justice are beyond man's comprehension. And finally, the messenger in the *Gesta,* like the one in the text of the *Qurʾān*, is not named. But the identity of the figure in the *Qurʾān* is established by *Ḥadīths* and Qurʾānic commentaries. Bukhārī, in a *Ḥadīth* on this passage in the *Qurʾān*, identifies the messenger as al-Khaḍir, "The Green One."

What on earth was a story such as this doing in a collection of tales for Christian moral instruction in the Middle Ages? But there it is, and its "moral" was not even Christianized in the *Gesta*. The necessity for absolute submission to the divine will without question, no matter how incongruent it may seem with human situations or man's point of view, is the prime tenet of Islam. In fact, the meaning of the word *Islam* is "submission" (to the divine will). The story has been further traced back to the Talmudic story in which Rabbi Jochanan, son of Levi, travels with Elijah. From the Arabian Jews, it was incorporated into the *Qur'ān*. Both the *Qur'ān* and Bukhārī's *Ḥadīths* and commentaries were brought with the Arabs to Spain, with the *Qur'ān* being translated into Latin at Cluny in the mid-twelfth century. The story next appears among the *exempla* of Jacques de Vitry, who has been credited with introducing it into Western Europe.[14]

The story of the hermit and the angel is not included in the Middle-English version of the *Gesta Romanorum*, but Latin versions of the *Gesta* were of course known in England. It reappears in the eighteenth century in Thomas Parnell's poem "The Hermit," which follows the story in the Latin *Gesta* fairly closely. Another eighteenth-century poet, Alexander Pope, believed that the tale was originally Spanish.[15] Pope was wrong, but not far wrong, for the tale undoubtedly entered Europe through Spain, if not through the *Qur'ān*, then certainly through the Jews of Spain.

Libro de Buen Amor

The Castilian *Book of Good Love*, completed around 1330 by Juan Ruiz, archpriest of Hita, is an episodic mixture of prose narrative and verse—some of it religious, some gay and satirical.[16] It includes everything from learned discourses on science to love to

[14] Clouston, *Popular Tales and Fictions*, pp. 24–28, traces the story from the Talmud to the *Gesta*.

[15] Parnell's poem is reproduced in the Swan translation of the *Gesta*, pp. 378–83. Pope's comments on the story are cited by Warton (*History of English Poetry*, I, 256–59), who discusses it at some length and disagrees with Pope.

[16] Juan Ruiz. *The Book of Good Love*, trans. Rigo Mignoni and Mario A. Di Cesare (New York, 1970). I have used the comments of Castro, *Structure of Spanish History*, pp. 392–451, for criticism and the significance of the work. For an analysis

beast fables to burlesque, like Byron's *Don Juan,* which one critic says contains "everything from flowerpots to chamber pots." The speaker and hero is found in the roles of rejected lover, seducer, and victim; yet he insists that his book has a high moral purpose. He explains in the prose preface that *buen amor* is from God, while *loco amor* is the sinful and worldly love of women. The purpose of his book, he says, is to show the dangers and evils of worldly love. But, he adds, since it is the nature of man to sin, if a man insists on pursuing wicked worldly love of women, he should be able to find means to assist himself in the book. Juan Ruiz was no Andreas Capellanus.

Following a prayer and several hymns on the joys of Mary, Ruiz proceeds to narrate his love affairs. First is a youthful love, in which the lady recites fables to him and leads him on only to reject him as a lover. For his next effort, he sends a friend to woo the lady but the friend gets her for himself. After an unsuccessful suit of a noblewoman, he laments having had only songs to offer her. He is disgusted with love. Don Amor (the God of Love) then appears to him in a dream and gives a discourse on the seven deadly sins, illustrating them with fables. He explains to Ruiz why he has failed thus far and how to succeed in the future—through the power of money and the employment of an old woman as a bawd. His advice is lavished with *fabliaux.* Following Don Amor's advice, Ruiz secures as a go-between the services of an old woman nicknamed Trotaconventos, whose name means, just as it suggests, "Convent-Trotter." (She is the direct ancestress of such later characters as La Celestina and Juliet's nurse.) With her help, he succeeds in seducing a widow who is pressured into this action by the old woman. But he soon forgets to flatter Trotaconventos with words and gifts and therefore loses his widow.

He travels to the Sierra where he meets, one at a time, four hideously ugly and clumsy mountain girls or shepherdesses. Each one feeds and shelters him, forces him to make love to her, and demands in return either a long list of gifts or marriage or both. The *zajal,* which Ruiz uses throughout the *Libro,* is particularly

of the metrics of the poetry in it, see Róque Esteban Scarpa, *Lecturas medievales españolas* (Santiago, Chile, 1949), pp. 392–93.

effective here as a means of relating his encounters with the shepherdesses. The whole section is, in poetic form and subject matter, a burlesque of earlier Provençal pastoral poetry and of Ibn-Quzmān of two centuries previous. When Ruiz returns to the city, he finds a procession of priests and clerics honoring the sacred image of Venus. There is a Rabelaisian carnival scene and a contest between Lady Lent and Don Carnal.

After two more unsuccessful attempts to woo widows, Ruiz presses suit, with Trotaconventos' help, on a nun. But the nun will agree only to a platonic love affair, and this is not quite to his taste. The episode with the nun is followed by an unsuccessful attempt to woo a Mooress, which gives Ruiz the opportunity to show off his knowledge of vulgar Arabic, and he does, by transcribing several Arabic words and phrases in with the Spanish. The book ends after the death of Trotaconventos and another affair.

The *Libro* is significant for its treatment of themes from European tradition (such as the debate between Sir Flesh and Dame Lent) with Arabic sensibility and literary forms. Its hero-narrator is related to the picaresque hero-narrator of the Arabic *maqāma* and many of its poems follow the Andalusian *zajal* form. The work is a thorough mixture of the two traditions, Christian-European and Hispano-Arabic.

Don Amor's appearance to the unsuccessful lover in a vision to give a discourse on the seven deadly sins, to explain to the lover why he has failed, to elaborate on love with the proper procedures for wooing a lady, and to illustrate his discourse with fables, *fabliaux*, and other tales, offers a model for the framework of Gower's *Confessio Amantis* of some sixty years later. Similarities between the *Libro* and the *Confessio* have not, as far as I have been able to determine, been hitherto pointed out. A detailed comparison of certain aspects of the *Libro* with corresponding ones of the *Confessio,* in spite of the differences in tone and narrator between the two works, should, if made, prove revealing, and not necessarily from the standpoint of attempting to show direct influence of one upon the other.

A comparison of the *Libro* with *The Canterbury Tales* has recently been made in an unpublished doctoral dissertation by Marion Hodapp, who points out the sad fact that there has been little contact between English and Spanish medieval scholars. Hodapp does not attempt to state a direct link between the works of Juan Ruiz and those of Chaucer, but concentrates on a comprehensive survey of similarities in their works and finds that both poets drew from a common stock of themes and traditions. Both, however, in drawing from the life around them, take liberties with tradition. Hodapp finds that, in spite of their differences, Juan Ruiz and Chaucer shared the same Western European literary heritage.[17]

El Conde Lucanor

Of the numerous works of Infante Don Juan Manuel (1282–ca. 1348), who was involved in crusades against the Moors and civil wars, most of which he disliked, only four survive. One of these, *El Conde Lucanor* (*Count Lucanor*), also called *Libro de Patronio* and *Libro de los Enxemplos,* like Juan Ruiz's *Libro de Buen Amor,* provides an example of the integration between Christian and Islamic cultures reflected in early Spanish literature.[18] Like Ruiz's work, many of its stories are from Arabic ones which the Infante was able to read in the original, and some of its stories contain phrases in colloquial Arabic written phonetically in Spanish.

El Conde Lucanor is a collection of fifty exemplary tales compiled between 1328 and 1334. Each time Count Lucanor asks a question of his counselor and instructor Patronio, Patronio replies with a tale, following which a short moral is given in verse. The *exempla* are drawn from those of Etienne de Bourbon and Jacques de Vitry and from Arabic sources. As might be expected, *Lucanor* shares tales in common with the *Disciplina Clericalis, Kalīlah wa Dimnah, The Seven Sages of Rome,* the *Arabian Nights,* the *Gesta Romanorum,* and local Spanish stories, which nationalize them.

17 Marion F. Hodapp, "Two Fourteenth-Century Poets: Geoffrey Chaucer and the Archpriest of Hita," *Dissertation Abstracts,* 29 (1968), 1897A (Univ. of Colorado).

18 A short but good discussion appears in Mérimée, *History of Spanish Literature,* pp. 67–68.

The Thousand and One Nights

The historian al-Masᶜūdi (d. 956) mentions in one of his extant works a Persian collection of tales called *Hazār Afsān* (*One Thousand Tales*) with its frame story of the king and the *wazīr's* daughter Shīrāzād and her slave girl Dīnāzād as one of the works (among which was *Kalīlah wa Dimnah*) translated from Pahlevi to Arabic under al-Manṣūr (754–55).[19] The author of the catalog of early Arabic literature called the *Fihrist* in 988 mentions the *Hazār Afsān* and calls it vulgar and insipid. It is generally assumed from the records of these two historians that the draft for the *Thousand and One Nights* was formed before the mid-tenth century and that its nucleus was the *Hazār Afsān*.

The *Nights* was a cumulative work which is thought to have assumed its present form between the twelfth and the fourteenth centuries. Beginning with the Persian stories and frame before the tenth century, materials from Baghdad (usually centering about the court of Hārūn al-Rashīd) were added between the tenth and twelfth centuries, and further materials from Egypt, such as the adventures of Aladdin (in Arabic, ᶜAlā al-Dīn) were added from the eleventh century on, especially in the thirteenth and fourteenth centuries. Among the groups of tales considered to be the oldest matter in the *Nights* and which may have formed part of the original *Hazār Afsān* were those of "The Fisherman and the Genie," "The Merchant and the Genie," "Qamar al-Zamān and Budur," and "The Enchanted Horse." Sir Richard Burton, in the terminal essay to his translation, considers the beast fables and the stories on the malice of women of the "Seven Wazīrs" group (*The Seven Sages of Rome* or *Sindibād* frame and stories) among the oldest matter in the *Nights*.

19 For the history of the *Arabian Nights*, I have used Hitti, *History of the Arabs*, p. 404; Nicholson, *Literary History of the Arabs*, pp. 456–58; Burton, *Thousand Nights and a Night*, VI, 3659, 3758–59, 3820; Joseph Campbell, ed., *The Portable Arabian Nights* (New York, 1952), pp. 5–6; and Mia I. Gerhardt, *The Art of Story-Telling: A Literary Study of the Thousand and One Nights* (Leiden, Netherlands, 1963), pp. 9 ff. The Gerhardt book is pedestrian. Night numbers and tale titles, except for those involving al-Khaḍir, are those of Campbell's "portable" edition for convenience of reference. Campbell's edition is based on Payne's, which Burton followed closely.

The Thousand and One Nights is mentioned by a Spanish poet of Granada, Ibn-Saᶜīd (1218–86), who is in turn quoted by an anthologist and historian of Spain, Abū-al-ᶜAbbās Aḥmad Ibn-Muḥammad al-Makkārī, in his *Windwafts of Perfume from the Branches of Andalusia the Blooming*. Evidently, then, the collection was known in some form in thirteenth-century Spain. The accumulation of its later Persian and Egyptian tales coincided in point of time with the accumulation and development of Arthurian matter, and there seems to have been some cross-fertilization between the *Nights* and Arthurian tales. Just as Oriental material appears, often unaccountably, in European tales and romances, European motifs appear in the *Nights*. In view of the probability of the *Nights* having been known in thirteenth-century Spain, a glance at some of its contents as a medieval collection of tales is in order.

The tales of the *Nights*, like *maqāmāt*, are a mixture of prose and poetry, but the language is for the most part the nonliterary or vulgar Arabic, which is why they have not been appreciated among the Arabs as literature as they have been in Europe. The overall frame-story of Shahrazād is too well known to need repetition. The *Nights* is, however, an illustration of the frame-story par excellence. Within the overall frame-story are many groups of tales in subordinate frames. The breakdown goes even farther. In the group "Jamasp and the Serpent Queen," for example, occur several tales which, in a complex structure, present the situation of a tale within a tale within a tale within a tale.

There are parallels in the *Nights* with Judeo-Christian tradition, Greek legends, Irish lore, and medieval European tales and romances. The Judeo-Christian tradition is represented in the *Nights* by a version of the apocryphal "Susanna and the Elders" in Night 394, and an analogue of the English morality play *Everyman* occurs in "The Angel of Death and the King of the Children of Israel" of Nights 463 and 464, in which the Angel of Death comes to the king, who first begs for time to put his affairs in order. When his request is denied, he asks who will accompany him. The angel replies that only his good works can come with him, but he, unlike Everyman, has none and so is taken to torment.

"The Voyages of Sindbad the Sailor" contains an interesting mixture of diverse materials. There are, for example, similarities between Sindbad's third voyage (Nights 546–50) and the Cyclops episode of Ulysses in the *Odyssey*.[20] Sindbad's first voyage (Nights 538–41) has been compared to the voyage of the Irish Saint Brendan.[21] In this voyage, Sindbad lands on an island which turns out to be a huge fish or whale. The same thing happens to Saint Brendan. The last incident in Saint Brendan's voyage involves his meeting the hermit Paul on a rock in the ocean, where he is fed by a lark and is to remain alive until Judgment Day. It has been suggested that the hermit represents a combination of Saint Paul the hermit, who is fed by a raven in the desert until his death, and Khaḍir, who sometimes appears as a hermit on a desert island where he is fed by a bird and is to live until Judgment.

Another parallel with Irish literature occurs in "The Second Calender's Tale," in which there is a contest involving a series of transformations between a princess and a genie. The latter becomes a lion and the princess changes a hair from her head to a sword and beheads him; the head becomes a scorpion and she becomes a serpent; the genie becomes an eagle and she a griffin, and so forth. The same pattern of transformations, the animals differing, is found in an early Irish tale.

The appearance of *The Seven Sages* in the "Seven Wazīrs" frame and tales within the *Nights*, as possibly being part of its oldest matter, was mentioned above. One of the tales in the "Seven Wazīrs," that of the merchant, his wife, and parrot, reappears, with minor modifications, in almost every major collection of medieval stories from the *Disciplina Clericalis* to *The Canterbury Tales*. Another story of *The Canterbury Tales* with analogues in the *Arabian Nights* is the "Squire's Tale," portions of which have parallels in Princess Dunya's dream of the fowler and the pigeons, in the history of King ʿUmar Ibn-al-Nuʿmān and

20 These are pointed out by Gustave von Grunebaum, *Medieval Islam*, pp. 298 ff.

21 Miguel Asín Palacios, *Islam and the Divine Comedy*, pp. 207–13, makes the comparison. Details here, including the observation on Saint Paul and Khaḍir, are from Asín Palacios.

his sons which involves a brother-sister marriage, and in the story of the enchanted horse.

There seems also to have been interchange between the *Nights* and chivalric-romance tradition in Europe. The convention in medieval romance of placing a sword between a sleeping couple to indicate a chaste relationship as found in *Tristan* and *Amis et Amyloun* was incorporated in "The Story of Prince Sayf al-Mulūk and Princess Badīᶜ al-Jamāl." An instance of the conversion of the beloved to Islam in order to marry is found in "ᶜAlī Nūr al-Dīn and the Frankish King's Daughter Maryam" (Nights 864–65) and in "The Man of Upper Egypt and his Frankish Wife." Such conversion was as popular in Arabic lore as it was in medieval Christian romances. A strange parallel with the grail stories occurs in one of the oldest and perhaps original tales of the *Nights*, that of "The Fisherman and the Genie," whose enchanted land which is restored when the spell is removed corresponds to the enchanted wasteland of many of the grail stories of Arthurian romance.[22]

Finally, there are several tales in the *Nights* in which al-Khaḍir in his Qurʾānic and *Ṣūfī* roles either appears or is mentioned. In "The Tale of Tāj al-Mulūk and the Princess Dunya," one of the analogues to Chaucer's "Squire's Tale," is an allusion to the episode of Moses and Khaḍir in the *Qurʾān* summarized above in connection with a similar story in the *Gesta Romanorum*:

> I marvel hearing people questioning of
> The Fount of Life and in what land 'tis found;
> I see it sprung from lips of dainty fawn,
> Sweet rosy mouth with green mustachio down'd:
> And wondrous wonder 'tis when Moses viewed
> That Fount, he rested not from weary round. (II, 761)[23]

These verses also suggest Khaḍir's connection with Alexander the Great in his legendary search for the Fountain of Life.

In "The Tale of Abū-Muḥammad Hight Lazybones," al-

22 Joseph Campbell, *Portable Arabian Nights*, p. 17. Others have pointed out the enchanted-wasteland correspondence.

23 Burton, *Thousand Nights and a Night*, II, 929, notes that the allusion is to the Qurʾānic story.

Khaḍir appears to Abū-Muḥammad while he is being flown by a *marīd* (an evil supernatural creature) to retrieve his bride who has been stolen by another *marīd*. He is forbidden to utter the name of Allah or the *marīd* will drop him. Abū-Muḥammad relates:

> But as we flew, behold, One clad in green raiment, with streaming tresses and radiant face, holding in his hand a javelin whence flew sparks of fire, accosted me, saying "O Abu Mohammed, say: —There is no god but *the* God and Mohammed is the Apostle of God; or I will smite thee with this javelin." (III, 1415)

Abū-Muḥammad complies; al-Khaḍir smites the *marīd* dead; and Abū-Muḥammad falls into the sea, is rescued by sailors, and later retrieves his bride.

He appears again in "The Adventures of Bulukiya" (III, 1989–90), within "The Tale of the Queen of Serpents," which is set in pre-Islamic times and includes prophecies of Muḥammad's coming. There are many fantastic creatures and a great deal of Persian magic in the tale, such as are found in the older portions of the *Nights*. In the tale, Bulukiya, of the Children of Israel, has read in Cairo a prophecy of Muḥammad's coming and goes in search of him. Along with the fantastic events of his travels, he meets also various angels and there are lengthy discussions of hell, punishment for unbelievers, and other aspects of Islamic theology. When Bulukiya is stranded on one of the islands in the story, al-Khaḍir comes to his rescue. Bulukiya asks how far it is to Cairo and Khaḍir tells him it is a ninety-five-year journey, but he will gladly carry him thence if he will pray to God for permission. Bulukiya prays, al-Khaḍir takes one step, and they are in Cairo. He then disappears.

In "The City of Brass" (IV, 2107–47), the Caliph has sent his *amīr* ("governor") Mūsā Ibn-Nuṣayr to North Africa to obtain some of the sealed bottles in which Solomon imprisoned rebellious *jinn* ("spirits"). Mūsā and his company arrive at the City of Brass and find outside the city many tablets with inscriptions warning about hoarding up treasures in this life. Once inside the city, they find all the people dead, including a beautiful maiden, above whom is an inscription explaining that the city was destroyed by a drought. Throughout the city are many inscriptions exhorting people to seek the ways of God and not worldly wealth. After Mūsā and his party have departed from it, they meet a tribe of blacks (descended from Ham) who are Muslims. Mūsā asks how they came to know of Islam when they have been cut off from all of the prophets, and the king explains that a great voice had spoken to them, saying that he was Abū-al-ᶜAbbās al-Khaḍir. Khaḍir taught them the religion and how to worship, and every Friday a great light would appear and Khaḍir's voice would be heard praising God. This story seems to be another version of "The Eldest Lady's Tale" (I, 183–94), in "The Porter and the Three Ladies of Baghdad," in which the people had refused Islam and were turned to stone.

Khaḍir plays a major role in "The Tale of ᶜAbdallāh Ibn-Fāḍil and His Brothers" (VI, 3527–72). During their travels, ᶜAbdallāh and his brothers come to a strange city. Only ᶜAbdallāh enters. He finds its inhabitants all have turned to stone except for one beautiful maiden, the former king's daughter. She tells him her story. Theirs had been a great empire, but the king and his people worshipped idols. Suddenly one day a tall man, whose hands reached below his knees, clad in green, and whose face illumined the area with its light, entered the palace. He warned the king to stop worshipping idols and exhorted him to embrace Islam. There was then a contest in which the idols were pitted against God. The idols failed, but the king still refused to accept Islam. The stranger next asked God to turn the people to stone. The princess, however, was converted and was spared. The stranger gave his name to her as Abū-al-ᶜAbbās al-Khaḍir. He instructed the princess in Islam, teaching her the *Qurʾān* and prayer rituals, and visiting her every Friday (the Islamic holy day). He had predicted ᶜAbdallāh's coming. She goes with ᶜAbdallāh to his brothers, whose jealousy separates them. Khaḍir later rescues the princess from the sea and establishes her in a foreign land, where he continues to visit her on Fridays. After ᶜAbdallāh finds her, al-Khaḍir returns them to ᶜAbdallāh's home.

Khaḍir as he appears in the *Arabian Nights* stories is tall and powerful, he is an agent of the supernatural, he appears in courts to hurl challenges, and he is green—all peculiarly similar to the green knight of the Middle-English *Sir Gawain and the Green Knight.* They could be related. The *Arabian Nights* was known in Spain, but its exact relationship to medieval European tales has not been determined. And it may never be determined because it is a complex relationship involving an interchange of materials and stories, most of which were transmitted orally.

Decameron

Boccaccio's *Decameron* of 1348–53 was apparently drawn from every available source or tradition, which, by the fourteenth century, included material taken over in European tradition from the East and from Arab Spain. It is not definitely known if Chaucer read or knew the *Decameron.* Several of Boccaccio's stories reappear in *The Canterbury Tales,* and both works have the frame of a traveling group, so there is speculation that Chaucer may have at least known about the *Decameron.* Suffice it to say that both Boccaccio and Chaucer were heirs to a literary tradition that had become eclectic and that the points of similarity between them illustrate not necessarily their direct contact with each other, but rather mutual access to the same source materials.

Among the many sources and analogues of the tales of the *Decameron* are the *Disciplina Clericalis, The Seven Sages of Rome,* "The Seven Wazīrs" of the *Arabian Nights, El Conde Lucanor,* John of Capua's *Directorium Humanae Vitae, Kalīlah wa Dimnah,* and Raymond of Bézier's *Kalilae et Dimnae* compiled from the *Directorium* and *Kalīlah.* The most frequently cited tale collections with analogues to Boccaccio's tales are the *Disciplina,* the *Gesta Romanorum,* and the Arabic "Seven Wazīrs," which contains considerably more analogous stories than *The Seven Sages.*

One of the tales, that of the lion's track (Day 1, Novel 5), has analogues in the "Seven Wazīrs" and in the last story in *El Conde Lucanor.* It is not likely that Boccaccio could have read either of these works in Arabic and in Castilian respectively; the story may therefore be one of many which were transmitted orally from Islamic Spain to Europe.

PART II—MIDDLE ENGLISH

Each of the major Latin source-books was eventually translated in some form into Middle English. The Middle-English version of *The Seven Sages of Rome* dates from 1330, that of the *Gesta Romanorum* from around 1440, and the *Disciplina Clericalis* also from some time in the fifteenth century. In addition, there were several tale collections composed in English, and these collections show vital links with Continental literature. In some there are connections with Spanish-Arabic literature and lore.

Purity

One of the four works of the anonymous poet of *Pearl* and *Sir Gawain and the Green Knight, Purity* is often viewed as a collection of biblical stories in English paraphrases. It is that, but it also contains elements neither English nor biblical. Written in alliterative verse, the work illustrates the theme of "purity" (refraining from any sin) with several biblical stories. It begins with a discussion of that portion of the Beatitudes in Matthew dealing with the pure in heart, then illustrates the theme of purity by the story of the rich man's banquet (in which one of the commoners invited appears directly from work in rags and dirty), Satan's fall, Eve's sin, Noah's flood, the destruction of Sodom and Gomorrah, and Belshazzar's feast.

The major source for *Purity* was the Vulgate Bible,[24] but the poet also used other sources, as in the destruction of Sodom and Gomorrah. This episode begins with a discussion of what love should be, compared to what the Sodomites have made of it. Abraham's bargaining with God, who finally agrees to save the city if ten righteous men can be found, is described. Then two angels, as handsome young boys, go into Sodom to Abraham's son Lot to warn him to flee the city the next morning, and Lot has to

[24] Robert J. Menner, ed., *Purity: A Middle English Poem,* xxxix. Citations to *Purity* are to the Menner edition.

defend them from the lust of his neighbors. When the evening meal is to be served, the angels ask that their food be prepared without leaven and salt, but Lot's wife salts the food in disregard of their request. The next day Lot, his wife, and two daughters flee the city and are warned not to look behind them. Lot's wife does look and is changed into a pillar of salt. The passage is followed by a reference to the *Roman de la Rose* and to the pearl as a symbol of purity, like Mary.

The two angels had asked that salt not be used because they were messengers of God, and it was a Jewish taboo to use salt in God's presence. There is then a sort of poetic justice in Lot's wife subsequently becoming a pillar of salt to be licked daily by beasts:

> For on ho standes a ston, and salt for þat oþer,
> And alle lyst on hir lik þat arn on launde bestes. (ll. 999–1000)

The idea of Lot's wife being licked by beasts in retribution for using salt in God's presence comes from Jewish lore; thus, it has been suggested that the poet may have known Hebrew, oral Jewish lore, or both.[25] It is an interesting suggestion and certainly not inconceivable in view of the wide variety of sources from which the poet can be shown to have drawn. The Jews were, after all, instrumental in disseminating Eastern scientific and philosophical learning from Arab Spain, along with Arab stories and tales, and their own Jewish lore.

The poet's discourse on ideal marital love (which the Sodomites had perverted) deserves quoting:

> I compast hem a kynde crafte and kende hit hem derne,
> And armed hit in myn ordenaunce oddely dere,
> And dyȝt drwry þerinne, doole alþerswettest,
> And þe play of paramorez I portrayed myselven;
> And made þerto a maner myriest of oþer,
> When two true togeder had tyȝed hemselven,
> Bytwene a male and his make such merþe schulde conne,
> Wel nyȝe pure paradys moȝt preve no better,
> Ellez þay moȝt honestly ayþer oþer welde;

25 Margaret Williams, trans., *The Pearl-Poet: His Complete Works*, pp. 39–40, makes this suggestion.

At a stylle stollen steven, unstered with syȝt,
Luf-lowe hem bytwene lasched so hote,
Þat alle þe meschefez on mold moȝt hit not sleke. (ll. 697–708)

This is not the same type of love as that between Lancelot and Guinevere or between Tristan and Isolt or that in Ibn-Quzmān and the troubadours where the lady is married and where marital love cannot exist. It is, rather, the type of love found in Ibn-Ḥazm and in Jean de Meun. Not only was courtly love (the adulterous variety) not natively Christian or Germanic, but neither was romantic and physical love in marriage, and besides, the early Church fathers, as C. S. Lewis shows in *The Allegory of Love,* had condemned marital love. The speaker in the above passage is God, and yet it is precisely because such love was antithetical to medieval Christianity with its monkish views of women that eschatological treatises and visions of strictly Christian origin could never associate an idealized beloved woman with virtue and the rewards of the afterlife. Such an association, as was seen in the preceding chapter, *was* characteristic of Islamic mystical, visionary, and eschatological writings. Both the use of the idealized maiden in *Pearl* and the passage in *Purity* cited above are, in their essence, of non-Christian origin and have earlier European predecessors chiefly in the Islamic literature of Arab Spain (and in the case of *Pearl,* in Dante's *Commedia* which probably owes some debt in this respect to Islamic concepts).

The type of love described in *Purity* is not often encountered in medieval literature. Some exceptions are the love between Parzival and his wife Condwiramurs in Wolfram von Eschenbach's *Parzival* and that between Arveragus and his wife Dorigen in Chaucer's "Franklin's Tale," both of which works have other connections with materials from Arab Spain. The romantic marital love in the "Franklin's Tale" is unique in Chaucer. By way of contrast, his remarks in the "Man of Law's Tale" are more typical of marital "love" in works reflecting the medieval Christian view. In this tale, on her wedding night, Custance must "leye a lite hir hoolynesse aside" (l. 713) and tolerate what is necessary in spite of being "holy."

The reference to "Clopyngel in þe compas of his clene Rose"

(l. 1057) in *Purity* is of course to Jean de Meun's portion of the *Roman de la Rose* which is by no stretch of the imagination either platonic or adulterous. (Jean de Meun pillories monkish views on chastity.) Jean's Rose is no wife of a noble, but a virgin, whom he must win by goodness and service (a concept already developed by Ibn-Ḥazm), as the poet of *Purity* seems to have been aware in the passage in which he mentions the work. Hence the poet's reference to the "clene Rose"—love itself was not, according to the passage quoted in *Purity*, considered evil by the poet, an attitude which can be regarded as generally atypical in English literature of the period.

In the section on Belshazzar's feast in *Purity*, the poet gives free rein to his fondness for elaborate descriptions of spices and jewels, which he also does extensively in *Pearl*. Here, in describing the jewels, ornaments, and the banquet table, he apparently borrowed from the description of the palace of the Great Khan in Cathay in *Mandeville's Travels* which had reached England by 1371. Other passages in which his descriptions follow those of Mandeville in many details are those of the Dead Sea (ll. 1020–48) and of the temple (ll. 1437 ff.).[26]

In *Purity* then, besides its biblical stories, are to be found marital love, the *Roman de la Rose*, *Mandeville's Travels*, and a Jewish legend. Such materials make for strange biblical paraphrases. Perhaps *Purity* too might be better regarded as a collection of tales than as a collection of paraphrases.

The Book of the Knight of La Tour Landry

Composed around 1371–72 by Geoffroy de la Tour, the Middle-English *Book of the Knight of La Tour Landry* is a collection of *exempla* and moral tales set in an instructive frame of the type of the *Disciplina Clericalis* and *El Conde Lucanor*. The narrator states that he employed two priests and two clerks to help him find *exempla* and that the book is for the instruction of his three

26 Similarities to *Mandeville's Travels* are pointed out by Menner, *Purity*, pp. xxxix–xli; and Williams, *The Pearl-Poet*, pp. 36–47. The "big fake" was one of the most popular travel accounts ever written. Composed in French around 1357, it had been translated into Latin and English before 1400, and 250 to 300 manuscripts in Middle English alone survive.

daughters. He addresses them from time to time within it, but there is no dialogue between father and daughters as there is between philosopher and student in the *Disciplina* and between prince and counselor in *Lucanor*.

The Knight of La Tour Landry is, in tone, in line with such English moral pieces as *The Cloud of Unknowing, Ancrene Riwle,* and Richard Rolle's *Mending of Life*. Those of its tales of Oriental origin have been Anglicized in their treatment, and its frame, not without interest, seems to be an adaptation of the instructive dialogue frame of the *Disciplina* and *Lucanor* to more of a straight narrative. In the latter portion of the book, the knight or narrator relates a disputation with his wife in which tales are told by each on aspects of love and how certain situations would be best handled by young girls.

Typical of the *Knight*'s treatment of Oriental and Moorish tales are those of Chapters 16 and 62.[27] The tale of Chapter 16 combines the story of the husband, his wife, and the telltale bird with another motif. The husband has caught an eel and brought it home. While he is away, the wife and her servant woman eat the eel, and when he returns, the magpie "squeals" on the wife. In revenge, she plucks out the bird's feathers. Afterwards, whenever the magpie saw a bald man, he would shriek, "Aha! You told about an eel, so now you're bald too!"

The story in Chapter 62, that of the roper, his wife, and her affair with a prior, is another reworking of a widespread Arab tale. An old lady helps the wife deceive her husband once he suspects her by switching the white and black wool with which he works. At another point in the story, when the husband rises from bed, he takes the prior's breeches instead of his own garment. The old lady and the wife then don breeches to pretend that everyone is wearing breeches. Finally, to stop the affair, he breaks both of his wife's legs, and when even this does not succeed, he slays his wife and the prior when he finds them together in the bed. In Arabic versions of the tale, used to illustrate the wiles and devices of women, the wife and the old woman always

[27] Citations are to *The Book of the Knight of La Tour Landry*, ed. Thomas Wright, *Early English Text Society*, 33 (1868).

succeed in deceiving the husband into thinking he was mistaken in his suspicions and there is no punishment or retribution for the wife. Geoffroy de la Tour has reworked the tale so as to point up not so much the devices of women, but the axiom that "crime does not pay" or "be sure your sins will find you out." Such reworked tales are interesting as illustrations of the adaptation of *fabliau*-type oriental materials to a more serious temperament.

Confessio Amantis

Some forty manuscripts exist of John Gower's *Confessio Amantis*, the earliest dating from 1390, and it was translated into several languages soon after it was written. Its frame, that of a lover confessing to and being absolved by Venus' chaplain Genius, has been observed as unusual because it revolves around courtly love but is at the same time set within a framework of the seven deadly sins,[28] a combination which had an earlier parallel in a portion of Juan Ruiz's *Libro de Buen Amor*. Divided into eight books, the stories within each of seven of the books supposedly relate to one of the deadly sins.[29] Books I through VI are concerned with pride, envy, wrath, sloth, avarice, and gluttony, and Book VIII with lechery. Many of the tales of Book VIII are incestuous ones, like that of Canacee and her brother Macarius in Book III, which Chaucer condemns in his "Introduction to the Man of Law's Tale" (ll. 77–80). Ironically, it seems to have been a tale of incest, with the heroine Canacee, which Chaucer began but broke off in "The Squire's Tale."

Book VII, "The Education of a King," permits Gower to display his knowledge of Aristotle, astronomy, astrology, law, theology, and ethics. Digressions to display an encyclopedic learning in such areas were common in vernacular literature of Europe after the twelfth-century translations. Gower does it in other books of the *Confessio*, Juan Ruiz does so in the *Libro de Buen Amor*, and other poets such as Jean de Meun, Wolfram von Eschenbach, and Chaucer do so extensively throughout their

28 Terence Tiller, trans., *Confessio Amantis*, by John Gower (Baltimore, 1963), p. 11.

29 Stories mentioned in the *Confessio* are those of *Confessio Amantis of John Gower*, ed. Reinhold Pauli, 3 vols. (London, 1857).

works. Such displays of learning appear to have been fashionable; they are abundant in most of the popular works and appear only sporadically in the less popular and more mundane ones of the thirteenth and fourteenth centuries.

The sources of the *Confessio* are varied. It includes stories from the *Gesta Romanorum* (such as the King of Hungary who is gracious to two pilgrims in Book I), from *The Seven Sages* (such as Virgil's mirror of Book V), from Trivet's *Anglo-Norman Chronicle*, from Livy, and from Ovid's *Epistles* and *Metamorphoses*. (Juan Ruiz, in his *Libro de Buen Amor*, also drew from Ovid as well as from Arabic sources.) Several of the tales of the *Confessio* are also found in *The Canterbury Tales*; examples are the tale of Florent (in Book I) and Chaucer's "Wife of Bath's Tale," the tale of Constance (Book II) and Chaucer's "Man of Law's Tale," the tale of Phoebus and Coronis (Book III) and Chaucer's "Manciple's Tale," and that of Appius and Virginia (Book VII) and Chaucer's "Physician's Tale." The sources used by Chaucer and Gower, however, were not always the same. Gower's tale of Appius and Virginia is apparently from Livy, while Chaucer's version is closer to that in Jean de Meun's *Roman de la Rose*.

Gower tended to draw largely from classical sources such as Ovid and Livy in the *Confessio*, but among his tales from other sources, some are apparently Oriental. One is of particular interest, that of Wise Petronella in Book I. In this story, King Alfonso of Spain poses three questions to a rival, the knight Don Pedro. Don Pedro's daughter Petronella answers them for the king, who is so impressed that he marries her and advances her father. One critic has made the observation, "The source of this tale appears to be untraceable."[30] Is it? Perhaps the exact source is not identifiable since it may have been oral, but the witty daughter of the Shahrazād type is common in Arabic literature. There are any number of Arabic stories, including several in the *Arabian Nights*, in which a maiden of humble birth (often of very poor parents and sometimes a slave) amazes a king by her

30 Tiller, *Confessio Amantis*, p. 93.

knowledge and intelligence as revealed through her ability to answer riddles that puzzle more noble minds. Usually the king marries her himself, but in some cases she is already in love with another and he bestows her on her beloved in marriage along with a quantity of gold and wealthy gifts, since such ability is greatly prized in a woman. A similar incident in real life is to be noted in the account of the slave girl Iᶜtimād al-Rumakiyya, who married King Muᶜtamid of Seville, which was incorporated as one of the stories in *El Conde Lucanor.* The setting of Gower's story in Spain and the use of King Alfonso suggest oral transmission of an Arab tale which would have been common in Spain with the Spanish setting substituted for an Eastern one.

Gower, like Chaucer, indeed, like most of the medieval poets and writers, did not stop to analyze the origin of his stories. Where the source was known, it might be cited, especially if citing it evinced erudition. Sometimes it was not, however, and since there were no copyright laws, it was of no import to them. Gower would certainly not be the first medieval writer to use materials from an Arabic or Oriental source in ignorance of their origin or original significance.

The Canterbury Tales

Chaucer's *Canterbury Tales,* most of which were composed in the last two decades of the fourteenth century, illustrate, perhaps more than any other work of medieval literature of the period the sort of eclecticism in literature which was characteristic of the encyclopedists of the thirteenth and fourteenth centuries. Like Boccaccio, Chaucer seems to have drawn from almost every conceivable source at the time. It is not, however, merely the number of sources and analogues of *The Canterbury Tales* or their diversity that makes them unique, but also the vivid and dramatic interaction among the pilgrims within the frame who relate the various tales. Even though the complete work was not finished, the frame itself, along with the various head and end links of the tales within it, provides a video tape of life in England in the late fourteenth century. Like the Archpriest of Hita, Chaucer drew not only from the literary traditions to which he was heir but also from the life around him.

Chaucer's works divide into two broad periods—a French period, during which a large proportion of his works was inspired by or derived from French literature; and an Italian period, during which he was influenced by Boccaccio, Sercambi, Petrarch, and others. They are often discussed in terms of their French and Italian influences. They will be discussed here, with a few exceptions, in terms of possible Spanish (including Arabic) influences.

Twelfth-century translations. Chaucer, like Gower and other contemporaries, frequently digresses to display his knowledge of the scientific works which poured into Europe in the twelfth century. In the description of the physician in the "General Prologue," for example, various medical authorities such as Galen, Razī, Ibn-Sīnā, and Ibn-Rushd are cited (ll. 429–34). In the "Man of Law's Tale" is an example of a Latinized Arabic term from astronomical treatises in the line "O Mars, o atazir, as in this cas!" (l. 305), the term *atazir* meaning "influence" being the Arabic *al-taʾthīr.*[31] A familiarity with treatises on alchemy in Latin translation can be seen in the "Canon's Yeoman's Prologue and Tale." Many other such references are scattered throughout *The Canterbury Tales.* A reference to "tables Tolletan" in the "Franklin's Tale" (l. 1273) is to the Toledan Tables of Alfonso X mentioned in Chapter II.

Travels to Spain. Some of Chaucer's pilgrims had been to Spain. It was mentioned earlier that among the many important points for pilgrimage in medieval Europe was the shrine of Saint James at Compostela in Spain. Chaucer's Wife of Bath, who, in the "General Prologue," is described as having made several excursions to Jerusalem, Rome, and Bologne, had also been "In Galice at Seint-Jame, and at Coloigne" (l. 466).

There is a reference to Spain in the "Pardoner's Tale" in a short discourse on the illegal mixing of Spanish and other wines:

> This wyn of Spaigne crepeth subtilly
> In other wynes, growynge faste by. (ll. 565–66)

[31] F. N. Robinson, ed., *The Works of Geoffrey Chaucer,* p. 693, points this out. The identification of the Toledan Tables is also from Robinson, p. 725.

Chaucer was of a vintner family. His father's business would have had French and Spanish connections, and Chaucer could have met men from these lands.[32] If he did, then the chances are he picked up bits of Spanish lore from them.

There is, in addition, good evidence that Chaucer himself visited Spain. Included in the 1966 *Chaucer Life-Records* is a document, signed by the King of Navarre and dated February 1365 (1366), granting a safe-conduct to "Geoffroy de Chauserre" for a period of just over three months. The document is cited by A. C. Baugh, who discusses its political ramifications with regard to the "Monk's Tale."[33] But besides the "Monk's Tale," a visit to Spain would have ramifications for the "Squire's Tale," which has similarities to some aspects of Arabic versions of the story which do not appear in its French analogues.

Views of the Saracens. Chaucer is very much a man of his day and age in his views of the Saracens, just as he is in his attitude toward the Jews in the "Prioress' Tale." The idea of anti-Semitism being an undesirable and bigoted prejudice was unknown in the fourteenth century[34] and it is very doubtful if Chaucer even questioned the prevailing attitudes towards either Jews or Saracens. In the "Tale of Sir Thopas" and in the "Man of Law's Tale" are to be found ideas associating the Saracens with idolatry which are characteristic of the *trouvère chanson-de-geste* tradition. In "Sir Thopas," Sir Olifaunt's swearing by Termagaunt (l. 810) is typical of French and Italian literary attribution of certain idols to the Saracens.[35] By way of contrast, in the "Man of Law's Tale" is a recognition of the *Qurʾān* and of Muḥammad as prophet when the Sultan's mother refers to

> The hooly lawes of our Alkaron
> Yeven by Goddes message Makomete. (ll. 332–33)

32 H. S. Bennett, *Chaucer and the Fifteenth Century,* Oxford History of English Literature (London, 1947), pp. 29–30, makes this suggestion.

33 Albert C. Baugh, "The Background of Chaucer's Mission to Spain," in *Chaucer und seine Zeit: Symposion für Walter F. Schirmer,* ed. Arno Esch (Tübingen, 1968), pp. 55–67.

34 See Joshua Trachtenberg, *The Devil and the Jews: The Medieval Conception of the Jew and Its Relation to Modern Antisemitism* (New Haven, 1943), for medieval attitudes towards and legends surrounding Jews.

35 Robinson, *Works of Geoffrey Chaucer,* p. 739, notices this.

A few lines later, however, in true *chanson-de-geste* tradition, the Saracens attribute their creation to "Mahoun" (l. 240).

The *Pearl*-poet follows this same tradition in *Patience*, a paraphrase of the story of Jonah. When the storm threatens to capsize the ship, before they seek Jonah, the sailors pray to their gods:

> But vchon glewed on his god þat gayned hym beste;
> Summe to Vernagu þer vouched avowes solemne,
> Summe to Diana deuout, & derf Nepturne,
> To Mahoun & to Mergot, þe mone & þe sunne,
> & vche lede, as he loued & layde had his hert. (ll. 164–68)

In having the sailors implore the help of such gods, the poet, like Chaucer, is borrowing from the convention of having Saracens cry out to nonexistent gods or idols. "Mahoun" in both Chaucer and the *Pearl*-poet is a corruption of Moḥammad, and in the latter the use of "Mahoun" and "Vernagu" represents, in typical medieval fashion, an anachronism of many centuries. It is not difficult to see how Chaucer and others, with such a lack of basic knowledge of Saracens or of their faith, could appropriate currently circulating Saracen stories and motifs, partly or entirely in ignorance of their origins.

Oriental tales. Many of *The Canterbury Tales* have Oriental analogues. Some of them had, by the time of Chaucer, become so widespread in Europe that it would be difficult to pinpoint Chaucer's exact source. The "Manciple's Tale," for example, of the man, wife, and telltale bird, is found in Ovid's *Metamorphoses*, the *Disciplina Clericalis, Directorium Humanae Vitae, Kalīlah wa Dimnah, The Seven Sages of Rome, The Book of Sindibād*, the *Arabian Nights*, Guillaume de Machaut's *Le Livre du Voir Dit*, Gower's *Confessio Amantis*, and a version of it in the *Knight of La Tour Landry*. A similar situation exists with regard to the "Merchant's Tale."[36] Chaucer was, of course, familiar with the major collections. He mentions Pedro Alfonso and quotes from the *Disciplina* in the "Tale of Melibee," l. 1189.

The Franklin's Tale. Chaucer refers to this tale, in its pro-

[36] See Germaine Dempster, "The Merchant's Tale," and James A. Work, "The Manciple's Tale," in *Sources and Analogues of Chaucer's Canterbury Tales*, pp. 333–56 and 699–722, respectively.

logue, as a Breton Lay, and the names of Arveragus and his wife Dorigen appear to be of Celtic origin. The tale itself, however, of the "damsel's rash promise," has numerous Oriental analogues, and although the source of Chaucer's tale is thought to have been Boccaccio (the tale appears in the *Filocolo* and in the *Decameron*), it is also to be found in Jean de Condé's *Chevalier à la Manche* and in *El Conde Lucanor*,[37] suggesting a Spanish route for its transmission to Europe.

The Monk's Tale. Among the Monk's instances of "modern tragedy" are two Pedros assassinated in 1379. One of these (l. 2391) was the King of Cyprus, Pierre de Lusignan, known to the English court. The other (l. 2375) was Pedro I, King of Castile and Leon, who was killed by his bastard brother Don Enrique de Trastamara after having been lured to the latter's tent.

Pedro I of Spain had come to the Black Prince at Bordeaux in 1366 to secure assistance against Don Fadrique and left his three daughters Beatrice, Constance, and Isabella with the Black Prince as security until 1371. In 1367, the Black Prince came to his assistance in Spain, accompanied by his marshal Sir Guichard d'Angle, a friend of Chaucer's. John of Gaunt, Chaucer's patron, married Pedro's daughter Constance in 1371 and for sixteen years assumed the title of King of Castile and Leon. In an attempt to enforce his claim, he assisted the Portuguese forces in their invasion of Castile in 1386. Chaucer's wife Philippa was attached to Constance's household in England.

Of the various accounts of Pedro I of Spain's death, Froissart (in that part of his chronicles of 1369–73), Machaut, and others criticized Pedro, while Chaucer's account agrees with that of the Spanish chronicler Pedro López de Ayala (1322–1407). Chaucer's source for his account in the "Monk's Tale" is not known. Suggestions have included Sir Guichard d'Angle, Constance, and the nobles with the Black Prince.[38] His precise source is perhaps not

37 Robinson, *Works of Geoffrey Chaucer*, pp. 721–22. The suggestion of a Celtic origin for the names is also Robinson's (p. 723).

38 Information on the two Pedros is from Haldeen Braddy, "The Two Petros in the 'Monkes Tale,'" *PMLA*, 50 (1935), 69–80; and Henry Lyttleton Savage, "Chaucer and the 'Pitous Deeth' of 'Petro, Glorie of Spayne,'" *Speculum*, 24 (1949), 357–75. See also Robinson, *Works of Geoffrey Chaucer*, p. 749.

as important as the fact that he had close connections with persons involved in Spanish affairs.

The Squire's Tale. This tale in Chaucer runs briefly as follows: Cambyuskan, king of "Tartarye," and Elpheta, his wife, have two sons, Algarsyf (the oldest) and Cambalo, and a daughter Canacee. At a birthday feast for Cambyuskan, a knight arrives in court on a steed of brass with gifts from the king "of Arabe and of Inde" (l. 1110), including the steed which flies and is worked by means of a pin and a sword with magical properties. Gifts for Canacee are a mirror in which one's foes are revealed and a ring which permits its wearer to understand the speech of fowls. Shortly after the feast, Canacee goes into the garden wearing her ring and hears a falcon lamenting her desertion by a tercelet she had agreed to love but who proved false. The narrator promises to tell later of how Algarsyf won his wife and how Cambalo won Canacee, and at this point the tale breaks off, unfinished by Chaucer.

The origin of the names in the "Squire's Tale" is unknown. Cambyuskan may represent the name Genghis Khan, and the names Elpheta and Algarsyf certainly look Oriental, although garbled.[39] The *Al* of Algarsyf is the Arabic and Persian definite article frequently attached to proper names. Haldeen Braddy observes of the name Elpheta that, in addition to being a star in the *Astrolabe,* it was known as a proper name and he points out a reference to "Elphita de la França" as a beautiful woman some fifty years after Chaucer's death in a Catalan *chanson* of Andrew Febrer. Referring to the "Monk's Tale," Braddy finds a connection between Chaucer and Catalonia "by no means farfetched."[40] The retention of peculiarly Arabic and Tartar or Mongolian names in Chaucer's tale points to sources in addition to the versions of the basic tale in Old French.

The Oriental setting of the tale was originally attributed by W. Skeat to the travels of Marco Polo,[41] and J. L. Lowes finds parallels with the fabulous letter of Prester John to Frederick

39 Robinson, *Works of Geoffrey Chaucer,* p. 718, thinks so too.

40 Haldeen Braddy, "Chaucerian Minutiae," *Modern Language Notes,* 58 (1933), 18–23.

41 Robinson, *Works of Geoffrey Chaucer,* p. 717.

and the gifts supposedly sent by Prester John of a ring, water from the Fountain of Youth, and a coat of salamander skin. Prester John is reported in the letter to have a fabulous mirror which reveals the approach of enemies. Lowes believes therefore that the setting and in part the fabulous gifts (but not the plot) were derived from Prester-John material, since a Latin version of the letter of around 1165 was known in England.[42] C. O. Chapman has noted parallels both in the setting and in the narrative between the "Squire's Tale" and *Sir Gawain and the Green Knight*, a point which will be of interest later.[43]

Especially Oriental in the plot of the tale are the arrival of gifts including the horse who flies, the Canacee and falcon episode, and the incest motif. The three known versions of the enchanted-horse story prior to Chaucer are Adènes le Roi's romance *Cléomadès* of a century earlier, Girard de Amiens' *Méliacin,* and the tale of "The Enchanted Horse" in the *Arabian Nights.* These have all been compared in detail with Chaucer's tale by H. S. V. Jones.[44]

In the *Cléomadès,* part of the scene is set in Spain. King Caldus has three daughters, and three knights from foreign lands come with gifts, one of which is an ebony horse which flies. The knights are then betrothed to the three daughters; the ugliest knight Crompart is to get the youngest and most beautiful daughter Marine, who turns to her brother Cléomadès for help in escaping a detested marriage. In another episode, when Cléomadès, after a journey on the horse, returns with his love Clarémondine, he leaves Clarémondine at the gate of Seville to go ahead and prepare a royal reception for her. Meanwhile the ugly knight Crompart steals her. The appearance of three knights at court (instead

42 John Livingston Lowes, "The Squire's Tale and the Land of Prester John," *Washington University Studies,* I (October, 1913), 3–18; and H. S. V. Jones, "The Squires' Tale," in *Sources and Analogues of Chaucer's Canterbury Tales,* pp. 357–76.

43 Coolidge Otis Chapman, "Chaucer and the *Gawain*-Poet: A Conjecture," *Modern Language Notes,* 68 (1953), 521–24.

44 See H. S. V. Jones's three articles: "Some Observations upon the Squire's Tale," *PMLA,* n.s. 13 (1905), 346–59; "*The Cléomadès,* the *Méliacin,* and the Arabian Tale of the 'Enchanted Horse,'" *Journal of English and Germanic Philology,* 6 (1907), 221–43; and "*The Cléomadès* and Related Folk-Tales," *PMLA,* n.s. 16 1908), 557–98. The discussion here follows Jones's findings in these three articles.

of one as in Chaucer), the horse and aerial journey, the betrothal of the unwilling youngest daughter to the ugliest visitor, and his stealing of a bride at the gate of the city where she has been left while a suitable reception is prepared are all paralleled in the *Arabian Nights.*

The *Méliacin* is set in Asia, and the three visitors are clerks (they are sages in the *Arabian Nights*). In two places where *Méliacin* differs from *Cleomadès,* it agrees with the *Arabian Nights*: in the trial by combat in which the hero is captured by the girl's father, and in the imprisonment of the hero beneath the cell of the ugly suitor. Jones decides from this that Chaucer's source was probably the *Cléomadès,* but the differences between them, including the Oriental-sounding names in Chaucer, have not been accounted for.

The tale of the enchanted horse almost certainly came into France and Europe through Arab Spain. Burton suggested Spain as the route by which it reached Europe; so did Clouston, in 1887. He was followed by Chauvin in 1898, who proposed as a source of *Cléomadès* and *Méliacin* a lost Spanish poem from an Old-Spanish translation of the *Arabian Nights.* Even Gaston Paris proposed that the French versions were from an oral Old-Spanish version. Jones's studies support the Spanish-Arabic suggestions of the earlier critics, and he concludes that there was probably a common source for the *Cléomadès* and *Méliacin* derived from a Spanish version of the *Arabian Nights* story combined with a lost Old-Spanish version of the story.[45]

The episode of Canacee and the falcon in Chaucer's tale (which is not in the Old-French versions) has also been identified as Oriental. There are two stories in the *Arabian Nights* with identical plots related to it. These are the stories of Tāj al-Mulūk and Princess Dunya and of Ardashir and Ḥayāt al-Nufūs, that of Princess Dunya being closest to the "Squire's Tale." Princess Dunya has turned against men as a result of hearing from a pigeon how her mate deserted her. Tāj paints pictures in her pa-

[45] Burton, *Thousand Nights and a Night,* III, 1630; Clouston, *Popular Tales and Fictions,* p. 373; Jones, "Some Observations upon the Squire's Tale," p. 349; and Jones, "The *Cléomadès,* the *Méliacin,* and the Arabian Tale," p. 243.

vilion depicting the male bird snared in a fowler's net which prevented his return, thus convincing the princess she was wrong to conclude that it was due to infidelity. Another parallel is to be noted between Canacee's governess and Dunya's nurse and confidante.[46] Still another parallel in the bird story, though not a very close one, can be found in the *Nibelungenlied* when, before she has met Siegfried, Kriemhild dreams that she has reared a falcon which two eagles tear to pieces before her eyes. When her mother, in interpreting the dream, tells her the falcon is a nobleman, she renounces all love just as Princess Dunya did.[47]

The incest motif is also found in the Dunya story, and a story close in outline to Chaucer's in the tale of King ʿUmar Ibn-al-Nuʿmān and his sons.[48] In the latter tale, the sister unwittingly marries her youngest brother, suggested in the "Squire's Tale" when the narrator announces his intention to relate later how Canacee was won by Cambalo (her youngest brother?). There is a reference in the "Man of Law's Tale" (ll. 78–79) to Canacee who loved her own brother, and it has been suggested that the incestuous development of the story was the reason that Chaucer dropped the tale. Incest does not appear in the French versions of *Cléomadès* and *Méliacin,* although it does in later Spanish ballads based on the story.

The conclusion that the tale in Chaucer—both the enchanted-horse and the falcon episodes—is of Arabic origin is almost unavoidable. Further, since the *Arabian Nights* was apparently known in Spain, versions of the tale which reached France and England were probably Spanish renditions, possibly both oral and written, of the tale of the *Nights,* which was, like most Arabic tale collections before printing, designed for oral recitation.

The Tale of Bereyn. The "Tale of Bereyn," added to some manuscripts of *The Canterbury Tales,* is no longer attributed to

46 Haldeen Braddy, "The Oriental Origin of Chaucer's Canacee-Falcon Episode," *Modern Language Review,* 31 (1936), 11–19, discusses the *Arabian-Nights* stories' similarities to the "Squire's Tale."

47 "The Nibelungenlied," trans. Helen M. Mustard, in *Medieval Epics* (New York, 1963), pp. 205–439.

48 Haldeen Braddy, "The Genre of Chaucer's *Squire's Tale,*" *Journal of English and Germanic Philology,* 41 (1942), 279–90, discusses the incest parallels.

Chaucer and belongs to the Chaucer apocrypha. The appearance of the tale is of interest, however, as another example of an Oriental tale which may have reached England by way of Islamic Spain. The story appears in all Eastern versions of the *Book of Sindibād* (*The Seven Sages of Rome*), including those in Spain; the story of the "Seven Wazīrs" in the *Arabian Nights*; and the *Libro de los Engaños e Asayamientos de las Mujeres* (the Old-Spanish translation of *The Seven-Sages-Sindibād* group of tales).[49]

Conclusion

Beginning in the early twelfth century in Europe, both the moral and the *maqāma*-type tale of Oriental provenance became well known, giving rise to extensive use of *exempla* and the spread of Oriental *fabliaux* and, at the same time, inspiring the creation of new tales in the countries of Western Europe, with a large, unaccountable number being spread through oral tradition. With the importation into Spain of an Arabic type of tale, the *maqāma*, containing a mixture of prose and verse and the appearance of such tales in Spain from the eleventh century on, came the concurrent appearance of the two types of Oriental frame story, the instructive and the dramatic, in Western Europe. An instructive dialogue or discursive type of frame appeared in the *Disciplina Clericalis* in England and later in *El Conde Lucanor* in Spain; examples of the dramatic frame in Spain are provided by the *Libro de los Engaños, Kalīlah wa Dimnah*, the *Libro de Buen Amor*, and the *Arabian Nights*. Recognition of the Oriental origin of the tale and frame story should therefore take into account the importation and composition of such tales and frames in Spain as well as in other countries of Western Europe, in that many of them may well have spread into Europe through Spain.

The major sourcebooks of the tale in the Middle Ages borrow heavily from each other. The earliest Latin collection, the *Disciplina Clericalis*, was compiled by a native of Spain who drew extensively from Arabic tales. Other compilations translated in

49 Clouston, *Popular Tales and Fictions*, pp. 104–105.

Western Europe which stem ultimately from Arabic and Persian sources are found in Spain, translated into Old Spanish or Castilian directly from the Arabic, eg., *The Seven Sages of Rome* and its counterpart the Spanish *Libro de los Engaños e Asayamientos de las Mujeres,* and the *Directorium Humanae Vitae* and its counterpart the Spanish *Kalīlah wa Dimnah,* with a Latin version from both of the latter two compiled in the early fourteenth century. The *Gesta Romanorum,* dating from between the late thirteenth and early fourteenth centuries, drew from most of the preceding collections, with some of its stories more closely related to the Spanish than to the Western-European Latin and Old-French versions. Some Oriental tales in the *Gesta,* such as that of "The Angel and the Hermit," appear to have been drawn from Spanish-Arabic or perhaps Jewish religious materials. Later tale collections, such as Boccaccio's *Decameron,* show a corresponding medley of sources, some of which seem to be ultimately of Spanish-Arabic provenance.

Oriental tales, along with more native material and tales from classical sources, reappear in Middle-English tale collections such as the *Confessio Amantis,* the *Book of the Knight of La Tour Landry,* and *The Canterbury Tales.* In the *Confessio* and *The Canterbury Tales* are, in addition, numerous digressions and essays on material of a scientific and philosophical nature which reached the Latin world through the translation efforts in Spain in the twelfth century. In *The Canterbury Tales,* in addition to Oriental tales which had become widespread by the end of the fourteenth century, the unfinished "Squire's Tale" is an example of an originally Persian story evidently brought into Spain with the *Arabian Nights* and subsequently reappearing in Old-French romances and finally in Chaucer.

In the many studies of sources and analogues to Western European tales, earlier Oriental analogues are frequently pointed out, and a few critical commentators have suggested Arab Spain as a route for transmission of many of the tales. But such tales are all too often lumped under the general heading of "Oriental," then labelled untraceable because they were Oriental and thus probably spread orally. It is to be hoped that more detailed studies will one day be made with regard to Spanish-Arabic tales and their relationship to "Oriental" tales in the other countries of Western Europe.

CHAPTER VI

ROMANCES

PART I—ENGLISH AND EUROPEAN ROMANCES

The eighteenth-century English critic, Thomas Warton, attributes all European romance to Arab Spain, under an extension of the premise that it would be logical to assume that medieval Spain disseminated literary as well as scientific influence.[1] But Warton also attributes the romance matter of Charlemagne to Arab Spain, and in doing so he credits Charlemagne with propagating Arab learning, which Charlemagne of course did not do. While Warton's observations that literary as well as scientific influence was exerted by Spain do seem to hold true for lyrics and tales of all types, they do not in the case of the romance per se, which was not as popular in all parts of Spain at an early date as it was in other countries of Western Europe. "Romance" in Spanish means the vernacular (as opposed to Latin), and the ballad (in the vernacular or popular tradition); the prose or long verse romance of medieval Europe is not native to Spain. Further, the medieval romance was a relative latecomer to written vernacular literature. It seems to be connected with the twelfth-century renaissance, but the connection was not a simple one and there do not seem to be sufficient grounds for attributing all European romance to the Arabic romance, even though the romance in Europe often shows Spanish-Arab influence within it.

A more rational account for the appearance of the romance and one more consistent with historical events is that of Urban Holmes who, in his survey of French literature up to 1300, attributes the birth of the French romance to the twelfth-century ren-

[1] Thomas Warton, *History of English Poetry*, I, 91–109.

aissance.[2] That is, the renaissance of scientific investigation and philosophical inquiry which resulted from the twelfth-century discovery and translation of manuscripts in Spain and Sicily provided an impetus for the vernacular romance. The romance in Old French, with the exception of *Aucassin et Nicolette,* is not a borrowed form, but one which began in France at a time when there was a wealth of material available from across the Channel and from below the Pyrenees for subject matter.

The medieval romance drew from the various traditions already in existence around it, from vision literature, lyric poetry, and *chansons de geste.* In many romances, including the Arthurian ones, were interpolated otherworld visions and voyages containing the Celtic and Oriental motifs differentiated in Chapter IV above.

The Provençal and Catalan troubadours were familiar with Arthurian heroes and tales, and both the poetry and the courtly-love tradition of the troubadours were gradually incorporated into the romance as it grew to overshadow the popularity of the epic or *chanson-de-geste* tradition. Love in the earlier romances is, as in the epic tradition, fairly rare, and when it occurs it is not particularly romantic. In the later romances, love comes to follow the precepts for courtly love as found in the troubadours. The Middle-English romances, even with native material, followed the trends established in Old-French romance but frequently anglicized to a large degree traditions developed in France which were not compatible with the English character. For example, it has been shown that the English romances modeled after French ones containing courtly love tended to deemphasize the love motifs and to add didacticism and an element of conscious piety.[3] Yet the prosody of the English tail-rime romances maintains the Provençal schemes which accommodate long stories.[4] The

2 Urban Tigner Holmes, Jr., *A History of Old French Literature: From the Origins to 1300* (Chapel Hill, 1937), p. 134.

3 Margaret Adlum Gist, *Love and War in the Middle English Romances* (Philadelphia, 1947).

4 Roger Sherman Loomis points out the French-lyric origin of the tail-rime stanza in *The Development of Arthurian Romance,* p. 134. A more detailed study of it is to be found in A. McI. Trounce, "The English Tail-Rime Romances," *Medium Ævum,* 1 (1932), 87–108, 168–82; and 2 (1933), 34–57, 189–98.

most frequent tail-rime forms are aaaBcccB of the *murabba*ᶜ and aaBccBddBeeB, the latter being the one which Chaucer reduces to utter absurdity in his parody of it in the "Tale of Sir Thopas."

One of the debts of the romance to the *Chanson-de-geste* tradition is reflected in the attitude toward the Saracens often found in medieval romances. The imputation of idolatry to Islam, a literary convention, had come into usage with the *chansons de geste,* illustrating the "official" views of Islam, that is, those propounded by the clergy which show a mixture of truth and fiction.[5] Among the earliest Christian writers to show an accurate knowledge of Islam was William of Malmesbury in his *Gesta Regum* (ca. 1120), in which Muḥammad is recognized as a prophet, *nam Saraceni et Turchi Deum Creatorem colunt, Mahomet non Deum sed eius prophetam destimantes,* which shows that an accurate assessment of Islam was possible when it was not more convenient and more dramatic to embroider accounts of Saracens as heathens, pagans, and idolaters. Far more common than William of Malmesbury's statements are views of Muḥammad as a traitor, the root of all evil, a schismatic (he is placed among the schismatics in the *Inferno*), and the worshipper of some thirty idols. A sympathetic treatment of the Islamic religion is found in Wolfram von Eschenbach's *Parzival,* but by way of contrast, in the last book of Lydgate's *Fall of Princes* (ca. 1440), Muḥammad is described as a false prophet, magician, and idolater who proclaimed himself the Messiah, married "Cardigan" (a corruption of the name of Muḥammad's first wife, Khadija), was epileptic and a drunkard, and died when, being drunk, he fell into a puddle and was devoured by swine.[6] Lydgate invented none of this fantasy, but was following an old, well-established tradition in

[5] Norman Daniel, *Islam and the West: The Making of an Image,* p. 309. William Wistar Comfort, in "The Literary Rôle of the Saracens in the French Epic," *PMLA,* 55 (1940), 628–59, has studied the official views of the Church on Islam and their relationship to the views found in the *chansons de geste* and romances. See also R. W. Southern, *Western Views of Islam in the Middle Ages* (Cambridge, Mass., 1962); and C. Meredith Jones, "The Conventional Saracen of the Songs of Geste," *Speculum,* 17 (1942), 201–25. The quotation of William of Malmesbury is from Southern, p. 35.

[6] Lydgate is cited by Samuel C. Chew, *The Crescent and the Rose: Islam and England during the Renaissance* (New York, 1937), pp. 398–400.

certain Latin writings on the life of Muḥammad and in the *chansons de geste.*

Saracens were from an early date confused with Saxons in literature, as in the twelfth-century *Chanson des Saisnes* of Jean Bodel, the work which also first delineated matters of Britain, France, and Rome.[7] Idols were imputed to both Saxons and Saracens in the *chansons,* a practice which continued down through the cycle plays and the English Renaissance. Examples of Saracen idolatry in Chaucer and in the *Pearl*-poet were seen in the preceding chapter.

In addition to being described as idolaters, Saracens were often portrayed in the epics and in later romances as giants. They were described as tall, hideous, huge, often misshapen, frequently as black Moors or Negroes, and usually with eyes as red as glowing coals (associated with ferocity). But, as one critic notes of the convention, "We find no such grotesque caricatures of humanity in Spanish literature; the reality was there too close at hand to permit of such treatment. But in France as later in Italy and England, distance lent enchantment, and the enchantment accounts for this grotesque type."[8] This is illustrated in the *Poema de Mío Cid,* the Spanish epic, in which we find no Archbishop Turpins slaying hundreds of the wretched heathens for the glory of Christendom. Rather there is the Cid (from the Arabic *Siyyid,* "Lord" or "Sir") attacking and raiding for treasure and glory of conquest and being friends with conquered Saracens as long as they pay tribute and are loyal to him. The idolatrous and monstrous heathen Saracens were for those who did not know them; and the more fantastic, the more imaginative the portrait painted of them, the more popular it would be with others who had no firsthand knowledge of the Arabs and Moors. After all, *Mandeville's Travels,* because of such inventions as people with no heads but with eyes in their shoulders and mouths in the center of their chests or those who had only one leg with a foot large

[7] The discussion of the Saracens and Saxons, their idolatry, and monstrous appearance follows Comfort, "Literary Rôle of the Saracens," pp. 630, 650–52; and Chew, *The Crescent and the Rose,* pp. 388–91.

[8] Comfort, "Literary Rôle of the Saracens," p. 652.

enough to serve as an umbrella,[9] was far more popular than Marco Polo's factual account of the peoples observed during his travels which were actually made. It is ironic that Mandeville's fictitious creations were believed while Marco Polo's honest observations were discredited, but much of the same desire to believe the fabulous is found in the views of the Saracens in the *chansons de geste* and romances.

Romance Tradition in Spain

The chivalric romance is generally of a later date in Spain than in other countries of Western Europe, possibly because of the popularity of Arabic-derived tales and fables in Spain which were only somewhat later replaced by the chivalric romance. Other Spanish romances, including Spanish Arthurian ones, date from the fourteenth century, and are called *novelas de caballerías,* rather than "romances," the term for ballads in Spanish. In general, Spain's romances, especially chivalric ones, show French and Arthurian influence, and, in turn, French romance tradition often reflects Spanish-Arabic motifs incorporated into the romance from other materials.

Historia del Caballero Cifar. The romance of *Cifar,* composed between 1299 and 1335, the oldest surviving book of chivalry in Castilian, has been characterized as "a strange mixture of the 'Golden Legend,' Arthurian romance and Oriental fable."[10] The name Cifar is the Arabic *Saffār,* "traveler," hence "Caballero Cifar" means "knight errant." Several Arthurian knights and stories are mentioned in it, showing the spread of matter of Britain south beyond France.

The first part of *Cifar* is based on the legend of Saint Eustace or Placidus, the Job-story of the man who loses all of his wealth, then his wife and two children, who are stolen by animals. It is related to the English *Syr Isambrace,* Chrétien's *Guillaume d'Engleterre,* and other stories of the cycle. There are motifs in

[9] *Mandeville's Travels,* ed. M. C. Seymour (Oxford, 1967), Chaps. 14, 19. These are only two of many monstrosities in Mandeville.

[10] J. B. Trend, "Spain and Portugal," in *The Legacy of Islam,* ed. Arnold and Guillaume, p. 37.

the *Cifar* drawn from *El Conde Lucanor*, the *Disciplina Clericalis*, and the matter of Britain. *Cifar* also includes interpolated tales and fables from the *Gesta Romanorum* and the *Libro de Buen Amor*.[11]

The Book of the Ordre of Chyualry. It was noted in Chapter II that such works as the *Alfonsine Tables* and the *Livre de Leschiele Mahomet* found their way to England, the latter in French. One of Raymond Lull's books written 1276–86, *Le Libre del Orde de Cauayleria*, also found its way to England in a French version. The original Catalan version is also extant, as are versions in Old French, Scots, and Middle English (but not Latin).[12] William Caxton printed an English version in 1485–86 and indicated that he translated his text from a French version, which was, in turn, translated from Catalan. One of the French manuscripts in which it appears contains in the same hand the *Traité Politique sur les Devoirs Respectifs des Princes & des Sujets*, from the *Secretum Secretorum*, a collection of materials on alchemy, magic, and mysticism, partially translated and partially invented during the translation period in Spain. The appearance of Lull's book in France and England is of interest as it indicates that transmission of materials from Spain and interchange with northern Europe did not end with the completion of the major translation efforts.

Romance Tradition in France and England

Most of the Middle-English romances have French originals. This is as true of Arthurian or native Welsh matter as it is of matter foreign to England, since Arthurian matter received its greatest development in France, whence it spread all over Europe and was reimported into England in the romance tradition. A vast body of Welsh Arthurian matter had poured into France begin-

[11] Charles Philip Wagner, "The Sources of *El Cavallero Cifar*," *Revue Hispanique*, 10 (1903), 4–104. María Rosa Lida de Malkiel, "Arthurian Literature in Spain and Portugal," in *Arthurian Literature in the Middle Ages*, ed. R. S. Loomis, pp. 406–18, points out Arthurian knights and stories in *El Cavallero*.

[12] The Middle-English text is reproduced in *The Book of the Ordre of Chyualry*, ed. Alfred T. P. Byles, *Early English Text Society*, 168 (1926). The discussion here follows Byles, pp. xi–li.

ning in the late eleventh century following the Norman Conquest of England, probably through oral transmission.[13] In France, at the hands of Chrétien de Troyes and others, these materials were woven into several cycles of romances. In addition, in the Middle-English romances derived from French originals and in a few for which no French original is extant, are to be noted an unusually large number of romances with Oriental sources and analogues, and even the Arthurian romances often contain Oriental matter. It would appear from this that France was a centralized recipient of Arthurian matter from the north and Spanish-Arab materials from the south, and that, as the romance was developed, Arthurian and Oriental materials were fused and disseminated throughout Europe from France. The large number of early Oriental analogues to many tales and motifs in French and English romances tends to support this thesis.

Incidentally, the Welsh belief that Arthur is not dead but will return has a parallel in the beliefs of two ancient schismatic groups of Muslims of the East called Shīʿites, who believe in an *Imām* (a hereditary prince and leader in spiritual matters as well as in battle) who disappeared and will some day return to lead the believers. There are two sects of the Shīʿites, *al-Sabʿiyya* ("Seveners," also called "Ismaʿīlites") who recognized seven *Imāms* or rulers from the time of Muḥammad, the seventh being Muḥammad Ibn-Ismaʿīl who disappeared in 770 and who will one day return, and *al-Ithnāʿashariyya* ("Twelvers") who await the return of the twelfth *Imām*, Muḥammad Ibn-Ḥasan, who disappeared in 870. It is a curious and probably unrelated parallel, but it suggests the fact that oriental lore was not incongruous or incompatible with that of Britain and Wales at the time when stories of all types were being woven together into romances.

Jean Bodel, in his *Chanson des Saisnes,* first classified the matters of the romance into those of Rome, Britain, and France. That of Rome included legends of Troy, Greece, Thebes, and

[13] R. S. Loomis, 'The Oral Diffusion of the Arthurian Legend," in *Arthurian Literature in the Middle Ages,* pp. 52–63. The sources and analogues listed by romance in Laura A. Hibbard, *Medieval Romance in England,* rev. ed. (New York, 1960), reveal Oriental matter and sources of Arthurian and other romances.

Alexander. The matter of Britain consisted of Arthurian stories, the cycles around such heroes as Gawain, Perceval, Lancelot, and Tristan; Arthur, like Charlemagne in the matter of France and like Hārūn al-Rashīd in the *Arabian Nights,* tended to be little more than a master of ceremonies. The matter of France centered around legends of Charlemagne and his twelve peers, represented by such Middle-English romances as the *Sowdone of Babylone, Sir Firumbas, Roland and Vernagu, The Sege of Melayne,* and *Otuel,* which, as their titles imply, are full of Spanish-Arabic motifs.

To the matter of Rome, most modern scholars add a group called "Graeco-Byzantine" and "adventure" romances, to which *Floire et Blanchefleur* is assigned. Some add a "matter of England," consisting of such English and Germanic legends as *Horn, Havelok,* and *Athelston,* and a "matter of Brittany," consisting of Breton lays, including those of Marie de France (in the mid-twelfth century) of *Sir Orfeo, Sir Degare, Lai la Freigne,* and *Emare.* Another grouping often found is one consisting of the Eustace-Constance-Florence-Griselda legends of persecuted queens and knights. Matter not clearly assignable to those delineated by Bodel or to Germanic legends thus tends to be grouped according to motif or plot of the story rather than to another group of matter assigned by origin, and much of the material so grouped is either apparently Oriental or has earlier Oriental analogues, indicating that in addition to a matter of Britain which reached France from the north, there may well have been a "matter of the East," much of which could have come through Spain into France to be fused with other romance materials. If this was true in the case of vision literature, lyric poetry, and tales, as it seems to have been, then it was likely true of certain romance materials, since the romance is indebted to the other genres.

The Erle of Tolous

Many of the Middle-English romances have Oriental or Spanish-Arab motifs, and several of them could probably be traced to Arab Spain in a more detailed study. *The Erle of Tolous* is an example of a romance built around an historical incident in southern France first recorded in Catalan chronicles, the earliest being near the end of the thirteenth century. As Catalonia preceded the rest of the Spanish peninsula in familiarity with Arthurian matter,[14] so it seems to have been involved in the interchange between Oriental materials and Arthurian and other European matter in European romance.

The *Erle* is a persecuted-wife story which in Catalan and in English versions concerns the Empress Judith, daughter of the Count of Bavaria and second wife of Louis the Pious (778–840). She was twice exiled from court and charged with relations with Bernard, count of Barcelona. Judith is proved innocent by combat, her champion being the earl or count of Toulouse. The use of a story from Catalan chronicles in a European romance is not unusual. Chaucer and Gower both use similar Spanish historical materials, as was seen in the preceding chapter.

Tristan and Isolt

Tristan, one of the the romances attached to Arthurian matter, was probably originally a Celtic elopement story whose chivalry and poetic sentiments were added in France, and is a good example of Celtic material developed in France into an Arthurian romance.[15] At some point in its development, however, certain Oriental motifs were added to it, motifs which had possibly spread through contacts between southern France and Spain. The Tristan story was well known to the Provençal and Catalan troubadours, with Tristan, as was remarked earlier, having been mentioned more often by the troubadours than any other Arthurian figure. As a result, as a study of the development of the Tristan legend has shown, "The composite legend reaching the romancers of the late twelfth century included not only Celtic tradition but elements from such heterogeneous sources as folk-tales, Arabic romance, and Oriental tales of trickery and deception."[16]

14 Malkiel, "Arthurian Literature in Spain and Portugal," p. 407.

15 Gertrude Schoepperle, *Tristan and Isolt: A Study of the Sources of the Romance* (London, 1913), II, 470–71.

16 Helaine Newstead, "The Origin and Growth of the Tristan Legend," in *Arthurian Literature in the Middle Ages*, p. 125. The two Oriental ruses are dis-

Two obvious examples of Oriental materials in *Tristan* are in the two ruses, Isolt's equivocal oath and the pretended innocent conversation between Tristan and Isolt in their tryst beneath the tree. In the first of these, Isolt escapes being burned with a red-hot iron by swearing that only her husband and the pilgrim who has just carried her (and who is Tristan in disguise) have ever held her in their arms. The rescue of a wife by her lover in disguise in a test of her fidelity is an ancient Oriental device originating in India.

The second ruse is accomplished when, in a meeting under a tree, Tristan and Isolt see a shadow beneath the tree and are aware that they are being spied upon; they therefore fake an innocent conversation for the benefit of their "chaperone." This episode was influenced by two Oriental *fabliaux*, both of which were very popular in Arabic sources and both of which were well known in twelfth-century France. One of the *fabliaux* is the tale of the enchanted tree, in which an adulteress who has had her lover while her husband was in a nearby tree watching the scene persuades her husband that what he has seen from the tree is an optical illusion; the other is the tale of the carpenter's wife, in which the wife and lover pretend to be carrying on an innocent conversation while the husband is spying upon them.

There is also an unusually close parallel between Tristan's marriage with Isolt of the White Hands and an eighth-century Arabic romance, *Qays wa Layla*.[17] Qays, separated from his wife Layla, marries another of the same name but then neglects her. When he becomes ill, he sends for his first wife and they die together soon after their reunion. The parallel is too close to be a matter of coincidence, although in the process of adaptation, of course, the story lost all traces of Islamic influence incidental to it.

---

cussed by Newstead, p. 131, and mentioned by Schoepperle, *Tristan and Isolt*, I, 212–13. The details here are from Newstead. The best recent study is Sigmund Eisner, *The Tristan Legend: A Study in Sources* (Evanston, 1969). Eisner notes the Eastern elements in *Tristan*.

17 Newstead, "The Origin and Growth of the Tristan Legend," pp. 131–32, discusses the *Qays-wa-Layla* parallel.

Aucassin et Nicolette

A unique example of the minstrel's art of the twelfth and thirteenth centuries survives in *Aucassin et Nicolette,* extant in a single Old-French manuscript of the thirteenth century, which also preserves the melody for the lyric portions.[18] It is in form a *chante-fable,* a regular alternation of prose narrative and lyric verse not native to European romance, but found in Arab romance and market-place tales of the *maqāma* type in Spain and in the *Arabian Nights* designed for recitation and singing in installments. Both the form and the romantic love story are generally recognized as Arab types, but how the story reached France in finished form is not known.

If the Provençal troubadours were influenced by the minstrel tradition in Spain, then *Aucassin* may well be the work of a French artist putting into use popular *maqāma* forms widely known in Arab and Christian Spain. The names of the hero and heroine are Arabic-derived: Nicolette is from *Nikaulis* (originally *Bilqīs*), a queen of Sheba, and Aucassin is the Arabic *al-Qāsim;* the story itself has many similarities to that of Prince Uns al-Wujūd in the *Arabian Nights.*[19]

One of the best-known passages in *Aucassin et Nicolette* is that in which Aucassin tells the viscount that he doesn't want to have anything to do with paradise because that's where the priests, the saints, the lame, the crippled, the ragged, and the naked go. He'd rather go to hell because that's where all the fun's going to be, with the clerks, the knights, the ladies, and of course his Nicolette. Besides its comic overtones, the passage also illustrates the basic incompatibility of romantic love with medieval Christianity and thus is a serious and slightly satirical recognition of that incompatibility.

18 See Eugene Mason, trans., *Aucassin and Nicolette and Other Mediaeval Romances and Legends* (New York, 1958), pp. xix–xx. Citations are to Mason's translation.

19 Samuel Singer, *Germanisch-Romanisches Mittelalter* (Leipzig, 1935), p. 159. (Part of Singer's work was originally published in 1918 as an essay entitled "Arabische und europäische Poesie im Mittelalter.")

Aucassin, like other romance heroes, meets a monstrous giant: "Tall he was, and marvellously ugly and hideous. His head was big and blacker than smoked meat; the palm of your hand could easily have gone between his two eyes; he had very large cheeks and a monstrous flat nose with great nostrils; lips redder than uncooked flesh; yellow teeth and foul" (p. 26). But the hideous giant is not a Saracen or a Moor! The author of *Aucassin et Nicolette* apparently knew Saracens first hand (Nicolette is a Saracen princess from Carthage). Further, Aucassin vanquishes him not by attacking him but with kindness, a most unchristian way to behave towards a hideous giant in the medieval-romance tradition.

Another peculiar passage in the work is the episode at Torelore where Aucassin and Nicolette find the king in childbed while the queen and other women of the realm are out fighting battles—with crab-apples, eggs, and cheeses for weapons. In Book II of Marco Polo's *Description of the World*, whose prologue states that it was written while he was in prison in Genoa in 1298, is a description of a similar custom in one of the provinces of the Kublai Khan in which after childbirth in a family, the father goes to bed and the woman then cares for both him and the infant.[20] If the minstrel-author of *Aucassin et Nicolette* knew of this passage in Marco Polo, however, then the manuscript would have to be dated a little later than the thirteenth century, perhaps very early in the fourteenth. At least the passage was probably influenced by some travel account of the custom, hence the attack on it.

The one word to describe *Aucassin et Nicolette* is "charming." Its author, however, was no naïve bumpkin, and part of its appeal lies in its tantalizing hints of familiarity with travel literature, *chanson-de-geste* tradition, and Arabic tales of the *maqāma* type.

Floire et Blanchefleur

Floire et Blanchefleur is often discussed in conjunction with *Aucassin et Nicolette*, since, like *Aucassin et Nicolette*, it too had

20 *The Adventures of Marco Polo*, ed. Milton Rugoff (New York, 1961), pp. 183–84.

Arab origins.[21] The story reached Western Europe in two forms, the original being an aristocratic one and the second a popular form for a less cultured audience. Both forms are found in Old French; the Middle-English versions, extant in four manuscripts dating from the second half of the thirteenth century, are based on the aristocratic form in Old French.[22] There are, as in the case of *Tristan and Isolt,* many references and allusions to the story among the Provençal poets, a good indication that the story reached Europe through Spain.

The Saracens in the tale attack a group of Christian pilgrims, after which the widow of one of the slain pilgrims is taken to Spain to serve the queen. In Spain she gives birth to a daughter, Blanchefleur, on the same day the Saracen queen (wife of King Felis of Spain) gives birth to a son Floire. The two are nursed by the Christian mother, they grow up together, and fall in love. Felis and his queen do not approve of the match, and in order to prevent their son from marrying the captive girl, they sell Blanchefleur as a slave and build an elaborate tomb to convince Floire that she is dead. But when Floire nearly dies from grief, they tell him the truth and he goes to search for Blanchefleur. He finds her in the harem of the Emir of Babylon and bribes the porter to smuggle him in to her in a basket of flowers. When the Emir discovers them, he condemns them to death. An argument then ensues between the lovers, each begging to die first so as not to be left behind after the beloved has gone, and the Emir, moved by their love, relents and marries them in a church.

The finding of a lost sweetheart in an Eastern harem, the hiding in a basket of flowers to gain admittance to the harem, and the garden setting of the Emir's palace are widely recognized as Arab motifs, with numerous parallels, including some among the stories of the *Arabian Nights.* Yet another parallel has been found in the Arabic story of ʿUrwa and her cousin Afrā who were in love.[23] The story is as follows: ʿUrwa's mother, discovering that

21 Singer, *Germanisch-Romanisches Mittelalter,* pp. 151–60, pointed these out.

22 Bruce Dickens and R. M. Wilson, eds., *Early Middle English Texts* (New York, 1951), p. 43. Hibbard, *Medieval Romance in England,* p. 184, *n.* 1, points out the many Provençal troubadour references to it.

23 Singer, *Germanisch-Romanisches Mittelalter,* pp. 160–63, discovered the par-

ᶜUrwa is in love with Afrā and desiring to save her for marriage to a rich man, sends her to a cousin for safekeeping. Meanwhile, her father rigs up an old grave and they convince Afrā that she is buried in it. She is then sold to a Syrian merchant. Afrā goes in search of her, finds her, and the story ends with the death of the two lovers.

The story of *ᶜUrwa wa Afrā* is found in the *Kitāb al-Aghānī* (*Book of Songs*) by Abū-al-Faraj al-Isfahānī, which Ḥakam II (961–76) in Spain had subsidized in order to obtain the first copy of it. In the same book of songs is also found the story of *Qays wa Layla*, the apparent original model for Isolt Blanchemain in the Tristan romance.

The inference is, I think, clear, and such descriptions as that of Wells who refers to *Floire* (Middle-English *Floriz and Blanche-flur*) as "the special Middle English representative of Byzantine influence in our period"[24] are much too general. The terms "Byzantine" or "Oriental," used to refer to the Arabic sources for these two stories when a Spanish-Arab route of transmission can be shown, are not only inadequate but misleading as well.

The marriage of the two lovers in a church at the end of the romance, with no mention of conversion of Floire, appears to be a not-too-careful reworking of an originally tragic ending. Conversion of one of the lovers was evidently not a part of the original, and this could be the reason for its not being added to the ending found in the Old-French and Middle-English versions. The church marriage without a conversion is indeed strange and simply not in the tradition of Western European romances involving marriages between Christians and Saracens, in which the conversion is almost always important. This inconsistency of

allels between the Arabic story of ᶜUrwa and Afrā and *Floire et Blanchefleur* as well as those between the story of Qays and Layla and that of Isolt Blanchemain and pointed out that both of the Arabic stories were in the *Kitāb al-Aghānī*. Other scholars, such as Ten Brink, Hibbard, Sands, and Dickens and Wilson, note "probable" Arab origins for the *Floire* story. See Hibbard, *Medieval Romance in England*, pp. 189–91; Singer, *Germanisch-Romanisches Mittelalter*, pp. 151–69; Dickens and Wilson, *Early Middle English Texts*, p. 43; and Donald B. Sands, ed., *Middle English Verse Romances* (New York, 1966), pp. 279–80.

[24] John Edwin Wells, *A Manual of the Writings in Middle English, 1050–1400*, p. 139.

Floire with European-romance tradition has not been pointed out before, to the best of my knowledge.

Another peculiarity in the romance as found in Old French and Middle English which has been overlooked by critics concerns the reason why marriage may have been forbidden between Floire and Blanchefleur. They were nursed by the same woman, which makes them foster siblings. In the Islamic religion, this is the same as blood kinship, and love between two children nursed by the same woman is considered just as incestuous as that between children of the same parents. The tale as it appears in Old French could thus also have been reworked from an Arab tale of incest (such as that in the "First Calender's Story," Nights 11–12, in the *Arabian Nights*), with the motif of the same nurse being retained since it would not have been recognized as incestuous in Christian tradition and with the ending being rewritten so that the two lovers could live happily ever afterwards.

Alexander the Great

Legends of Alexander were popular in medieval Europe from a very early date. The origin of the Latin Alexander histories, legends, and romances was probably the Pseudo-Callisthenes version of Alexander of the fourth century, the earliest extant Latin manuscript of which dates from the ninth century.[25] It was followed in the tenth century by Presbyter Leo's Latin *Historia Alexandri Magni (Historia de Proeliis)*, from which were derived numerous twelfth- and thirteenth-century romances and histories of Alexander. The Alexander story is extant in Middle English in three alliterative fragments and a prose *Life* of the fourteenth century and in three fifteenth-century versions.[26]

In most of the Alexander stories (but not in the early Middle-

[25] See I. Friedlaender, *Die Chadhirlegende und der Alexanderroman* (Leipzig, 1913). The discussion of the Alexander legends here follows Friedlaender.

[26] The early texts are published in *Alexander and Dindamus*, ed. Walter W. Skeat, *Early English Text Society*, Extra Series 31 (1878); *The Wars of Alexander*, ed. Walter W. Skeat, *Early English Text Society*, Extra Series 47 (1886); *Kyng Alisaunder*, ed. G. V. Smithers, *Part I: Text, Early English Text Society*, 227 (1952), and *Part 2: Introduction, Commentary, and Glossary, Early English Text Society*, 237 (1953); and *The Prose Life of Alexander*, ed. J. S. Westlake, *Early English Text Society*, 143 (1913).

English fragments) is some mention of a quest of Alexander for eternal life. This quest in Eastern developments of the story occurs in Alexander's travels in Asia after he has conquered the civilized world and goes in search of the Spring of Life. At some point in the quest, Alexander's cook Andreas, preparing to wash and cook a dead fish, immerses it in a spring and the fish comes to life and swims away. Alexander, to punish the cook, has a stone tied to his neck and has him tossed into the spring. Andreas is then changed into a sea demon in the spring. In other versions of the quest, the cook jumps into the spring to retrieve the fish and becomes immortal. He is then named al-Khaḍir, "The Green One," who causes grass to grow wherever his feet touch, and who is to live until the Day of Judgment.

Khaḍir is first connected with the Alexander story in Qurʾānic commentaries on *Sura* 18 (in which Khaḍir's appearance has been noted in a previous chapter). In this instance, in verses 59–63, when Moses and the unnamed servant of the Lord are traveling together, the servant forgets the fish he had brought for food and it escapes to the sea. Bukhārī and other commentators of the ninth century identified the servant in the episode as Khaḍir, with Moses here appearing in lieu of Alexander in the earlier stories.

The Qurʾānic account and its commentaries have been traced to three main sources, the Gilgamesh epic, Alexander romance, and the Jewish legend of Elijah and Rabbi Joshua ben Levi, all of which involve the eternal-life idea. The Qurʾānic account was then followed by accounts by many tenth-century Persian theologians, epic poets (such as Firdausī), historians (such as Ṭabarī), and later Persian writers, in which Alexander's cook loses the fish when it comes to life in the spring, jumps in, drinks of the water, and becomes immortal. It is the Spring of Life for which Alexander had been searching, but he is denied it, because only one mortal was destined to drink from it and become immortal, and that was Khaḍir.

Both lines of the Alexander story, that descended from the Latin version of Presbyter Leo and that from the East incorporating Khaḍir, seem to have converged in Spain, as evidenced by the *aljamiado* (Spanish language in Arabic script) version found in a sixteenth-century manuscript.[27] In this version, Alexander the Great is, as in many of the Persian and Arabic versions, confused with Alexander Dhū al-Qarnayn ("the double horns"). He travels with the angel Rafael ("Zāyēfīl" in the manuscript), and as a traveler he calls on two men for help, one who can answer any question whose answer is to be found in booklore and the other, Khaḍir, who is the source of knowledge imparted directly from God. Khaḍir's role here seems to have been influenced by his role in *Ṣūfī* mysticism, for which he was well known in Spain. There is also an early sixteenth-century manuscript in the British Museum in which Alexander Dhū al-Qarnayn is confused with Alexander the Great, and in which Alexander goes in search of the Life Spring with Elisa (Elias) and Khaḍir as his companions. With this, we find Khaḍir in England.

The Grail

The grail, a mystical vessel used at the Last Supper and in some accounts used to catch the blood of Christ at the Crucifixion, appeared in Arthurian romance in the late twelfth century. Most of the grail texts were composed in a fifty-year period, 1180–1230. There are eight texts of Arthurian knights in quest of the grail: Chrétien de Troyes' *Perceval* with its four continuations; the *Queste del Saint Graal, Lancelot,* and *Estoire del Saint Graal* in the Latin Vulgate Cycle; the French prose *Perceval* and *Perlesvaus*; the *Peredur* in the *Mabinogion*; and Wolfram von Eschenbach's *Parzival.* All but the *Peredur* were composed on the Continent.[28]

The grail itself in these various accounts changes from the dish of the Last Supper to a chalice containing Christ's blood, to a platter of gold and jewels, or to a stone; it may be borne by a procession of maidens or it may glide into a hall on a beam of light; and it may hold a single wafer or a severed head swimming in blood. The various treatments of it differ considerably, but in

[27] See Andrew Runni Anderson, "The Arabic *History of Dulcarnain* and the Ethiopian *History of Alexander,*" *Speculum,* 6 (1931), 434.

[28] R. S. Loomis, *The Grail: From Celtic Myth to Christian Symbol* (New York, 1963), pp. 3–6.

most accounts it is associated with a maimed fisher king and a wasteland.

Theories as to the origin of the grail as it appears in twelfth-century romance are as varied as the accounts of the grail. Among the significant theories are those of R. S. Loomis, who proposes that it originated in pagan Irish legends; Jessie L. Weston, in vegetation rites; M. A. Murray, in the Coptic rite of Egypt; and A. E. Waite, in Christian mysticism.[29] Probably, like much romance material, the grail stories grew from an amalgamation of Celtic, Christian, and perhaps Eastern sources, legends, and myths, whose original significance was lost but of which just enough of the original outlines remain to puzzle scholars seeking to establish a single source for the grail and the quest of it in romance. Whatever their origin, the grail stories were, along with Arthurian matter from Wales, woven in France into the grail quest of the romances.

Integrated into a few of the grail stories is the account of Joseph of Arimathea who supposedly caught Christ's blood in the grail, was imprisoned for twenty years during which time he was miraculously fed, and on gaining his freedom, brought the grail with him to England, where he traveled to convert the people to Christianity. There is nothing in Irish or Welsh lore to account for the Joseph story. It is not native to English, Irish, or Welsh tradition. Nor is it found in all of the quest stories, but in only two of the early texts, Robert de Boron's metrical *Joseph* (c. 1190–1200) and the Vulgate *Estoire del Saint Graal* which borrowed from Robert de Boron's *Joseph*.[30]

No one knows where Robert found the Joseph story or the idea for it. A similar evangelization story, that of Saint James the

[29] Loomis, *The Grail*; Loomis, *Celtic Myth and Arthurian Romance* (New York, 1926); Loomis, *Wales and the Arthurian Legend* (Cardiff, 1956); Jessie L. Weston, *From Ritual to Romance* (New York, 1957); Weston, *The Quest of the Holy Grail* (London, 1913); Margaret A. Murray, "The Egyptian Elements in the Grail Romance," in *Ancient Egypt*, ed. Flinders Petrie (New York, 1916), pp. 1–14, 54–69; and Arthur Edward Waite, *The Holy Grail* (New York, 1961). (Jessie Weston's *From Ritual to Romance* first appeared in 1920. Waite's book also appeared earlier.)

[30] These are Loomis' observations in *The Grail*, p. 3; *Wales and the Arthurian Legend*, p. 19; and *Celtic Myth and Arthurian Romance*, p. 145.

Apostle coming to Spain to Christianize it, had been known for centuries, and it could be that exposure to the Saint-James legend through pilgrimages to Compostela in Spain, where James was purported to be buried, inspired the invention of a similar legend of Joseph and England. There are obvious similarities between the two legends, and Compostela had, partly through Cluniac efforts, become an important site.

In addition to possible Spanish-Christian inspiration for the basic story of Joseph of Arimathea, there may have been Spanish-Arabic or Hebrew influences. The names in the *Estoire* of the Vulgate Cycle (Josue, Aminadap, Jonas, Ysaies) show an Hebraic origin,[31] and in a passage in a fourteenth-century manuscript written by the monk John of Glastonbury (the Joseph story was later connected to Glastonbury which had been identified with Avalon) occurs a peculiarly Islamic reference to Jesus. The passage purports to be from *libro Melkini, quo fuit ante Merlinum.* It states that Joseph of Arimathea is buried at Glastonbury and that his sarcophagus contains two cruets with the blood and sweat of Jesus: *"Habet enim secum Joseph in sarcophago duo fassula alba et argentea, cruore prophetae Ihesu et sudore perimplete."* This translates as, "For Joseph has with him in his sarcophagus two white and silver cruets, filled with the blood and sweat of the prophet Jesus."[32] To find reference to Jesus as a prophet by a Christian monk is startling. The "prophet Jesus" is a term which would only be used by a member of the Hebrew faith in which Jesus is considered a minor prophet or by a member of the Islamic faith in which he is considered a major prophet. It is particularly characteristic of Islamic references to Jesus.

Since the appearance of the grail and Joseph of Arimathea stories coincided with the major translation period of scientific works in Spain, and Spanish Jews as well as Muslims often played a vital role in the translation and transmission of such material, such a passage as this is not really surprising, although one critic

31 Loomis, *Celtic Myth and Arthurian Romance,* p. 145.

32 The Latin version is Hearne's edition, quoted in Murray, "The Egyptian Elements in the Grail Romance," p. 68; the translation is Robinson's, quoted in Loomis, *The Grail,* pp. 260–61. Murray cites the passage for its Islamic reference to Jesus, p. 60.

finds it "a cryptic effusion, the latinity of which excites as much wonder as the content."[33] Its crypticism may be due to Islamic and/or Hebrew influences and transmitters of portions of the story if it was inspired by that of Saint James of Spain.

The grail story was, in turn, popular in Spain. In addition to a translation of the French *Estoire* in the late thirteenth century, there was a Portuguese version of Joseph of Arimathea and a Catalan story of the grail in the fourteenth century.

Parzival

Although Wolfram von Eschenbach's *Parzival*, written between 1197 and 1215, draws from traditional Arthurian material and the grail quest of Chrétien de Troyes, it adds new themes and ideas to such material. Wolfram acknowledged Chrétien as a source, but not as his sole source, for *Parzival*. Chrétien was not, for example, the source for the first two and the last three books.[34] The first two books relate the adventures of Parzival's father Gahmuret and his marriage to a Moorish queen in North Africa who bore him a son Feirifiz. (The latter's mixed blood was reflected in a black-and-white-spotted complexion.) Near the end of *Parzival*, Feirifiz is converted, marries a Christian maiden of the grail, and departs for India. His son will be Prester John, and one of Parzival's sons will be Lohengrin. Wolfram is tying in several unrelated legends with his Parzival story.

As source material for the grail, Wolfram mentions, in addition to Chrétien, one Kyot of Provence, who, in turn, supposedly obtained his information in Toledo in a manuscript written by the "heathen Flegetanis." Neither Kyot nor Flegetanis has been identified, and they are generally thought to have been nonexistent, notwithstanding much obviously Spanish-Arabic-derived material in *Parzival*. In my opinion, Wolfram's Kyot did exist as a person, although no specific identity for him can be proposed. Suffice to note that there are two Kyots mentioned in *Parzival*,

33 Loomis, *The Grail*, p. 261.

34 This is discussed in Helen M. Mustard and Charles E. Passage, trans., *Parzival*, by Wolfram von Eschenbach (New York, 1961), p. xxii. My discussion of *Parzival* follows my article, "Wolfram's 'Flegetanis,'" in *The Southern Quarterly*, 11 (January, 1973), 157–66.

one the Provençal source and one a Kyot, Duke of Catalonia, whose daughter was Sigune. Provence during the twelfth century, the period of the troubadours, was connected culturally and politically with Aragon, and it may be that the reason that no Provençal Kyot who fits Wolfram's remarks has been identified is that Wolfram's Kyot was from Aragon or Catalonia. The suggestion of a northern or eastern Spanish identity for Kyot is offered here as one yet to be explored. But Flegetanis *can* be identified, at least tentatively.

Parzival is different from other grail stories in many respects—most noticeably in its geography, its treatment of love, its description of the grail, and its inclusion of scientific lore, all of which suggest Spanish influences. Wolfram's story takes place in Europe, Asia, and Africa as opposed to the Britain and Wales of other grail accounts. The hermit Trevrezent's travels in Book IX, like those of Gahmuret in Books I and II, include real geographical locations in Spain, North Africa, and the Near East. (The names *Trevrezent,* like Ṭrabzon, a town in Turkey, and *Gahmuret,* among others, are suspiciously Eastern sounding.) The vegetation in *Parzival* is subtropical with mention of olive branches, as found in Spain and Provence, and it in no way matches the usual Britain and Wales settings of other grail stories. There are, further, several Spanish kings and noblemen included among Wolfram's characters. Thus, part of the geography and some of the characters are Spanish.

The love in *Parzival* is not the courtly, adulterous variety of most romances. It ranges from the childlike (Obilot and Gawan) to sensual love (Gawan and Antikonie) to love sight unseen (Gramoflanz and Itonje) to marital love (Parzival and Condwiramurs), and it is almost always highly romantic. It resembles the love in Ibn-Ḥazm's *Dove's Neck-Ring* more closely than does the love of most of the other Arthurian romances. Even the guardians of the grail are married and their marriages are love matches, which is in sharp contrast to other grail guests imposing conditions of celibacy. The love in *Parzival* is thus more Andalusian than French or German.

In accounts of the grail prior to Wolfram's, the grail is a cup, vessel, or platter. In Wolfram it is a stone attended by twenty-five maidens and guarded by a military order called Templeisin. A wafer is placed on the stone every Good Friday by a dove. There is a wounded knight connected with the grail castle and a wasteland in Wolfram's version as in other versions. The stone, the wounded knight, the castle, and the wasteland invite comparison to a fifteenth-century English carol:

> Lully, lulley; lully, lulley;
> The fawcon hath born may mak away.
> He bare hym vp, he bare hym down,
> He bare hym into an orchard brown.
> In that orchard ther was an hall,
> That was hangid with purpill and pall.
> And in that hall ther was a bede;
> Hit was hanged with gold so rede.
> And yn that bed ther lythe a knyght,
> His wowndes bledying day and nyght.
> By that bedes side ther kneleth a may,
> And she wepeth both nyght and day.
> And by that beddes side ther stondith a ston,
> 'Corpus Christi' wretyn theron.

Many critics have suggested a connection between this poem and the grail because of the hall with purple (grail castle), the brown orchard (wasteland), and the wounded knight, but E. K. Chambers calls such a connection "a wild conjecture" because a grail poem should contain a grail vessel and there is none in the poem.[35] There is no vessel in the poem, but there is a grail in it in the form of the stone with writing on it, like the grail in Wolfram's story.

The grail has miraculous feeding properties, in addition to which, Wolfram's stone, the "*Wunsch von pardîs,*" the "*lapsis exilis,*" has other miraculous properties. It is the power by which the phoenix is burned and restored; messages appear on its edges and disappear when they have been read; and no one who looks upon it can die or age for a week thereafter. Its description is

[35] Edmund K. Chambers, *English Literature at the Close of the Middle Ages*, p. 112. The lyric is from Chambers, pp. 11–12.

evocative of some of the fabulous accounts in treatises on alchemy, magic, and astrology and in lapidaries translated from Arabic to Latin in the twelfth century.

"*Ichne kan decheinen buochstap*" ("I do not know any letters"), says Wolfram.[36] He then proceeds in several later passages to bombard his audience with lists of material which were translated into Latin in eleventh- and twelfth-century Spain. He may have known no Latin and may have been reciting information he had gotten by heart orally, but then he may have been using the device of self-conscious negation found later in Chaucer. "I don't know the colors of rhetoric," says Chaucer in the "Nun's Priest's Tale," and then he displays every device of rhetoric taught in the schools of his day, concluding with a rousing parody in grand style of the lament for Richard I by the rhetorician Geoffrey de Vinsauf whose work on rhetoric was one of the standard textbooks. In fact, whenever Chaucer says "I don't know 'thus and so,' " we can expect a seemingly learned discourse on "thus and so" to follow. So it was with Wolfram.

Wolfram professes ignorance, then displays an unbelievable amount of learning through the hag Cundrie, a linguist, scientist, and sorceress:

der meide ir kunst des verjach,
alle sprâche sî wol sprach,
latîn, heidenisch, franzoys,
si was der witze curtoys,
dîaletike und jêometrî:
ir wâren ouch die liste bî
von astronomîe
si hiez Cundrîe:
surziere was ir zuoname. (VI, 312: 19–27)

The translation reads, "The maiden was so learned that she spoke all languages, Latin, Arabic, French [*Heidenisch* or "heathen" meant Arabic]. She was versed in courtesy, in dialectic, and in geometry; she also knew the science of astronomy. Her name was

[36] *Parzival,* in *Wolfram von Eschenbach,* ed. Karl Lachmann, 7th ed. (Berlin, 1952), Book II, 115: 27. Citations to *Parzival* are all to this edition.

Cundrie; her surname was Sorceress." In Books XV and XVI, Cundrie displays some of her learning. For example, there is a long list of gems and minerals (XVI, sec. 791) in which some of the names are Arabic. It is undoubtedly from one of the works translated into Latin during the preceding century. Cundrie's naming of the planets in Book XVI (782: 1–12) is surprising in that the names she gives for the seven planets are Germanicized Arabic terms. The sun is *Samsî* (Arabic *al-Shams*), the moon is *Alkamêr* (Arabic *al-Qamar*), Saturn is *Zvâl* (Arabic *Zuḥal*), and so forth.[37] Wolfram may not have been a Latin scholar, but where then did he find his Arabic terms, especially in astronomy, if he did not get them from someone who had read them in Arabic? True, Wolfram may have attributed to his Kyot and Flegetanis legendary material on the grail which he had actually obtained from another source; but at some point, he must have come into contact with then-current Spanish-Arabic scientific and pseudo-scientific treatises, perhaps through a person who had read them in the original or through a troubadour who knew of them through contacts with Spain and Arabic-reading or Latin-reading acquaintances.

Somebody had to bring the Arabic terms to Germany, just as somebody had to introduce an Arabic word for green into the German language. Parzival's father, Gahmuret, when he goes into the service of the Baruch, Caliph of Baghdad, is described as wearing emerald-green silk riding gear. The word used for "emerald green" is *achmardi*, the Arabic *asamardī*,[38] a strange word to find in Middle-High German. And finally, somebody had to translate the astronomical and astrological treatises and lapidaries Wolfram cites so copiously.

Kyot, Wolfram's purported source for the grail story, is mentioned in some six passages in *Parzival*. The longest passage includes a description of the "heathen Flegetanis," whose work Kyot is supposed to have read in Arabic. The passage is as follows:

[37] Mustard and Passage, trans., *Parzival*, p. 435, *n.* 5, call attention to the Arabic terms.

[38] This word is pointed out by Singer, *Germanisch-Romanisches Mittelalter*, p. 165, and others.

Kyôt der meister wol bekant
ze Dôlet verworfen ligen vant
in heidenischer schrifte
dirre âventiure gestifte.
der karakter â b c
muose er hân gelernet ê,
ân den list von nigrômanzî.
es half daz im der touf was bî:
anders waer diz maer noch unvernumen.
kein heidensch list möht uns gevrumen
ze künden umbe des grâles art,
wie man sîner tougen inner wart.
ein heiden Flegetânîs
bejagte an künste hôhen prîs.
der selbe fisîôn
was geborn von Salmôn,
ûz isrâhelscher sippe erzilt
von alter her, unz unser schilt
der touf wart vürz helleviur.
der schreip fon des grâles âventiur.
Er war ein heiden vaterhalp,
Flegetânîs, der an ein kalp
bette als ob ez waer sîn got.

. . . .

Flegetânîs der heiden
kunde uns wol bescheiden
ieslîches sternen hinganc
unt sîner künfte widerwanc;
wie lange ieslîcher umbe gêt,
ê er wider an an sin zil gestêt.
mit der sternen umbereise vart
ist gepüfel aller menschlîch art.
Flegetânîs der heiden sach,
dâ von er blûwechlîche sprach,
im gestirn mit sînen ougen
verholenbaeriu tougen.
er jach, er hiez ein dinc der grâl:
des namen las er sunder twâl
imme gestirne, wie der hiez.
"ein schar in ûf der erden liez:
diu vuor ûf über die sterne hôch.
ob die ir unschult wider zôch,
zît muoz sîn pflegen getouftiu vruht

> mit alsô kiuschlîcher zuht:
> diu menscheit ist immer wirt,
> der zuo dem grâle wirt gegert."
> Sus schreip dervon Flegetânîs. (IX, 453: 11–455: 1)[39]

The translation reads:

> Kyot, the well-known master, found in Toledo, discarded, set down in heathen writing, the first source of this adventure. He had first to learn the *abc*'s, but without the art of black magic. It helped him that he was baptized, else this story would still be unknown. No heathen art could be of use in revealing the nature of the Grail and how its mysteries were discovered.
>
> A heathen, Flegetanis, had achieved high renown for his learning. This scholar of nature was descended from Solomon and born of a family which had long been Israelite until baptism became our shield against the fire of Hell. He wrote the adventure of the Grail. On his father's side, Flegetanis was a heathen, who worshipped a calf as if it were his god. . . .
>
> The heathen Flegetanis could tell us how all the stars set and rise again and how long each one revolves before it reaches its starting point once more. To the circling course of the stars man's affairs and destiny are linked. Flegetanis the heathen saw with his own eyes in the constellations things he was shy to talk about, hidden mysteries. He said there was a thing called the Grail whose name he had read clearly in the constellations. "A host of angels left it on earth and then flew away up over the stars. Was it their innocence that drew them away? Since then baptized men have had the task of guarding it, and with such chaste discipline that those who are called to the service of the Grail are always noble men." Thus wrote Flegetanis of these things.[40]

From the passage above, several facts can be ascertained about Flegetanis. First, he was possibly of Jewish and "pagan" origin, since the calf-worshipping idea could, in the medieval mind, apply to any non-Christian religion, including Zoroastrianism and Islam. Secondly, he knew astronomy and/or astrology, and read certain mysteries (of the grail, according to Wolfram) in the stars. Finally, he wrote in Arabic ("Heathen") and a manuscript

39 Other passages in which Kyot is mentioned are: VIII, 416: 20–30; VIII, 431: 2; XV, 776: 10; XVI, 805: 10; and XVI, 827: 1–14.

40 The translation is from Mustard and Passage, trans., *Parzival*, pp. 243–44.

of his work(s) was in Toledo, the major center for translation of such works in the twelfth century.

An Arabic astrological origin for the grail story cannot be considered unless an outline for it should be discovered in one of the prologues in the hundreds of astrological and necromantic manuscripts of the twelfth century. But Wolfram's connection of the grail with an Arab origin cannot be passed over. Treatments of the grail story prior to Wolfram tended to be highly mystical, and Wolfram's treatment of it indicates that he either did not understand the materials with which he was working (hence a stone instead of a dish, platter, or cup) or that the idea for the grail actually did originate in astrology. He appears to have been familiar, at least second or third hand, with treatises on astrology and alchemy and lapidaries translated in Spain and southern France. There was a large quantity of such treatises of a pseudo-scientific nature and they are characteristically mystical and state in their prologues that they are expounding intimate philosophical secrets of astrology, of the philosopher's stone, of alchemy, or of necromancy.[41] As Wolfram's lists of gems and planets could have been known only through translations from Arabic, it is not difficult to see how he might have attached the (to him unfamiliar) mystical grail to the idea of mystical knowledge found in "heathen" astrological manuscripts in Toledo.

This leads one to suspect that Flegetanis may have been one of the astronomer-astrologers whose works were translated in Spain and France (and Sicily) shortly before Wolfram composed his *Parzival.* The question is, which one? He would, it seems, have to have been one of the well-known ones, perhaps so well known that Wolfram could have gained some knowledge of his works without having read them himself in Latin, and one whose name has some similarity to "Flegetanis," if it is a corruption of a real Arab or Persian name.

Alfraganus meets these conditions. His name with the definite article removed, *-Fraganus,* is similar enough to Wolfram's "Flegetanis," assuming the usual medieval garbling of Arabic and

41 See, for example, some of the prologues and *incipits* of astrological treatises reproduced in Charles Homer Haskins, *Studies in the History of Medieval Science.*

Persian names, to have been its original. He was one of the most widely known and most frequently quoted in medieval Europe of all of the astronomers and astrologers whose works were translated in Spain and Sicily. Dante borrowed heavily from Alfraganus' *Liber de Aggregationibus Scientie Stellarum et Principiis Celestium Motuum* in the *Vita Nuova* and *Convivio*; and in the *Convivio*, in quoting measurements and movements of the planets, Dante mentions Alfraganus' *liber*, with which he was familiar.[42] Alfraganus may also be the "Frigidilles" cited by Gower in the *Confessio Amantis*.[43]

There were actually two men known as "Alfraganus" in medieval Europe. The first of these was the astronomer Abū-al-ᶜAbbās Aḥmad Ibn-Muḥammad Ibn-Kathīr al-Farghānī of Transoxania (d. after 863) who worked under al-Maʾmūn in Baghdad. His *De scientia astorum* was translated into Latin by John of Seville in 1137 and by Gerard of Cremona before 1172. Both of these translators worked in Toledo. The work was widely diffused in Europe and there are numerous manuscripts of it.[44]

The second "Alfraganus" was misnamed Alfraganus in translation. This was the astrologer Abū-Bakr ᶜUmar Muḥammad Ibn-al-Farrukhān al-Ṭabarī (d. 815), from Tiberias (Israel and Jordan). He is also referred to as Omar Alfraganus Tiberiadis in many manuscripts, including those of John of Seville, who translated his *De natiuitatibus*, a work of pure astrology. The astrologer Alfraganus was repeatedly quoted by Arabic and Latin writers and was also repeatedly mistaken for the astronomer Alfraganus, who did not write on astrology per se. The confusion of the two men is a well-known medieval error.

John of Seville himself wrote on astrology in addition to his many translations. John was, incidentally, of Jewish origin. The two al-Farghānīs lived and worked in Persia and were of Persian,

[42] Paget Toynbee, "Dante's Obligations to Alfraganus in the *Vita Nuova* and *Convivio*," *Romania*, 24 (July, 1895), 413–32, cites Dante's references to Alfraganus.

[43] J. S. Tunison considers "Frigidilles" a confused and unidentified reference in Gower in *The Graal Problem: From Walter Map to Richard Wagner* (Cincinnati, 1904), pp. 108–109, *n*. 9.

[44] See Francis J. Carmody, *Arabic Astronomical and Astrological Sciences in Latin Translation: A Critical Bibliography* (Berkeley, 1956), pp. 38–39, 113–15; and George Sarton, *Introduction to the History of Science*, I, 567–68.

and possibly also of Jewish or mixed, extraction. They worked under Muslim patronage, as Jewish scientists writing under Muslim patronage were the rule rather than the exception, but their works were translated into Latin in Toledo and other centers in southern Europe.

It is my belief that Wolfram's Flegetanis is Alfraganus, either the astrologer or the astronomer, or, more likely, a confused blending of the two. The works of both men were sufficiently widely known for one to have been able to glean a surface knowledge of either of them without having read their works in Latin translation. A study of extant manuscripts, at least of their prologues, of the astronomer and the astrologer and of the works either correctly or incorrectly attributed to them might yield further clues about the strange Oriental magical properties and characteristics of the grail Wolfram describes in *Parzival*.

Conclusion

The romance tradition in Old-French literature dates from the period of the major translation efforts in Spain. As it replaced that of the older *chanson-de-geste* or epic tradition in the twelfth century in France, it incorporated motifs such as descriptions of the Saracens as idolatrous and as huge, deformed black men from the *chansons de geste*. At the time of the birth of the romance, there was a new lyric poetry, a new romantic and courtly-love concept, and many Oriental *contes* and fables being spread by the troubadours who had come into contact with the poems and stories of Andalusia, and these, along with visions of the afterlife with particularly Islamic motifs in their Oriental aspects, all provided materials for the romance to draw upon.

A large influx of Celtic lore had reached France from the north beginning in the late eleventh century and with the Celtic lore were Arthurian stories. The two traditions, Andalusian and Celtic, were then fused in France, and, as a result, the Arthurian and other romances frequently contain Andalusian motifs.

Spanish-Arabic material is evident not only in romances which have retained their initial oriental outlines such as *Aucassin et Nicolette* and *Floire et Blanchefleur*, but also in Arthurian romances whose basic story is Celtic, such as *Tristan and Isolt.* Even the grail story seems to be a mixture of diverse traditions, with Wolfram von Eschenbach's treatment of it perhaps the best example of such a mixture, one which shows the tremendous impact of the new learning brought into Europe with the translations.

In the literature covered thus far, a very ancient mythical Persian figure, "the Green One," has been encountered in the poetry of Andalusia, in Islamic mystic writings, in the *Qur'ān*'s commentaries, in the *Arabian Nights,* and in legends and romances of Alexander the Great. Let us now compare this figure with the green knight in an explication of the Middle-English romance *Sir Gawain and the Green Knight,* a character for whom no prototype in Welsh, Irish, English, or French literature has been found.

PART II—*SIR GAWAIN AND THE GREEN KNIGHT*

One of the few definite and incontestable observations which can be made concerning *Sir Gawain and the Green Knight,* one of the most fascinating works of the late medieval period, is that it is an aristocratic romance. It is an alliterative work, but not entirely so, for it also uses rime in each stanza. It is a religious work; that is, many of the events within it have a clearly religious significance; and yet it is not by any stretch of the imagination (outside that of the Robertsonian critical school) primarily concerned with ecclesiastical proselytizing. Its religious elements function within a festive setting, and the religious tone of the poem is tempered with a boisterous spontaneity, a genuine appreciation of the fun in life with no apologies for it. For example, when Sir Gawain has struck the green knight's head off,

> Þe fayre hede fro þe halce hit to þe erþe,
> Þat fele hit foyned wyth her fete, þere hit forth roled.
> (ll. 427–28)[45]

[45] *Sir Gawain and the Green Knight,* ed. J. R. R. Tolkien and E. V. Gordon; 2nd ed., ed. Norman Davis (London, 1967), hereinafter referred to as Davis, ed., *Sir Gawain.* All citations to the poem are to this edition.

There is more than a touch of humor, to use the words of Burton Raffel, in "the terrified knights of the Round Table, frantically kicking at the chopped-off head as it rolls at them" like a football.[46] Such humor is characteristic of the poet. In *Patience* when, during the storm, the sailor seeks Jonah, he finds him

> Slypped vpon a sloumbe-selepe, & sloberande he routes.
> Þe freke hym frunt with his fot, & bede hym ferk vp. (ll. 186–87)

The sailor finding Jonah lying asleep, "slobbering and snoring" and nudging him with his foot and telling him to "ferk up" is not exactly biblical. Difficult as the language of *Sir Gawain* is, its humorous touches can still be felt, as some of the more recent critics of the poem point out.

But, like *Pearl, Sir Gawain and the Green Knight* has been subjected to many limiting critical evaluations which tend to restrict the poem's theme(s) to a particular allegorical interpretation. And, like the *Pearl, Sir Gawain* does not lend itself to such interpretation. The poem has further been reduced to a moralizing homily (with the facts in the romance's story appropriately distorted to fit the sentence) by modern patristic exegetes, dissipated into a spray of ancient Celtic motifs (whether such motifs actually existed or not) by the Celtists, and seen by the myth-and-ritual critics as a song and dance of a journey into the realm of the dead (because the green knight was green and corpses may turn green in decaying). The poem does seem to harken back in some respects to ancient myths,[47] it does draw from certain Celtic tales, and it is certainly a Christian work. The poet has drawn from all of these areas, but he seems also to have drawn from other areas which have not been recognized by the Celtists, Patrists, and mythologists.[48] And even if all of the sources of the poem were to

46 Burton Raffel, trans., *Sir Gawain and the Green Knight* (New York, 1970), p. 12. Another recent critic who emphasizes the humor in the poem is Larry D. Benson, *Art and Tradition in Sir Gawain and the Green Knight* (New Brunswick, 1965).

47 In addition to containing remnants of vegetation myths, the poem also seems to evidence vestiges of a prehistoric conflict between matriarchal and patriarchal rituals, as demonstrated by Sally P. Kennedy, "Vestiges of Rule Ritual in *Sir Gawain and the Green Knight*," Diss. Univ. of Tenn. 1968.

48 Morton W. Bloomfield, "*Sir Gawain and the Green Knight*: An Appraisal," *PMLA*, 76 (1961), 7–19, summarizes the criticism of *Sir Gawain* up to that year. His

be identified, the fact would remain that *Sir Gawain* is, like *Pearl,* more than the mere sum of its sources.

Structure and Prosody

Sir Gawain and the Green Knight is a study in balance and symmetry. It is divided into four sections or "fyttes," the challenge, the arrival, the sojourn, and the rendezvous.[49] The first and third sections are set in Arthur's and Bercilak's courts, respectively, at the Christmas season, and the settings are appropriately those of feasting and merrymaking. The second and fourth sections are primarily set in the wilderness and include Sir Gawain's journey to Bercilak's castle and his subsequent visit to the green chapel. There are further parallels among the poem's sections in the arming of Sir Gawain (which occurs twice), his journey to the castle and to the green chapel, the descriptions of the green knight's castle and of the green chapel, the three temptation scenes and the three strokes of the axe, and Gawain's two confessions, one to a priest and one to the green knight.[50] In addition, the balance between description and action is carried out within each section, as in the meaningful alternation between the temptation and hunting scenes in the third section.

The verse of *Sir Gawain* is basically four-stress alliterative, and the stanzas or strophes vary in length from twelve to thirty-seven lines.[51] Each strophe concludes with a device called a bob and wheel, the bob consisting of one or two words written in the

---

study has been supplemented by Raffel in the introduction to his translation and by Neil D. Isaacs in the afterword to Raffel's work. Raffel and Isaacs also provide some evaluation of the criticism.

49 The section titles are those of Henry Lyttleton Savage in *The Gawain-Poet: Studies in His Personality and Background.*

50 Donald R. Howard, "Structure and Symmetry in *Sir Gawain,*" in *Sir Gawain and Pearl,* ed. Robert J. Blanch, p. 202. For discussion of the parallels in significance between the animals hunted and the bedroom scene of the three temptations of Sir Gawain by the lady, see Savage, *The Gawain-Poet,* pp. 35–37, and Raffel, trans., *Sir Gawain and the Green Knight,* pp. 29–30.

51 Detailed discussion of the metrics can be found in Marie Borroff, *Sir Gawain and the Green Knight: A Stylistic and Metrical Study* (New Haven, 1962). See also Benson, *Art and Tradition in Sir Gawain,* pp. 110–29; and Isaacs, afterword to Raffel's translation, pp. 141–42.

margin to the side of the last line of the alliterative strophe, and the wheel being the four short, rimed alliterative lines which follow it. For example, in the strophe in which the green knight first appears, the description of his color is given in the wheel. He is in form and feature

> . . . ful clene;
> For wonder of his hwe men hade,
> Set in his semblaunt sene;
> He ferde as freke were fade,
> And overal enker-grene. (ll. 146–50)

With the bob, a change in meter is signaled, and the wheel follows in the shorter lines, which are alliterative but end-rimed in the pattern aBaBa. With this device, the poet can build up to a climax in each stanza. He often reserves his most dramatic or startling moments, as in the first mention above of the green knight's color, for the bob and wheel. The rhythm of the wheel is basically *tum*-ta-(ta)-*tum*-ta-*tum*-(ta), although this too sometimes varies, possibly due to scribal copying. Occurring as it does at the end of each strophe, the rhythm could easily, if recited, tend to add a tone of flippancy which, in spite of the humor and wit in the poem, is not at all in keeping with its general tone. And this would destroy the climactic effect otherwise possible in an abrupt change in meter. If the wheel (and bob) were sung, however, the danger of a light tone due to the shortness of the rimed lines would be avoided. It is to be noted also that while the number of alliterative verses preceding the bob and wheel varies greatly from strophe to strophe, the number of verses in the bob and wheel, one plus four, is invariable, whether the strophe it concludes is a long or a short one.

Alliterative poetry was oral, recitative poetry, but the bob and wheel of each stanza in *Sir Gawain* could have been, and in my opinion very probably were, sung. If so, the poem is the only example of this type, suggesting an alternation between recitative and singing, which has survived in Middle English. As early as 1925, Robert M. Garrett noticed the alternation between the purely alliterative verses and the short, rimed bob and wheel as "so very curious a reminiscence of the cante-fable form of *Aucassin and Nicolette*,"[52] itself a unique survival of the form in Old French. The manuscript in which *Aucassin et Nicolette* is found also preserves the music. *Sir Gawain* does not, but it is to be remembered that the manuscript of *Sir Gawain* is generally conceded to be a scriptorium-produced copy and not the original of the poem. It is my suggestion therefore that *Sir Gawain* is a Middle-English representative of the *chante-fable* form with its regular alternation between recitative and song. *Aucassin et Nicolette*, the only other known Western European survival of the form, has been recognized as an adaptation of Arab minstrelsy of the type epitomized by the *maqāma*, which had been popular in Spain.

Religious and Festive Elements

Sir Gawain is, as many critics have noted, primarily a festive poem,[53] the festivals with which the poem is associated being Christmas and the New Year, with their attendant religious significance. The poem is thus religious in a festive and joyful sense as well as in a personal sense in which prayer, confession, penance, and various moral virtues are emphasized. The religious elements, both festive and personal, are essential to the poem, but its theme cannot be neatly tacked down to a particular virtue or to any one of the seven deadly sins.

The action of the poem, both in the opening scene at Arthur's court and in Gawain's journey to seek the green chapel a year later, occurs at the Christmas season, and the scenes at Arthur's and Bercilak's courts involve feasting, merrymaking, gifts, kisses, and games. The green knight even offers his challenge to Arthur's court as a Christmas game:

52 Robert Max Garrett, "The Lay of Sir Gawayne and the Grene Knight," *Journal of English and German Philology*, 24 (1925), 128.

53 John Speirs, *Medieval English Poetry: The Non-Chaucerian Tradition*, p. 219; Benson, *Art and Tradition in Sir Gawain*, p. 248; and Raffel, trans., *Sir Gawain and the Green Knight*, p. 24. A recent study along this line is that of Martin Stevens, "Laughter and Game in *Sir Gawain and the Green Knight*," *Speculum*, 47 (1972), 65–78.

Here is no mon me to mach, for myȝtez so wayke.
For þy I craue in þis court a Crystemas gomen,
For hit is ȝol and Nwe ȝer, and here are ȝep mony. (ll. 282–84)

After the green knight has been beheaded and has picked up his head, mounted, and left the court, Arthur soothes Guinevere:

> Dere dame, to-day demay yow neuer;
> Wel bycommes such craft upon Christmasse,
> Laykyng of enterludez to laȝe and to syng. (ll. 470–72)

John Speirs, in calling *Sir Gawain* "a midwinter festival poem," finds the green knight related to "the Green Man—the Jack in the Green or the Wild Man of the village festivals of England and Europe," who is "a descendant of the Vegetation or Nature god . . . whose death and resurrection are the myth-and-ritual counterpart of the annual death and rebirth of Nature." He argues that the winter of the poem is "implicitly enchantment," that the beheading is a "ritual contest" between Sir Gawain and Bercilak, and that the green knight's description implies vegetation, since he is "a recrudescence in poetry of the Green Man."[54] Bercilak may derive from a green vegetation figure (which will be discussed later), but Speirs goes much too far in insisting that the poem is therefore a ritualistic nature celebration in midwinter. There is no annual beheading of the green knight, as this only occurs once in the poem, and there is no restoration of a wasteland to greenness and fertility at his beheading as would be expected in a ritualistic enactment of the death-and-rebirth cycle. The poem was, further, written for an aristocratic, courtly audience, not for participants in a village festival. It would seem therefore more in keeping with the poem itself to attribute its festive elements to the Christmas and New Year season which it was very likely written to celebrate.

Chaucer's "Squire's Tale" is also a festive poem, celebrating "Cambyuskan's" birthday. C. O. Chapman, conjecturing that Chaucer may have used *Sir Gawain* as a model (but not as the

[54] Speirs, *Medieval English Poetry*, pp. 219–25; and Speirs, "*Sir Gawain and the Green Knight*," *Scrutiny*, 16 (1949), 274–300.

source) for portions of his tale, points out several similarities between the opening portions of both works. Both poems open in a royal hall on a festive occasion; a strange knight whose appearance astonishes the hosts in both stories rides in suddenly; and the knights in the two halls think the strange knight (in *Sir Gawain*) and the strange mechanical horse (in the "Squire's Tale") are "from Fairy."[55] No one has, incidentally, suggested that the "Squire's Tale" although it is unfinished, represents a village or nature festival. Chapman's observations are also of interest in that the "Squire's Tale" is an Arab-Persian story which probably reached Europe through Spain, as mentioned in Chapter V. The points of similarity between the opening portions of Chaucer's and the *Gawain*-poet's tales pertain to festival stories; in this the two works are very similar, but the stories themselves are not related to each other.

The more personal religious aspects of the poem can be seen in the testing of Gawain, the two confessions, the penance, and the green chapel. That Gawain is being tested is apparent, but it is not always clear why he is being tested. In the initial challenge in Arthur's court, the test seems to be for both bravery and the ability to keep one's word even if it means death; the same two virtues seem to be involved when Gawain's guide, on the way to the green chapel, offers to cover for him if he wishes to back out of his rendezvous. At Bercilak's castle, the test seems to involve chastity and again the ability to keep one's word in the exchange of winnings. Finally, at the green chapel, both bravery and patience (in the broad sense in which it is used in the poem *Patience*) seem to be involved.

Gawain's failures of the various tests are equivocal. He is brave, but not enough to keep from flinching at the first axe-stroke. He makes the rendezvous as he had agreed, but he fails to live up to his word in the exchange of winnings by not yielding up the green girdle the lady had given him. At the denouement, when Bercilak has explained the preceding occurrences to him, Gawain admits to two sins as reasons for his taking and concealing the "magic"

[55] Coolidge Otis Chapman, "Chaucer and the *Gawain*-Poet: A Conjecture," pp. 522–23.

belt: "Corsed worth cowarddyse and couetyse boþe" (l. 2374), he exclaims. In covetousness, cowardice, and in failure to keep his "trawþe," Gawain seems to have been motivated, however, by the desire to preserve his life. One critic concludes from this that Gawain was guilty of *cupiditas*, or self-love,[56] a conclusion not inconsistent with the poem's facts.

In his study of the significance of the pentangle or endless knot on Gawain's shield, George Englehardt believes that since the pentangle represents whole or unending virtue, the "moral of the poem" emerges from the testing of Gawain as "the perfect knight."[57] One might ask, "What moral?" But Gawain does seem to be tested as an ideal Christian knight. Two other critics, Paul Delany and Douglas Moon, in attempting to deal with Gawain's being tested, find it necessary to distort the poem. Delany believes that the unnamed guide who tries to dissuade Gawain from going on to the green chapel is the green knight in disguise, and Moon, following Mother Angela Carson and R. S. Loomis, argues that the green knight's unnamed wife and Morgan le Fay are the same person.[58] But the language of the poem is not so obscure as to admit such speculations as these to the realm of possibility. It should be sufficient simply to observe that Gawain is tested; as a human being, he naturally falls short of the ideal for the perfect Christian knight.

Gawain's shortcomings lead to the two confession scenes and to his penance, in the form of the axe-nick and his wearing the green girdle as a symbol of his shame.[59] His first confession (ll. 1876–84) is to a priest who absolves him although he has accepted

56 David Farley Hills, "Gawain's Fault in *Sir Gawain and the Green Knight*," *Review of English Studies*, 14 (1963), 129–30.

57 George J. Englehardt, "The Predicament of Gawain," *Modern Language Quarterly*, 16 (1955), 218–25.

58 Paul Delany, "The Role of the Guide in *Sir Gawain and the Green Knight*," in *Critical Studies of Sir Gawain and the Green Knight*, ed. Donald R. Howard and Christian Zacher (Notre Dame, 1968), pp. 227–35; Douglas M. Moon, "The Role of Morgain la Fée in *Sir Gawain and the Green Knight*," *Neuphilologische Mitteilungen*, 67 (1966), 39–40; Mother Angela Carson, "Morgain la Fée as the Principle of Unity in *Gawain and the Green Knight*," *Modern Language Quarterly*, 23 (1962), 5; and Loomis, *Wales and the Arthurian Legend*, p. 89.

59 See John Burrow, "The Two Confession Scenes in *Sir Gawain and the Green Knight*," in *Sir Gawain and Pearl*, ed. Blanch, pp. 123–34.

the green girdle from the lady. And yet, although some of the poem's critics would argue otherwise, it seems to have been a valid confession:

> And he asoyled hym surely and sette hym so clene
> As domezday schulde haf ben diȝt on þe morn. (ll. 1883–84)

After all, the confession occurred *before* Sir Gawain had failed to keep his word, *before* the green knight returned from the hunt. One does not confess to and do penance for a sin in advance of committing it, and nothing is said of indulgences in the poem. The second confession is made to the green knight himself.

That Bercilak was the second one to whom Gawain confessed is a matter of special interest. It shows that his strange, ambiguous role in the poem is in many respects a religious one. He has the double function of serving as an instrument to illustrate the Old Testament blow for a blow of Moses' law and of acting as a sort of hermit-priest to whom Gawain confesses and from whom he receives penance to illustrate Christian grace of the New Testament. After Gawain's confession, Bercilak absolves him:

> Þou art confessed so clene, beknowen of þy mysses,
> And hatȝ þe penaunce apert of þe poynt of myn egge,
> I halde þe polysed of þat plyȝt, and pured as clene
> As þou hadeȝ neuer forfeted syþen þou watȝ fyrst borne.
> (ll. 2391–94)

The fact that the green knight is associated with a chapel and the fact that he hears Sir Gawain's confession and gives penance indicate that his is a definitely religious role in the poem. The location of his chapel is Hautdesert, or "high wilderness." It represents an hermitage, in which an errant knight could both hear Mass performed by its hermit and make confession to him, and although Bercilak is a non-Christian and a supernatural figure, the supernatural being is being used in a particularly Christian role.[60]

The supernatural elements of the poem, such as the green

[60] G. V. Smithers, "What *Sir Gawain and the Green Knight* is About," *Medium Ævum*, 32 (1963), 172, 184.

knight's replaceable head, seem never to outweigh the Christian elements but, rather, to serve them. Several observations about the green knight might be made. He appears suddenly in Arthur's court to offer a challenge; he is a knight; he is associated with a chapel, the name and appearance of which indicate that it is an hermitage. As a messenger of Morgan le Fay, he does not initiate the beheading game although he does test Gawain with his wife; in his hearing Gawain's confession and giving penance, he dramatizes the means to divine grace; and, finally, only at the end does he reveal his name and the meaning of the preceding events. His role in *Sir Gawain* is thus not consistent with that of the typical green man of village festivals, even though he may be a distant cousin, because of his predominantly religious, Christian-oriented role in the poem.

Morgan le Fay

Morgan le Fay's role in the poem is a minor but still an organic one.[61] The poet has used magic and Christianity side by side, not an unusual practice in Arthurian legends. There are, however, no green giants in Christian theology or legends, and the green knight is not portrayed as an angel. The poet must therefore account for his coming to Arthur's court and testing Gawain somehow, and since he cannot place him within the known hosts of heaven or Christian saints, he simply uses a person known for magic, Morgan le Fay, who also functions to help tie the story in with more traditional Arthurian matter. Through the expediency of Morgan, the poet can account for the green knight's ini-

61 For arguments that Morgan le Fay plays a major role in the poem, see Alan M. Markman, "The Meaning of *Sir Gawain and the Green Knight*," in *Sir Gawain and Pearl*, ed. Blanch, pp. 159–75; Denver Ewing Baughan, "The Role of Morgan le Fay in *Sir Gawain and the Green Knight*," *Journal of English Literary History*, 17 (1950), 241–51; T. McAlindon, "Magic, Fate, and Providence in Medieval Narrative and *Sir Gawain and the Green Knight*," *Review of English Studies*, 16 (1965), 121–39; Moon, "The Role of Morgain la Fée"; and Carson, "Morgain la Fée as the Principle of Unity." For arguments to the contrary, see J. R. Hulbert, "Syr Gawayne and the Grene Knyȝt," *Modern Philology*, 13 (1916), 433–62, 689–730; George Lyman Kittredge, *A Study of Gawain and the Green Knight* (Cambridge, Mass., 1916); and Albert B. Friedman, "Morgan le Fay in *Sir Gawain and the Green Knight*," in *Sir Gawain and Pearl*, ed. Blanch, pp. 135–58.

tial reason for coming to Arthur's court by making him her emissary. The second test did not need to be accounted for, and the poet has included no specific justification for it, just as there is no reason stated outright for Gawain's refusal of the lady's advances and no real explication by the narrator of the penance and confession in the poem. Morgan's jealousy of and dislike for Guinevere and the desire to frighten her out of her wits are not important here. But by giving her such selfish, petty motives, the poet maintains a continuity with Gawain's statement shortly preceding Bercilak's announcement of Morgan's motive. Gawain says that woman is the cause of man's troubles. Morgan was known for being beautiful when she was benevolent and old and hideously ugly when malevolent.[62] Her ugliness in *Sir Gawain* could thus be related to her malevolent motives in sending Bercilak to Arthur's court, but not necessarily. One critic, noticing that there is always an ugly hag in all of the Perceval stories of Arthurian romance, holds "the Loathly Lady to be always, and in every guise, connected more or less closely, with Gawain."[63] It is to be noted also that in *Sir Gawain* she only appears in the company of Bercilak's beautiful lady, almost like the traditional *duenna* as found in the *Roman de la Rose,* who functions both to protect her young charge and to assist a deserving and courteous lover in attaining her. She does not actively function in this role in *Sir Gawain,* but there are suggestions of her being associated with the old governess—she only appears with the lady, and Gawain is obliged to pay his respects to her (he does not recognize her as his aunt) and does so.

Courtly Love

In the third section of the poem, as soon as Bercilak has departed for the hunt, his lady steals in to Gawain's chamber, softly shuts and locks the door, and comes to the bed where Gawain, having seen her, pretends to be asleep. The conversation has hardly begun when the lady announces:

[62] See Lucy Allen Paton, *Studies in the Fairy Mythology of Arthurian Romance,* 2nd ed. (New York, 1960), p. 151.

[63] Jessie L. Weston, *The Legend of Sir Perceval,* II (London, 1909), 199.

Ʒe are welcum to my cors,
Yowre awen won to wale,
Me behouez of fyne force
Your seruant be, and schale. (ll. 1237–40)

The scene is repeated on the following two mornings, with the lady becoming more persistent each time. Gawain resists her offers of love, but the reason for his resistance is not clear. It could relate to the bargain Gawain had made with Bercilak, to the reversal of roles of wooer and wooed, to Christian chastity as opposed to courtly love, or to a conflict between ideals within the courtly-love tradition itself.

Because of the bargain to exchange winnings, Gawain is caught in a comically impossible predicament. If he rejects her outright, he will damage his reputation as a courteous lover who would be expected to comply with her wishes. But if he yields to her, he will have certain difficulty in carrying out the exchange of winnings agreed upon with Bercilak (in a possible scene which we are supposed to imagine but not mention), and even if he could do so, he would have to reveal his love, a cardinal sin for the courtly lover. Yet, in analogues of the story in which there is an exchange of winnings between the lover and the husband, one of which appears in the *Arabian Nights*, the lover is quite willing to deceive the husband and win his wife. Gawain deceives Bercilak with the girdle which he accepts and conceals, but will go no further.

Attention has been called to the lady's assuming the role normally played by the knight in a typical courtly-love situation, and by reversing the roles, making the whole ritual slightly ridiculous.[64] This is possible, but then a reversal of roles in courtly love did not necessarily involve ridicule. In Wolfram von Eschenbach's *Parzival*, for example, Gahmuret, Parzival's father, is actively wooed, claimed, and won by Herzeloyde, and there is nothing at all comic or ironic in her doing so, even when she offers her service as the lover would normally do. Further, the woman's taking the initiative is a Celtic custom. In primitive Celtic lore,

[64] J. F. Kiteley, "The *De Arte Honeste Amandi* of Andreas Capellanus and the Concept of Courtesy in *Sir Gawain and the Green Knight*," *Anglia*, 79 (1961), 12–15.

women almost invariably do the wooing, and, as Briffault has shown in his study, *The Mothers*, they "do so with a directness and a determination that ignore rebuffs." [65]

The conflict between courtly love and the Christian ideal of chastity involved in the bedroom scenes is obvious. This may have occurred to Gawain, but then he had a reputation for being courteous, which included being known as a skillful lover in the courtly tradition. It was seen in Chapter III that by the time the troubadours and romance-writers flourished, courtly love had crystallized into a formulaic ritual in which the lady was always either married or in a situation which made marriage impractical. In other Arthurian stories in which Gawain is prominent, he acts in accordance with the formalized tradition. He was not known for chastity, and he would not be expected to reject Bercilak's lady. But he does reject her. It has been suggested that Gawain's situation is related to the "Potiphar's-Wife" tale in which the young man's rejection is motivated by loyalty to her husband;[66] but Bercilak is not Gawain's father, his lady is not Gawain's stepmother as in the "Potiphar's-Wife" stories, and they have known each other for only one day.

Because of Gawain's renown as a not-so-platonic lover, the lady's ideas of courtly love, and his rejection of her advances, a conflict seems to exist among values or standards within the courtly-love tradition itself. The tradition within which the lady is acting, in addition to pre–courtly love Celtic tradition, is that of Ibn-Quzmān, of troubadours and romance writers, in which the lady is married and of higher station than her suitor. Yet one of the factors contributing to Gawain's refusal seems to have been her being married. He does not wish to "be traytor to þat tolke þat þat telde aȝt" (l. 1775). As a known lover, then, he appears to be acting in accordance with an earlier courtly-love tradition, that found in Ibn-Ḥazm and in Jean de Meun, in which the lady must not be married. Such a clash between values within the courtly-love tradition itself would partially explain Gawain's

65 Robert S. Briffault, *The Mothers: A Study of Sentiments and Institutions* (New York, 1927), III, 441.

66 Benson, *Art and Tradition in Sir Gawain*, p. 44.

refusal of the lady's advances. And, although not consistent with Gawain's reputation in other Arthurian romances, his refusal could also be a result of his acting in accordance with the Christian ideal of chastity. The poet does not fully explicate the refusal, perhaps because there was more than one consideration involved and because the conflicts of interests and of traditions would not permit a simple explanation.

Sources and Analogues

There are three elements in the plot of *Sir Gawain* which scholars have isolated and traced to older versions. These are the beheading challenge, the chastity test, and the exchange of winnings. The earliest study of sources for *Sir Gawain* was that of George Lyman Kittredge in 1916, which remains standard, although it has since been supplemented by many shorter studies.

Kittredge showed that the beheading challenge was of Celtic origin, having first apeared in two versions of the "champion's bargain" in the Middle-Irish narrative *Fled Bricrend* (*Feast of Bricriu*), the earliest manuscript of which dates from 1100. The hero of the story is Cuchulinn, and his being willing to submit to a return blow the next day is important. Like many other Celtic stories, the champion's bargain was further developed not in Celtic but in Continental stories. This has led Kittredge to propose a lost French work incorporating the beheading story as the immediate source for *Sir Gawain*.[67] Scholars today are reticent about the theory of a lost French source, but if the green knight is related to the Arabic green figure al-Khaḍir, then a French source would have been the logical place for such a mixture of Arabic and Celtic elements to have occurred first, as it occurred in other Arthurian stories.

Among the earliest French versions of the story are *Le Livre de Caradoc* and *La Mule Sanz Frain*, both dating from around the turn of the thirteenth century.[68] The challenge in *Caradoc*,

67 Information on the beheading challenge is taken from Kittredge, *A Study of Gawain*, and from Davis, ed., *Sir Gawain*, pp. xv–xx.

68 Benson prints the beheading challenge of *Caradoc* in an appendix to his *Art and Tradition in Sir Gawain*.

which appears in the first continuation of Chrétien de Troyes' *Perceval*, is fairly close to that in *Sir Gawain*. It is set on a feast day; a knight rides into Arthur's court to offer his challenge; and the return blow is set for a year later when he returns to the court. The challenge and setting are altered in *La Mule Sanz Frain* by Paien de Maisières, in which Gawain travels to a revolving castle, and after beheading a churl or villain (not a knight), must return for his blow the next day. The villain is tall, bushy-haired, and "black like a Moor." His appearance here as a typical Saracen ogre suggests a non-European, non-Celtic origin for the challenger. Heinrich von dem Türlin's *Diu Crône* of around 1210 is based on the account in Paien's *Mule*. In another French version of the story, *Hunbaut*, of the first half of the thirteenth century, the challenger is again a tall, ugly, black villain. But in *Hunbaut*, Gawain avoids a return blow by seizing the villain's head after striking it off; when he cannot get his head back, the villain dies.

Two late French prose versions of the story which were noticed by Kittredge are *Perlesvaus* and *Perceual le Galloys*, the latter dated around 1530. Lancelot, rather than Gawain, is the hero of *Perlesvaus*, in which there is a return blow the next year, not by the knight Lancelot beheaded, but by his brother who is also beheaded. In connection with the beheading, a wasteland is restored and repeopled, an element which, along with an annual beheading, clearly indicates a vegetation ritual. William Nitze, noting the appearance of the beheading challenge in both *Sir Gawain* and *Perlesvaus* and the connection of the latter with vegetation rites, proposed a similar vegetation ritual origin for the green knight.[69] His theory was followed up by that of Speirs mentioned earlier. There is, however, no wasteland restoration and no annual beheading in *Sir Gawain* as in *Perlesvaus*. In *Perceual le Galloys*, the challenger is the father of the hero. This version is remarkable in that the challenger, while not green, is dressed in green satin.

All of the extant English analogues of the beheading challenge are later than *Sir Gawain*. One of them is the *Carl of Carlisle*,

69 William A. Nitze, "Is the Green Knight Story a Vegetation Myth?" *Modern Philology*, 33 (1936), 351–66.

appearing in two manuscripts, one dated around 1450 in couplets, and the Percy-Folio manuscript of around 1650, in which the story is written in tail-rime stanzas. The carl asks Gawain to behead him not as a challenge, but in order to disenchant him. After being beheaded, he becomes a handsome knight. In *The Turk and Gawain,* which is found only in the Percy-Folio manuscript, the Turk, like the carl, asks Gawain to behead him in order to release him from an enchantment which had turned him into a Turkish dwarf. In the *Turk,* as in *La Mule Sanz Frain,* the chief antagonist has been made into an Oriental character, a good indication that the original character in this role may have been Oriental. *The Green Knight* (in the Percy Folio) and "The Ballad of the Green Knight" are both late and somewhat corrupt versions of *Sir Gawain and the Green Knight.*

A Celtic origin for the chastity test has also been pointed out in the Irish story of Cuchulinn and Blathnat (wife of Curoi). A crude later version of it appears in the French romance *Yder,* and Gawain is tested with the carl's wife in the *Carl of Carlisle,* in which he is subsequently given the carl's daughter.

Unlike the beheading challenge and the chastity test, the exchange of winnings is non-Celtic and first appears in a twelfth-century *fabliau.* It does not occur in any other Arthurian narrative. The only extant analogues of it are in the Latin poem *Miles Gloriosus* of the late twelfth century (believed to be from the Loire Valley) and in the *Arabian Nights,* and it reappears in the fourteenth century in one of Giovanni's *Novelles.*[70] In the *fabliau,* a poor knight becomes the partner of a rich merchant and they agree to exchange winnings. The wife of the merchant helps the knight deceive him and they rob him of his treasure. The husband is then driven out and the wife marries the knight. The *Gawain*-poet is thought to have been familiar with the *fabliau* in some form.

When Gawain is dressed and armed to leave Arthur's court,

[70] Hulbert, "Sir Gawayne and the Grene Knyȝt," pp. 699–701. Laura Hibbard Loomis, "Gawain and the Green Knight," in *Arthurian Literature in the Middle Ages,* ed. Loomis, p. 537, points out that the *fabliau* does not appear in other Arthurian stories.

two strophes (ll. 619–99) are devoted to a description of his shield with its "pentangel" and the significance of the figure:

> Hit is a syngne þat Salamon set sumquyle
> In bytoknyng of trawþe, bi tytle þat hit habbez,
> For hit is a figure þat haldez fyue poyntez,
> And vche lyne vmbelappez and loukez in oþer,
> And ayquere hit is endelez; and Englych hit callen
> Overal, as I here, þe endeles knot. (ll. 625–30)

The poet then explicates its five angles and sides in terms of the five senses, the five fingers, five social virtues, five wounds of Christ, and five joys of Mary.

The pentangle, though R. S. Loomis has attempted to derive it from a wheel in order to show a Celtic origin for it,[71] is neither Celtic nor Christian in origin, and the only European literature in which it appears prior to *Sir Gawain* are books of magic and necromancy associated with Solomon; Dante's *Convivio*, where it is used to illustrate man's natural perfection; and the *Geometria Speculativa* of Thomas Bradwardine, Archbishop of Canterbury (ca. 1349), where it is described as a geometric figure.[72] It was, however, almost exclusively a figure of magical significance and one with Semitic connotations. In this connection, Margaret Williams states that "the pentangle on Gawain's shield can be traced back through Jewish legends from Spain to Byzantium, and from there back to the East where it is found on Babylonian pottery."[73] It seems to have reached Western Europe in the many works on magic and necromancy which entered Europe along with scientific lore during the twelfth-century translation in Spain and Sicily, in which, as mentioned in earlier chapters, Jewish scientists, philosophers, and translators played a major role. William of Auvergne, Bishop of Paris (first half of the thirteenth century) condemns the figure as one of several "execrable

[71] Roger Sherman Loomis, "More Celtic Elements in *Gawain and the Green Knight*," *Journal of English and Germanic Philology*, 42 (1943), 168–69.

[72] Richard H. Green, "Gawain's Shield and the Quest for Perfection," in *Sir Gawain and Pearl*, ed. Blanch, pp. 186–87; Davis, ed., *Sir Gawain*, p. 93.

[73] Margaret Williams, trans., *The Pearl-Poet: His Complete Works*, p. 60. See also Hulbert, "Sir Gawayne and the Grene Knyȝt," pp. 721–25; and Vincent Foster Hopper, *Medieval Number Symbolism* (New York, 1938), p. 124.

consecrations and detestable invocations and images."[74] The *Gawain*-poet has thus converted a rather notorious magical symbol to Christian use.

The Green Knight

The poet devotes a great deal of attention to the description of the strange knight and actually emphasizes his green color and reemphasizes it in several passages, with similes and other comparisons, such as "grene as þe gres and grener hit semed/þen green aumayl on golde glowande bryȝter" (ll. 235–36). Other than gold trim, the only nongreen color about him is his "rede yȝen" (l. 304), which he rolls ferociously.[75] It was noticed in Part I of this chapter that Saracens in romance tradition, borrowing in turn from that of the *trouvère chansons de geste,* were often portrayed as having red eyes, associated with ferocity.

No one seems to know what to make of the green knight because of his color. Studies of his origin have attempted to associate him with winter, vegetation, a monster herdsman, death, and the Lord of Hades. The green knight appears in none of the earlier versions of the beheading challenge. Since the challenge is known to be of Celtic origin, Loomis attempts to account for his color with the explanation that "one of the Irish words for gray, *glas,* also may mean green." This permits him then to associate the knight with Welsh figures who wore gray and to suggest that the green knight was a personification of winter.[76]

Other critics, such as Nitze and Speirs, associate the green knight with a vegetation figure. He may originally have been such a figure, but he does not resemble the "green man" or "Jack-in-the-Green" of medieval Europe with whom he has been identified by proponents of the vegetation theory. As Benson points

[74] William of Auvergne is quoted by Lynn Thorndike, *A History of Magic and Experimental Science,* II, 280. Richard H. Green, in his article in *Sir Gawain and Pearl,* ed. Blanch, pp. 265–66, *n.* 10, points out Thorndike's discussion of the pentangle and other symbols.

[75] Robert B. White, Jr., in "A Note on the Green Knight's Red Eyes," *English Language Notes,* 2 (1965), 250–52, suggests that red eyes in medieval physiognomy were associated with strength, courage, and manliness.

[76] Loomis, *Celtic Myth and Arthurian Romance,* p. 59; and Loomis, *Wales and the Arthurian Legend,* p. 87.

out, the stock figure of the literary green man is a youth clad in green leaves, who has neither green skin nor a long, flowing green beard. Sir James Frazer's study of festivals—in which the village green man, often confused with Saint George, appears—further illustrates the figure's appearance as a youth clad in leaves.[77] I have already mentioned that *Perlesvaus*, one of the analogues of *Sir Gawain*, is patterned on ancient vegetation rituals. Ananda Coomaraswamy shows, by comparing the ritual to Vedic tradition, that, in connection with the beheading, irrigation and repopulation are also essential elements of such ritual,[78] but these elements are not to be found in *Sir Gawain*.

It has also been suggested that the green knight represents a literary wild man or monster herdsman. Alice Buchanan derives Bercilak from the Irish *Bachlach*, "Herdsman," the name of the challenger in *Fled Bricrend*, since such a wild man usually appears more often in literature and art than the green man.[79] But, in addition to being ferocious, Bercilak is a knight, and one to be admired as much as feared, a point often overlooked by critics who associate him with vegetation or herdsman figures.

Just as green was associated with life, rebirth, and vegetation in the Middle Ages, it also seems to have been associated, according to some views, with death and the Celtic otherworld. This has led to proposals that the green knight represents death or the devil and the poem a descent to the otherworld.

A connection between the "yeoman" as a devil in Chaucer's "Friar's Tale" and the green knight, since the former is dressed in green, has been suggested.[80] In the "Friar's Tale," the summoner meets a yeoman in the forest who wears "a courtepy of grene" (l. 1382). But he wears green not because he is a devil but because he wishes to appear as a yeoman, and green was worn by

77 Benson, *Art and Tradition in Sir Gawain*, p. 63; James George Frazer, *The Golden Bough*, 3rd ed., II (New York, 1911), 75–84, 324–48.

78 Ananda K. Coomaraswamy, "*Sir Gawain and the Green Knight*: Indra and Namuci," *Speculum*, 19 (1944), 109.

79 Alice Buchanan, "The Irish Framework of *Gawain and the Green Knight*," *PMLA*, 47 (1932), 316.

80 Garrett, "The Lay of Sir Gawayne and the Grene Knight," p. 129. See also D. W. Robertson, Jr., "Why the Devil Wears Green," *Modern Language Notes*, 69 (1954), 470–72.

yeomen, as, for example, by the knight's yeoman in the "General Prologue" to *The Canterbury Tales*. The stranger tells the summoner he is also a "bailly" (l. 1396) and that he comes from "fer in the north contree" (l. 1413). He does not reveal that he is a fiend from hell until later (l. 1448), when he brags about the disguises he can assume. There have been other arguments, such as that of Dale Randall, that the green knight represents a fiend from hell.[81]

A. H. Krappe concludes that the green knight is the Lord of Hades, and Heinrich Zimmer develops Krappe's conclusion, with the thesis that the green knight represents death and his beautiful wife represents life. He bases his opinion in part on the fact that pale green is the "color of livid corpses."[82] (It is also the color of my carpet.) The most expansive treatment of *Sir Gawain* in this light is that by Hans Schnyder, who views the poem as an allegory of a descent to the otherworld.[83] But, as in the case of the life or vegetation figure, none of the advocates for interpreting the green knight as a representative of death or the devil has been able to produce a single literary representative of such a figure.

It might be well at this point to recapitulate some of the findings on *Sir Gawain* before proceeding further. Of the three component parts of the plot of *Sir Gawain*, two of them, the beheading challenge and the chastity test, are of Celtic origin, although, as in the case of much Celtic material, they were developed in romances on the Continent. The third part, the exchange of winnings, derives from an Oriental *fabliau* written in Latin, found in France in the twelfth century and in the *Arabian Nights*, suggesting that it may have reached Europe through Spain. The pentangle on Sir Gawain's shield, for which the poet gives an elaborate Christian explication, was a figure associated with

[81] Dale B. J. Randall, "Was the Green Knight a Fiend?" *Studies in Philology*, 57 (1960), 479–91.

[82] Alexander Haggerty Krappe, "Who *Was* the Green Knight?" *Speculum*, 13 (1938), 215; and Heinrich Zimmer, *The King and the Corpse* (New York, 1948), 76–77. Géza Róheim, in *Animism, Magic, and the Divine King*, pp. 291–92, finds the green knight's holly branch a death symbol.

[83] Hans Schnyder, *Sir Gawain and the Green Knight* (Bern, 1961).

Solomon and magic and apparently came to be known in Europe during the translation of scientific and pseudo-scientific works in Spain and Sicily of the twelfth century.

Next, the prosody of *Sir Gawain* may be a development of the *chante-fable* form of Arab and Persian provenance as exemplified by the Old-French *Aucassin et Nicolette.* The poem itself is festive and predominantly of a religious nature, in regard to its Christmas and New Year settings and its personal religious elements, and the green knight functions in a religious role in the poem.

Finally, the green knight seems to have been substituted for the monster herdsman of the Irish version of the beheading challenge. He is neither green nor a knight in any version of the story prior to *Sir Gawain.* His being foreign to the Celtic story is also suggested in his evolving in certain versions of the story into a deformed Turk and a black Moor and in his having in *Sir Gawain* the red eyes often attributed to Saracens in romance and *chanson-de-geste* tradition. Although he may be derived ultimately from a vegetation figure, he does not resemble the European "green man" in *Sir Gawain,* and the poem lacks other motifs associated with vegetation rituals. Suggestions that he represents a wild man, death, or the devil are not entirely satisfactory to account for him either. As a figure with religious-type functions, he appears in connection with a chapel (which resembles an hermitage), he hears Gawain's confession, and he gives penance in the form of an axe stroke.

Since there are other apparently Oriental borrowings in *Sir Gawain and the Green Knight,* and since no Celtic or Western European figure from whom the green knight could undoubtedly derive has been found, surely a possible Oriental source for him is worth investigating. Whereas no European green figure has been found who resembles the green knight, there is such a figure in Persian and Arabic lore who bears a striking resemblance to him. This is al-Khaḍir, "the Green One," who is associated with ancient vegetation myths, who is both frightening and benevolent, and who is a noble and religious figure. Sometimes, acting as a messenger, he rides into court to offer a challenge. He does not always reveal his identity and, like Bercilak, he never reveals it or explains events at his initial appearance.

Khaḍir

Khaḍir is a pre-Islamic figure whose history and genealogy are quite complex.[84] As incorporated into Islamic writings, he had evolved from the composite mixture of a large number of diverse legends. Apparently having come into the Islamic sphere through Persian legends, he has been identified by Burton as a Wazīr to Kaykobad, who founded the Kayonian dynasty in the sixth century B.C. He appeared as a contemporary of Alexander the Great in some legends, and in others as a contemporary of Adam, Noah, and Moses; and he was later confused with such figures as Elijah and Saint George. It was Khaḍir's being immortal and a vegetation figure which probably led to his being confused with Saint George, who, in the legends of his martyrdom, revived each time he was slain. In fact, Baring-Gould refers to Saint George as a "Christianized Semitic god," who is none other than a manifestation of the older Khaḍir.

In his having attained immortality and at the same time becoming green in color and causing the grass to grow wherever he treads, all of which were accounted for by drinking from the Spring of Life in the Alexander legends, his kinship to ancient vegetation figures is apparent. And as a vegetation figure, al-Khaḍir could well be, as Baring-Gould has suggested, a descendant of the Babylonian Tammuz, the Phoenician Adon or Baal, the Syrial Baal, and the Egyptian Osiris, all of whom are seasonally put to death and revive and who then spend half of their time in heaven and half in the nether world. Their deaths were occasions of wailing and seeking for them on earth, and as these were reenacted, they evolved into elaborate rituals. Similarities between such rituals and those of later Europe in celebrations in-

[84] Information on Khaḍir's background is from the *Encyclopedia of Religion and Ethics*, VII, 693; Mark Lidzbarski, "Wer ist Chadhir?" *Zeitschrift für Assyriologie und Verwandte Gebiete*, 7 (1892), 104–16, whose view (not generally accepted) is that Khaḍir derives from Babylonian and not Persian legends; Richard F. Burton, trans., *The Book of the Thousand Nights and a Night*, III, 2009; and Sabine Baring-Gould, *Curious Myths of the Middle Ages*, pp. 290–91.

volving Saint George and/or the leaf-clad youth representing the "green man" have been shown by Sir James Frazer. Very likely the Persian and Islamic Khaḍir is a cousin of the European "green man." His appearance in both the Near East and Western Europe and his connections with some of the oldest vegetation myths and cults suggest that al-Khaḍir was originally an Indo-European nature god who, through various metamorphoses to render him compatible with the later monotheistic religions, somehow survived. When he was appropriated by the *Ṣūfīs* and other Islamic writers, Khaḍir did not lose all of his vegetation characteristics, and even in his appearance as a representative of mystic divine knowledge, he remains green. Bercilak resembles his cousin Khaḍir much more closely than he does more distant vegetation-figure relatives such as the "Jack-in-the-Green."

Khaḍir's appearance in the literature of medieval Spain has been noticed in earlier chapters. He was involved in an episode in the *Qurʾān,* which was translated twice in the twelfth century, at Cluny by an Englishman and at Toledo by a Spaniard, and he was discussed by the Qurʾānic commentators, most notably Bukhārī, who was known to Mark of Toledo, one of the *Qurʾān*'s translators. Khaḍir had a special importance for the *Ṣūfīs,* who were active in Spain, as illustrated by his appearance twice in the Spanish mystic Ibn-ʿArabī's *al-Futūḥāt al-Makkiyya,* a forerunner of Dante's *Divina Commedia.* Also, as a representative of both divine knowledge and vegetation, Khaḍir was familiar to Spanish-Arab poets of the twelfth century and is alluded to in their poetry which contains other themes later appearing in Old-French poetry. The story of the hermit in the Continental *Gesta Romanorum* which closely resembles the Qurʾānic account in which Khaḍir travels with Moses has been remarked upon, along with Khaḍir's role in several tales of the *Arabian Nights,* a cumulative work which was, in some form, also known in Arab Spain. Finally, he has been seen to have been connected with the Spring of Life in the legends of Alexander the Great, in which he reappears in an *aljamiado* manuscript and in an English one on Alexander of the early sixteenth century.

Tale Number LXXX in the Continental *Gesta Romanorum*

of the hermit and the unnamed angel with its strong resemblance to the Qur'ānic account of Moses and Khaḍir has been noticed by Clouston as having previously appeared among the *exempla* of Jacques de Vitry in the thirteenth century.[85] Several of his *exempla* recur in the *Gesta*. Further, according to Clouston, Thomas Bradwardine, who did not know the *Gesta Romanorum* story of the hermit, cited the story from Jacques de Vitry in his *De Causa Dei Contra Pelagium*, a work with which the *Gawain*-poet seems to have been familiar as evidenced by his treatment of the Pelagian controversy in the *Pearl*. In the *Encyclopedia of Islam*, three possible sources for the Qur'ānic story are discussed: the Gilgamesh epic, in which Gilgamesh travels to seek his ancestor who has eternal life; the Alexander romances, in which Khaḍir attains immortality in the Spring of Life; and a legend in the Jewish Talmud, in which Rabbi Joshua ben Levi, traveling in company with Elijah, is shocked by the actions of the latter in a series of events which appear to be injustices. The Qur'ānic story thus may be, as Clouston believes, drawn from the Jewish legend, but the Jewish account too could have been known in Spain. Clouston also suggests that Jacques de Vitry introduced the story into Europe and that he, in turn, must have obtained it from Syria. The story had, however, preceded Jacques in Europe in the two Latin translations of the *Qur'ān* of the twelfth century, and there is no need to attempt to trace the story to Syria when it was accessible in the Cluniac *Qur'ān*.

The story in the *Qur'ān, Sura* XVIII, Sections 9 and 10, and in the *Gesta Romanorum*, Tale Number LXXX, has some similarities to *Sir Gawain and the Green Knight*. In all three accounts, a mysterious stranger who represents a higher authority (God and Morgan le Fay respectively) appears suddenly. A journey or quest is then involved (Moses, the hermit, and Sir Gawain). The travelers are tested in the *Qur'ān* and *Gesta* with regard to being able to accept events that appear unjust but are manifestations of God's will which is beyond human understanding. Sir Gawain is being tested for keeping a bargain which he does not have to

85 See W. A. Clouston, *Popular Tales and Fictions*, pp. 21–28. The *Gesta* story and the Qur'ānic account are outlined in Chapter V above.

keep and which he thinks will cost him his life if he keeps it. Like Moses and the hermit, he does not understand the nature of the test resulting from the initial challenge; hence his impatience when the green knight has swung the axe twice without touching him:

> Gawayn ful gryndelly with greme þenne sayde:
> "Wy! þresch on, þou þro mon, þou þretez to longe;
> I hope þat þi hert arʒe wyth þn awen seluen." (ll. 2299–2301)

After the nick on his neck with the third stroke, Gawain leaps to his feet, ready to fight, but the green knight merely looks at him somewhat askance, as a prize fighting-cock would look at a bantam rooster whose feathers were ruffled. He then explains the bargain and prior events to Gawain. Likewise, it is only at the end of the Qurʾānic and *Gesta* accounts, when the traveler can tolerate no more, that an explanation is given by the mysterious stranger. Lastly, Khaḍir's not always being recognized as "the Green One" is paralleled in Bercilak's not being recognized by Sir Gawain as the green knight when Gawain arrives at his castle.

It is in his appearance to *Ṣūfīs* in their writings that Khaḍir develops into a forerunner of the green knight. Farid al-Dīn ʿAṭṭār, a twelfth-century Persian poet, compiled a collection of lives of Muslim mystics, in which several of the episodes in the lives involve mysterious appearances of Khaḍir. A typical account from Farid al-Dīn is given below in A. J. Arberry's translation:

> Ibrāhīm Ibn-Adham (d. 782), King of Balkh, was one day having a general audience. "Suddenly a man with aweful mien entered the chamber, so terrible to look upon that none of the royal retinue and servants dared ask him his name; the tongues of all clove to their throats." He approaches Ibrāhīm's throne, and when asked what he wants, replies that he has just alighted "at this caravansai." Ibrāhīm replies that it is not a caravansai. The stranger asks who possessed the throne before him and Ibrāhīm replies "My father." "And before that?" "My grandfather." And so on, until the stranger remarks, "Then this is a caravansai, since, as soon as one man leaves, another enters, and he too leaves for another." Ibrāhīm is shaken. He gives up his kingdom and wealth and becomes a pilgrim. On his way to Mecca, he calls on

God, and Khaḍir then comes and explains to him the visit of the stranger and identifies himself, Khaḍir, as that stranger.[86]

The account of the Persian poet is remarkable in that the basic pattern of it recurs in later accounts of Khaḍir as he appears in the *Arabian Nights*. He is green, he arrives suddenly in a royal court, the courtiers are awestruck and speechless at his aspect, he is not an independent agent but a messenger (of God), he exemplifies divine knowledge and teaching, and he does not reveal his identity or the purpose of his startling appearance until later. There are thus parallels between this account of Khaḍir's appearance, some of the accounts of his appearance in the *Arabian Nights*, and the appearance of Bercilak in Arthur's court with his later explanation and identification of himself to Sir Gawain at the green chapel. Khaḍir, like Bercilak, represents much more than merely a primitive vegetation figure.

In the *Arabian Nights*, Khaḍir is alluded to in "The Tale of Tāj al-Mulūk and the Princess Dunya" as a green vegetation figure connected with Alexander the Great's quest for the Spring of Eternal Life and with Moses' journey in the *Qur*ʾ*ān*. This same tale contains one of the analogues to Chaucer's "Squire's Tale." Khaḍir is one of the characters in "The Tale of Abū-Muḥammad Hight Lazybones." He is but a very minor figure in the tale, but he appears, dressed in green, as a supernatural servant of God who challenges the hero. In three other tales, "The Adventures of Bulukiya" (within "The Tale of the Queen of Serpents"), "The City of Brass," and "The Tale of ʿAbdallāh Ibn-Fāḍil and His Brothers," al-Khaḍir plays a major role.[87]

Several things are remarkable in each of these last three tales. The tales involve travel or a quest of the hero; in one of them it is a quest for knowledge of Muḥammad and the religion (as Moses sought knowledge in the Qurʾānic episode in which Khaḍir accompanied him). Also, religious indoctrination, theol-

[86] Farid al-Dīn ʿAṭṭār, *Muslim Saints and Mystics*, trans. A. J. Arberry (Chicago, 1966), pp. 62–67.

[87] The *Arabian-Nights* stories involving Khaḍir are outlined and discussed in Chapter V above.

ogy, and didacticism, while usually rare in the *Arabian Nights*, become significant in these tales. Tales involving al-Khaḍir tend to be loaded with didacticism. Further, Khaḍir functions as a messenger or emissary (as does the green knight in *Sir Gawain*), rarely appearing of his own volition. And finally, he is associated with the supernatural, but it is a good force. He does not assist the wicked and he requires proof of faith in God (as the green knight requires honesty and courage of Sir Gawain) or else he instructs people in the Islamic faith.

In the tale of ᶜAbdallāh Ibn-Fāḍil, al-Khaḍir enters dramatically into the king's court with a challenge (conversion to Islam and the contest between God's power and that of the idols), just as the green knight rides into Arthur's court with a challenge. He is tall, powerful, awe-inspiring, and admirable, like the green knight in *Sir Gawain*. He appears on Fridays (holy days), just as the green knight appears at Christmas. Khaḍir, although he has a green countenance and green clothing and is ultimately a vegetation figure, does not function as such a figure in any of these tales in which he functions as a religious figure. The people of the two dead cities (the City of Brass and the city in which the inhabitants have been turned to stone) are not restored, any more than winter disperses or a land is repeopled with the green knight's beheading. The green knight therefore appears to share attributes with al-Khaḍir as he appears in the *Qurʾān* and in the *Arabian Nights*. In fact, because of the quasi-religious functions of both green figures, Bercilak resembles al-Khaḍir much more closely and in more respects than he does a mere village "Jack-in-the-Green" or any of the other mythical figures with whom some critics have associated him.

Conclusion

Sir Gawain and the Green Knight, a festive poem informed by definite religious elements, is, like *Pearl*, unique in Middle-English poetry because of the vast array of traditions from which the poet has drawn and because of the manner in which these traditions are combined to create two works unlike any other in the Middle-English period. The short, rimed bob and wheel at the end of each alliterative strophe in *Sir Gawain* is evocative of the Arabic-derived *chante-fable* form, and, if these short lines were sung, as they would appear to have been, *Sir Gawain* is the only *chante-fable* in Middle English known to survive.

Sir Gawain combines Celtic and Eastern motifs in its plot. The beheading challenge and chastity test have been shown to be of Irish origin, while the exchange of winnings seems to have been influenced by an Arabic *fabliau* current in the twelfth century in France. In addition, the pentangle of Sir Gawain's shield was a well-known magical and Semitic symbol which reached Western Europe during the twelfth century when many treatises on magic and necromancy were translated in Spain and Sicily along with scientific works.

Many suggestions have been made as to the derivation of the green knight and his symbolic function in the poem. Among these are a vegetation figure, a wild herdsman, a personification of winter, death, and the Lord of Hades. None of these figures, however, is entirely satisfactory to explain the green knight, who appears to be of much greater complexity. His closest literary predecessor is al-Khaḍir, "the Green One," of Arabic and Persian lore, who, like the green knight, is a composite of ancient vegetation ideas and later religious meanings and functions. A widely-known figure, al-Khaḍir had appeared among *Ṣūfī* writings, in the *Qur'ān*, in an *exemplum* of Jacques de Vitry, in the *Gesta Romanorum* (although he is not named in the last two), in the *Arabian Nights*, in early Spanish-Arab poetry, and in legends of Alexander the Great. In view of the many influences of Arab Spain on European vernacular literature, Khaḍir as he was known in Islamic Spain may be the ancestor of the Middle-English green knight, who, in being appropriated for use in Christian-Arthurian literature, lost many of his Oriental characteristics and acquired a more Celtic appearance.

Many critics have commented upon the large number of Oriental figures and stories in Arthurian romances. Since the originally Celtic Arthurian stories were actually formulated into the romances in France, it is not difficult to see how Oriental materials could infiltrate them through the many contacts between

Spain and France. Kittredge is then justified in proposing a lost French source for *Sir Gawain and the Green Knight*. If the story was known in France, it could easily have been exposed to stories involving Khaḍir and *fabliaux* involving exchanges of winnings from Spain, and it may be, like *Tristan and Isolt*, another Arthurian romance whose Celtic elements have been "contaminated" with Arabic lore.

CHAPTER VII

spain to england

Since the rapid development of vernacular literature in Western Europe coincided in point of time with the translation and transmission of scientific and philosophical works from the ancient Greeks and later Persian, Hindu, and Arab scholars through Spain and Sicily, there was naturally at the same time cultural and literary as well as scientific and philosophical interchange between Islamic and Christian civilizations in Western Europe. Beginning in the late eleventh century and extending through the mid-thirteenth, massive translation projects in Spain and Sicily were undertaken. A center for translation was established at Toledo which drew scholars and churchmen from all over Europe, and Toledo became known as a great international center of learning. Roger II had a similar one in Sicily. Additional centers were established in other cities of Spain and southern France. Through the translations, Europe came into contact with a wealth of learning, not all of which was of a purely scientific or philosophical nature.

Within Spain itself, the Arab culture over some seven centuries (from 711 to 1492) integrated with the Christian culture, an integration which is reflected in the vocabulary and syntax of the Spanish language and in the development of Spanish poetry from Arabic models. Not only were the Arabs' dress and customs emulated by their Christian neighbors, but their alphabet was also used for the Spanish language. A form of literature developed called *aljamiado,* which consisted of a Romance dialect of medieval Spain written in the Arabic script, and many Mozarabic or Christian Spaniards, including some of the ecclesiastics, were more adept at reading and writing Arabic than Latin.

There is strong evidence that the rise of lyric poetry and the courtly-love tradition in Provence, followed by other countries of Europe, owed its inspiration to the vulgar Arabic poetry of Spain, which had developed into forms quite different from the traditional Arabic prosody of the East, and to Ibn-Ḥazm's treatise on love. From as early as 900 the *muwashshaḥ* form of poetic composition, peculiar to Andalusia, is known to have been in existence. It was soon followed by its offspring the *zajal*, from which the *murabbaᶜ* rime (aaaBcccB) later appeared in Provençal troubadour lyrics and even later in English lyrics and other poetry. Themes as well as forms in Andalusian poetry were to be adapted by the troubadours. Poems on chess as a game of fortune and on the marguerite or daisy, two favorite themes in Old-French literature of the thirteenth and fourteenth centuries, are found in Spanish-Arabic poetry from the eleventh century. Similarly, courtly love as it appears in the early Provençal troubadours and later European literary works predates all of these in Andalusia. Ibn-Ḥazm's treatise on love, *The Dove's Neck-Ring*, written in 1022, spells out almost all of the major premises and formulae for courtly love which later characterize troubadour lyrics and later appear in literature throughout Europe.

Two peripheral theories which have been proposed to account for the rise and development of courtly love point to Arab Spain. These are the theory of courtly love being a by-product of the Albigensian heresy and that which suggests that courtly love was an outgrowth of the conflict between Aristotelianism and Islam among the Arab philosophers. Neither of these theories is sound from the point of view of an historical cause-and-effect relationship. Courtly love no doubt affected Albigensian rhetoric, but it is highly doubtful if it could have caused or inspired the heresy. That courtly love was not a philosophical by-product is illustrated by the fact that the troubadours who appropriated it were not scholars. They were working within a folk tradition, not a learned one. This is reflected in their adaptation of the *zajal* of Andalusia for rimed poetry. The *zajal* was not a recognized literary form in Classical Arabic but was, rather, a folk form, a vulgar form, to which the troubadours could easily have had access. The theories of Denis de Rougemont and A. J.

Denomy—ascribing troubadour courtly love to the *Ṣūfī* influences on the Albigensians or to Spanish-Arab philosophers, respectively—while not entirely plausible, do show a recognition of some connection between the troubadours and the Arabic poetry of Spain. The troubadours' very name was taken from the Arabic word *ṭarraba*, and their admittedly Saracen instruments, along with their Arabic names transliterated into vernacular European languages, were brought into Europe through Spain.

Both the courtly love and rimed lyric poetry of medieval Europe can be traced directly to Arab Spain. Neither romantic love nor end rime was native to the Germanic temper of medieval Europe, while both the courtly-love tradition and short, lyric poetic forms are to be found in Arab Spain over a century before the Provençal troubadours flourished. Courtly love conflicted with medieval Christianity, whether it was concerned with earlier romantic and marital love or with the later stylized adulterous love. After the Albigensian Crusade, courtly love was then appropriated to religious use, particularly in the cult of the Virgin, as had been done earlier in Spain.

The Islamic *Ṣūfīs* (mystics) were active in Spain from the tenth century; one of the greatest of the Islamic mystics, Ibn-ᶜArabī, was a native of Spain. The *Ṣūfīs* were instrumental in appropriating lyrical love poetry for mystical use long before its appearance in lyrics honoring Mary and Christ. Islamic and *Ṣūfī* influence is especially detectable in Latin and European vernacular visions of the afterlife from the twelfth century on. Such motifs as the raging river of hell, spanned by a soul-bridge, *al-Sirāṭ*, an astronomical paradise, and a hell structured according to the sin or crime to be expiated are particularly Islamic and particularly evident in European visions dating from the twelfth century and later. Even the *Vision of Tundale*, supposedly written by an Irish Monk in 1149, contains many Islamic eschatological motifs and ideas, as do other Irish visions and voyages to the otherworld. Such Islamic works as the *Livre de Leschiele Mahomet* on the afterlife were found all over Europe during and after the translation period in Spain.

Characteristic of *Ṣūfī* eschatological writings was the use of a beautiful beloved maiden who appeared in a vision of the afterlife to impart divine knowledge, to teach, and, when appropriate, to chastise the visionary and urge him to renounce worldly pleasures in order to win her as his bride in paradise. This maiden, quite different from the Celtic fairy mistress who lures a mortal lover to the otherworld, was totally foreign to medieval Christianity. The *Ṣūfīs* were also largely responsible for the development of an ancient vegetation figure, al-Khaḍir, "the Green One," into a representative of divine mystical knowledge whose mission was often to appear unannounced in a court to challenge unbelievers. Both the maiden and "the Green One" could have served as models for the Pearl maiden and the green knight of the Middle-English *Pearl*-poet's two major poems. A large quantity of Islamic otherworld material is also known to have been incorporated into many romances, which drew from Spanish-Arabic materials as well as from native French and Celtic matter.

The Oriental tale and the fable, like lyric poetry and afterlife visions, as they appeared in Western Europe, had connections with Arab Spain. Arabic and Persian *exempla, fabliaux, contes,* and collections of tales within a frame story were disseminated all over Western Europe through Spain. The major Latin tale sourcebooks of the Middle Ages, the *Disciplina Clericalis,* the *Directorium Humanae Vitae, The Seven Sages of Rome,* and the *Gesta Romanorum,* all contain large numbers of Arab and Persian tales, many of which are direct translations and several of which can be shown to have penetrated Europe through Spain. Hence, in the later tale collections such as Don Juan Manuel's *El Conde Lucanor,* Boccaccio's *Decameron,* Gower's *Confessio Amantis,* and Chaucer's *Canterbury Tales,* are to be found a diversity of tales of Oriental as well as of Classical and native European lineage. All of the major European Latin collections of tales either have Arabic counterparts in Spain or contain tales which could have reached the West only through Spain.

With the rise of the romance tradition which competed with and replaced the older epic *chansons de geste* in twelfth-century France, Arthurian matter, of Celtic origin, was brought into France from across the Channel, where it met a corpus of Spanish-

Arab lore from below the Pyrenees. As a result, many of the medieval romances, including those of the Arthurian and grail groups, reflect Oriental motifs from visions and tales of Arab and Persian origin.

Two obviously Oriental romances are those of *Aucassin et Nicolette* and *Floire et Blanchefleur*. The latter contains within it a story, that of a fake tomb to prevent two lovers from marrying by convincing one that the other is dead, which is similar enough to the Arabic romance, *ʿUrwa wa Afrā*, to have been drawn from it. Fusion of Celtic and Oriental materials in Arthurian romance can be seen in *Tristan and Isolt*, in *Parzival*, and in *Sir Gawain and the Green Knight*. The story of Isolt Blanchemain in *Tristan*, in which the lover marries a lady of the same name as his beloved from whom he is separated, neglects her, and is reunited with his true beloved just before death, is similar to the Arabic story of *Qays wa Layla*, which was, along with *ʿUrwa wa Afrā* (the *Floire* story) in the *Kitāb al-Aghānī* (*Book of Songs*), brought into Spain in the tenth century. There are, in addition, two oriental ruses incorporated in the story of *Tristan and Isolt* from Arabic *fabliaux* current in France in the twelfth century. These were the tryst beneath the tree and the oath of Isolt which includes Tristan in disguise. Another Arabic *fabliau* appears in the exchange of winnings in the Middle-English *Sir Gawain and the Green Knight*, whose green knight has close parallels with the green figure, al-Khaḍir, in Arabic lore. In a different vein, Wolfram von Eschenbach's *Parzival* contains a wealth of materials from newly translated Arabic scientific manuscripts, from lapidaries and astronomical treatises, with many Arabic terms simply Germanicized. His Provençal "Kyot" has not been identified to date, but his "Flegetanis" was probably Alfraganus, a name well known in astronomy and astrology following the translations in Spain and Sicily. Thus, we find materials from both Arabic scientific writings and folklore in the romances and tales of Germany, France, and England.

England was very much involved in the translation efforts of the twelfth century and several English scholars traveled to Spain and Sicily to study and to participate in the translations themselves. The first translation of the *Qurʾān* into Latin was done by an Englishman, Robert of Ketton. Many scientific treatises were later to appear in English libraries. These included lapidaries, treatises on the astrolabe, treatises on astronomy, Alfonso X's Toledan Tables, and other documents. Even after the translation period, Spanish works in Catalan appeared in England, an example of which is Raymond Lull's *Book on the Order of Chivalry*, translated from Catalan into Old French and Middle English.

English lyric poetry, afterlife visions, tales, and romances, all incorporated in their development the Continental traditions in these genres. Provençal troubadour poetic forms and rime schemes are apparent in the English lyrics and in the early English drama cycles which were later developing in England than in France. Such poetic themes as courtly love, chess, and the marguerite, found in Andalusian poetry of the eleventh century and later reappearing in Old-French romances and lyrics, in turn, from France reached England.

The vision literature of England reflects a mixture of native trends, including Celtic ones, and Islamic motifs from the Continent. The Irish monk's *Vision of Tundale* even suggests in its Latin prologue that it was found in a "barbarous" tongue, and because of its many Islamic eschatological motifs, that "barbarous" tongue was no doubt Arabic. The maiden in the *Pearl* relates to *Ṣūfī* visions which develop the theme of the beloved appearing in a vision to expound on paradise and theological precepts. An Old-French translation from Catalan (and in turn from Arabic) of the *Livre de Leschiele Mahomet*, describing Muḥammad's ascent in a vision to an astronomically structured paradise, also appears mysteriously in England.

The major Continental Latin sourcebooks for tales of various types set in instructive or dramatic frames were well known in England, and such collections as *The Seven Sages of Rome* and the *Gesta Romanorum* were translated into Middle English. The *Disciplina Clericalis*, composed in England in the eleventh century by the Spanish Jewish immigrant Pedro Alfonso, is replete with Arabic stories. Fourteenth-century English collections such as Gower's *Confessio Amantis* and Chaucer's *Canterbury Tales* draw from eclectic sources—Celtic, French, Arabic, Latin, and Italian. Like the story in the *Erle of Tolous*, some stories in both the *Confessio* and *The Canterbury Tales* appear to have been woven from events described in Catalan chronicles, and many of the stories in both have Oriental, specifically Arabic, analogues. Chaucer's "Squire's Tale" has analogues in the French *Cléomadès* and *Méliacin*, tales of the enchanted horse, and relates further to the Arabic version of the story (in the *Arabian Nights*), of Persian origin, probably known in Spain through the *Arabian Nights*.

The romance tradition of medieval England was, like English poetry and drama, heavily influenced by Old-French literature, often in turn influenced by Spanish-Arabic works. *Floire et Blanchefleur*, for example, a romance with definite earlier Arabic analogues, reappears in Middle-English translation from the French. The Alexander legends and romances which appeared in English as well as Continental versions also show Oriental influences. One sixteenth-century English manuscript of Alexander's quest for the Spring of Eternal Life incorporates al-Khaḍir, usually confined to Eastern versions of the Alexander legend. Arthurian matter, as it was reimported from France, no longer contained purely Celtic stories, but had been infused with Oriental lore in France. An example is the Tristan story and possibly that of the green knight. Finally, matter of France, as it appears in Middle-English romances seems, like that of England, to have absorbed Saracen motifs. Such romances include the *Sowdone of Babylone, Sir Firumbras, Roland and Vernagu, The Sege of Melayne*, and *Otuel*. These Middle-English Charlemagne romances, like many other works mentioned here, have scarcely been touched upon.

The Middle-English *Pearl* and *Sir Gawain and the Green Knight* have been chosen for more detailed study here because they are not usually considered to be related to southern Continental traditions. But even in these two peculiarly northern English works can be discerned traces of influences ultimately from Andalusia.

Because they do not seem to imitate the more cosmopolitan

and more classical aspects of Chaucer's and Gower's works, because they were not written in the fashionable London dialect of southern England, and because they reflect more of the older native English alliterative prosody as opposed to imported French forms, the *Pearl*-poet's works are sometimes viewed as not having been within the mainstream of fourteenth-century literature. And yet the poet's works evidence a familiarity with an appreciable amount of the religious and vernacular literature of his day. He draws from both Celtic legends and Continental literature and he uses the older alliterative verse along with end rime. In the *Pearl,* he not only combines alliteration with end rime, imported into England through France through Provence, but also incorporates stanza-linking devices adapted by the Provençal poets from the Andalusian *muwashshaḥ* and *zajal* which also provided models for the major Provençal rime schemes. In *Sir Gawain and the Green Knight,* he concludes each alliterative strophe with a short rimed bob and wheel which may have been sung following the recitative of the long, purely alliterative verses of the strophe, in the manner of the French *chante-fable,* adapted in turn from the Arabic-Persian *maqāma* (an adventurous tale in prose and verse), as modified by the refrain form of the *zajal.*

Both the *Pearl* and *Sir Gawain* have elicited considerable comment as to their meanings. Critics of the two poems have studied the Celtic, French, and Christian-ecclesiastical elements in them, and still the poems evade explication as typical medieval English poetical representatives of these elements. Perhaps the reason for this is that neither the Pearl maiden of *Pearl* nor the green knight of *Sir Gawain* relates to traditional Celtic, English, French, or Christian lore. The *Pearl* maiden has literary predecessors only in Islamic eschatological visions and treatises and in Dante, who was heir, indirectly, to the Islamic tradition; and the green Knight bears a much closer resemblance to al-Khaḍir as he had evolved in Islamic literature than to a simple green-clad youth, a wild man, or a representative of death. When cognizance is taken of the Arabic and Persian literary heritage to Western Europe along with the scientific one through Spain, it would seem that one of the reasons that earlier models and literary predecessors for the Pearl and for the green knight have not been found is that critics have stopped short. They have not looked quite far enough to the south.

It should be realized that the *Pearl*-poet's heritage, like that of other fourteenth-century writers, included not only Christian writings, not only Celtic legends, not only French and Arthurian romances, but also, indirectly, Arabic literature, a large proportion of which entered Europe through Spain. The *Pearl*-poet mixed English alliterative verse with French end rime, the medieval love vision with a personal elegy and the eschatological vision; and he appears also to have combined a Persian-Arabic vegetation and religious figure with Celtic legends, and the heavenly maiden of the *Ṣūfī* afterlife with the Christian Apocalypse. He was therefore working within a conglomeration of oral and written literary traditions, all of which need to be recognized in evaluating his works. And with recognition of the true diversity of his raw materials, we can do justice to his artistry in critical appraisals. He has combined so many diverse motifs in *Pearl* and in *Sir Gawain and the Green Knight* and has synthesized them in such a manner as to leave to posterity two works which are broadly symbolic in their suggestions and meanings and which thus remain provocative.

Let this be like the last chapter in Samuel Johnson's *Rasselas*, a "Conclusion in Which Nothing Is Concluded," for it has not been my purpose here merely to see how many earlier Arabic potential sources could be found for various medieval works, but rather to suggest that the contributions of Arabic Spain to medieval European and English literature have been too long neglected or passed over. And if our assessment of the belles-lettres of the Middle Ages is to be reasonably accurate, we must take cognizance of their debts and relationships to the literature of the Iberian Peninsula. Spain was, after all, not a remote province in Tibet or Argentina or Australia or Siberia, and it is surely time the scholars and students of medieval literature stop treating it as such and follow the example of our historians who would never dream of viewing Spain as insignificant, remote, or culturally isolated from France and other countries of Europe in the Middle Ages. A great deal of further research into the relationships among Spanish-Arabic and other medieval literatures still could and should be done before we can "get it all together." I have but scratched the surface.

Bibliography

Abbott, Claude Colleer. *Early Mediaeval French Lyrics.* London: Constable & Co., 1932.

Alatorre, Margit Frenk, ed. *Lírica hispánica de tipo popular.* Colección Nuestros Clásicos, 31. Mexico: Universidad Nacional Autónoma de México, 1966.

Alexander and Dindamus. Ed. Walter W. Skeat. *Early English Text Society,* Extra Series 31 (1878).

Alfonso X. *Antología de Alfonso X, el Sabio,* ed. Antonio G. Solalinde. Buenos Aires: Colección Austral, 1940.

Alfonso, Pedro. "Peter Alphonse's *Disciplina Clericalis,*" ed. William Henry Hulme. *Western Reserve University Bulletin,* 22, No. 3 (1919).

ᶜAlī, Maulānā Muḥammad, trans. and ed. *The Holy Qurʾān: Arabic Text, Translation and Commentary.* Rev. ed. Lahore, Pakistan: Aḥmadiyyah Anjuman Ishāᶜat Islām, 1951.

Alonso, Damaso, and Jose M. Blecua, eds. *Antología de la poesia española: Poesia de tipo tradicional.* Madrid: Editorial Gredos, 1956.

Anderson, Andrew Runni. "The Arabic *History of Dulcarnain* and the Ethiopian *History of Alexander.*" *Speculum,* 6 (1931), 434–45.

Arberry, Arthur J. *Arabic Poetry: A Primer for Students.* Cambridge: Cambridge Univ. Press, 1965.

———, trans. *Moorish Poetry: A Translation of "The Pennants," an Anthology Compiled in 1243 by the Andalusian Ibn-Saᶜīd.* Cambridge: Cambridge Univ. Press, 1953.

———. *Sufism: An Account of the Mystics of Islam.* London: George Allen and Unwin, 1950.

Arnold, Thomas Walker. *The Preaching of Islam: A History of the Propagation of the Muslim Faith.* 3rd ed., 1935; rpt. Lahore, Pakistan: Sh. Muḥammad Ashraf Kasmiri Bazar, 1965.

Arnold, Thomas Walker, and Alfred Guillaume, eds. *The Legacy of Islam.* Oxford: Oxford Univ. Press, 1931.

ᶜAṣi, Mīshel, ed. *Ājmal al-Muwashshaḥat*. Beirut: Dār al-Manhār li al-Nashar, 1968.

Asín Palacios, Miguel. "Abenmasarra y su escuela." *Discurso de recepción*. Madrid: Real Academia de la Historia Memorias, 1914.

———. *Islam and the Divine Comedy*, trans. Harold Sunderland. London: John Murray, 1926.

ᶜAṭṭār, Farid al-Dīn. *Muslim Saints and Mystics*, trans. Arthur J. Arberry. Chicago: Univ. of Chicago Press, 1966.

Baldwin, Charles Sears. *Medieval Rhetoric and Poetic*. New York: The Macmillan Co., 1928.

Baring-Gould, Sabine. *Curious Myths of the Middle Ages*. New York: University Books, 1967.

Baughan, Denver Ewing. "The Role of Morgan le Fay in *Sir Gawain and the Green Knight*." *Journal of English Literary History*, 17 (1950), 241–51.

Becker, Ernest J. *A Contribution to the Comparative Study of Medieval Visions of Heaven and Hell, with Special Reference to the Middle-English Versions*. Baltimore: John Murphy Co., 1899.

Bédier, Joseph. *Les Fabliaux*. 6th ed. Paris: Librairie Ancienne, Honoré Champion, Editeur, 1964.

Bennett, H. S. *Chaucer and the Fifteenth Century*. Oxford History of English Literature. London: Oxford Univ. Press, 1947.

Benson, Larry D. *Art and Tradition in Sir Gawain and the Green Knight*. New Brunswick: Rutgers Univ. Press, 1965.

———. "The Authorship of *St. Erkenwald*." *Journal of English and Germanic Philology*, 14 (1965), 393–405.

Blanch, Robert J., ed. *Sir Gawain and Pearl: Critical Essays*. Bloomington: Indiana Univ. Press, 1966.

Bloomfield, Morton W. "*Sir Gawain and the Green Knight*: An Appraisal." *PMLA*, 76 (1961), 7–19.

———. "Symbolism in Medieval Literature." *Modern Philology*, 56 (1958), 73–81.

The Book of the Knight of La Tour Landry. Ed. Thomas Wright. *Early English Text Society*, 33 (1868).

The Book of the Wiles of Women. Trans. John Esten Keller. Univ. of North Carolina Studies in the Romance Languages and Literatures, No. 27. Chapel Hill: Univ. of North Carolina Press, 1956.

Borroff, Marie. *Sir Gawain and the Green Knight: A Stylistic and Metrical Study*. New Haven: Yale Univ. Press, 1962.

Braddy, Haldeen. "Chaucerian Minutiae." *Modern Language Notes*, 58 (1933), 18–23.

———. "The Genre of Chaucer's *Squire's Tale*." *Journal of English and Germanic Philology*, 41 (1942), 279–90.

———. "The Oriental Origin of Chaucer's Canacee-Falcon Episode." *Modern Language Review*, 31 (1936), 11–19.

———. "The Two Petros in the 'Monkes Tale.'" *PMLA*, 50 (1935), 69–80.

Brenan, Gerald. *The Literature of the Spanish People*. 2nd ed., 1953; rpt. New York: Meridian Books, 1957.

Briffault, Robert S. *The Mothers: A Study of the Origins of Sentiments and Institutions*. 3 vols. New York: The Macmillan Co., 1927.

———. *The Troubadours*, ed. Lawrence F. Koons. Bloomington: Indiana Univ. Press, 1965.

Brittain, F. *The Medieval Latin and Romance Lyric to A. D. 1300*. Cambridge: Cambridge Univ. Press, 1937.

Brockelmann, Carl. *History of the Islamic Peoples*, trans. Joel Carmichael and Moshe Perlmann. New York: Capricorn Books, 1960.

Brown, Carleton F. "The Author of *The Pearl* Considered in the Light of his Theological Opinions." *PMLA*, 19 (1904), 115–53.

———, ed. *English Lyrics of the XIIIth Century*. Oxford: Oxford Univ. Press, 1932.

———, ed. *Religious Lyrics of the XIVth Century*. 2nd ed. Oxford: Oxford Univ. Press, 1952.

Browne, Edward G. *A Literary History of Persia*. 2 vols. New York: Charles Scribner's Sons, 1902 and 1906.

Bryan, W. F., and Germaine Dempter, eds. *Sources and Analogues of Chaucer's Canterbury Tales*. 1941; rpt. New York: Humanities Press, 1958.

Buchanan, Alice. "The Irish Framework of *Gawain and the Green Knight*." *PMLA*, 47 (1932), 315–38.

Buckler, F. W. *Harunu'l-Rashid and Charles the Great*. Cambridge, Mass: The Mediaeval Academy of America, 1931.

Burton, Richard F., trans. *The Book of the Thousand Nights and a Night*. 6 vols. 1886; rpt. New York: Heritage Press, 1934.

Campbell, Joseph, ed. *The Portable Arabian Nights*. New York: Viking Press, 1952.

Campbell, Killis. "A Study of the *Seven Sages* with Special Reference to the Middle English Versions." *PMLA*, n.s. 7 (1899), 1–107.

Carmody, Francis J. *Arabic Astronomical and Astrological Sciences in Latin Translation: A Critical Bibliography*. Berkeley: Univ. of California Press, 1956.

Carson, Mother Angela. "Morgain la Fée as the Principle of Unity in *Gawain and the Green Knight*." *Modern Language Quarterly*, 23 (1962), 3–16.

Castro, Américo. *The Structure of Spanish History*, trans. Edmund L. King. Princeton: Princeton Univ. Press, 1954.

Chambers, Edmund K. *English Literature at the Close of the Middle Ages*. Oxford History of English Literature. Oxford: Oxford Univ. Press, 1945.

Chambers, Edmund K., and F. Sidgwick, eds. *Early English Lyrics: Amorous, Divine, Moral, and Trivial*. 1907; rpt. London: Sidgwick and Jackson, 1921.

Chapman, Coolidge Otis. "Chaucer and the *Gawain*-Poet: A Conjecture." *Modern Language Notes*, 68 (1953), 521–24.

———. "The Musical Training of the *Pearl* Poet." *PMLA*, 46 (1931), 177–81.

Chaucer, Geoffrey. *The Works of Geoffrey Chaucer*, ed. F. N. Robinson. 2nd ed. Boston: Houghton Mifflin Co., 1961.

Chaytor, H. J. *The Troubadours and England*. Cambridge: Cambridge Univ. Press, 1923.

Chew, Samuel C. *The Crescent and the Rose: Islam and England during the Renaissance*. New York: Oxford Univ. Press, 1937.

The Cloud of Unknowing and the Book of Privy Counselling. Ed. Phyllis Hodgson. *Early English Text Society*, 218 (1958).

Clouston, W. A. *Popular Tales and Fictions*. Detroit: Singing Tree Press, 1968.

Colledge, E. *The Mediaeval Mystics of England*. New York: Charles Scribner's Sons, 1951.

Comfort, William Wistar. "The Literary Rôle of the Saracens in the French Epic." *PMLA*, 55 (1940), 628–59.

Conley, John. "*Pearl* and a Lost Tradition." *Journal of English and Germanic Philology*, 54 (1955), 332–47.

Cook, Arthur Bernard. "The European Sky-God." *Folk-Lore*, 17 (1906), 141–73.

Coomaraswamy, Ananda K. "*Sir Gawain and the Green Knight:* Indra and Namuci." *Speculum*, 19 (1944), 104–25.

Corbin, Henry. *Creative Imagination in the Ṣūfism of Ibn-ᶜArabī*, trans. Ralph Manheim. Princeton: Princeton Univ. Press, 1969.

Coulton, G. G. "In Defence of the Pearl." *Modern Language Review*, 2 (1907), 39–43.

Cruz Hernández, Miguel. *Historia de la filosofia española: Filosofia hispano-musulmana*. Madrid: Asociación Española para el Progreso de las Ciencias, 1957.

Daniel, Norman. *Islam and the West: The Making of an Image*. 1960; rpt. Edinburgh: Edinburgh Univ. Press, 1962.

D'Ardenne, S. R. T. O. "The Green Count and *Sir Gawain and the Green Knight*." *Review of English Studies*, n.s. 10 (1959), 113–26.

Denomy, Alexander J. *The Heresy of Courtly Love.* 1947; rpt. Gloucester, Mass.: Peter Smith, 1965.
Dickens, Bruce, and R. M. Wilson, eds. *Early Middle English Texts.* New York: W. W. Norton & Co., 1951.
Dillon, Myles. *Early Irish Literature.* Chicago: Univ. of Chicago Press, 1948.
Dozy, Reinhart, and W. H. Engelmann. *Glossaire des mots espagnols et portugais dérivés de l'arabe.* 2nd ed., 1869; rpt. Amsterdam: Oriental Press, 1915.
Eisner, Sigmund. *The Tristan Legend: A Study in Sources.* Evanston: Northwestern Univ. Press, 1969.
The Encyclopedia of Islam. Ed. M. Th. Houtsma, T. W. Arnold, and others. 4 vols. London: Luzac & Co., 1913–34.
Encyclopedia of Religion and Ethics. Ed. James Hastings. 13 vols. New York: Charles Scribner's Sons, 1951.
Englehardt, George J. "The Predicament of Gawain." *Modern Language Quarterly,* 16 (1955), 218–25.
Entwhistle, William J. *The Spanish Language.* London: Faber & Faber, 1936.
Esch, Arno, ed. *Chaucer und seine Zeit: Symposion für Walter F. Schirmer.* Tübingen: Max Niemeyer Verlag, 1968.
Eschenbach, Wolfram von. *Wolfram von Eschenbach,* ed. Karl Lachmann. 7th ed. Berlin: Walter de Gruyter & Co., 1952.
Farmer, Henry George. *A History of Arabian Music.* 1929; rpt. London: Luzac & Co., 1967.
Frazer, James George. *The Golden Bough.* 3rd ed. 12 vols. New York: Macmillan & Co., 1911–15.
Friedlaender, I. *Die Chadhirlegende und der Alexanderroman.* Leipzig: Druck und Verlag, 1913.
García Gómez, Emilio. *Cinco poetas musulmanes.* Buenos Aires: Espasa-Calpe Argentina, 1945.
———. *Las jarchas romances de la serie árabe en su marco.* Madrid: Sociedad Estudios y Publicaciones, 1965.
———. "Un precedente y una consecuencia del 'Collar de la Paloma.'" *Al-Andalus,* 16 (1951), 309–30.
———. *Al-Shiʿr al-Āndalusī,* trans. Ḥusayn Muʾnis. 2nd ed. Cairo: Maktabat al-Nahḍa al-Miṣriyya, 1952.
———. *Todo Ben Quzmān.* 3 vols. Madrid: Editorial Gredos, 1972.
———. "Veinticuatro jarchas romances en muwashshaḥas árabes." *Al-Andalus,* 17 (1952), 57–127.
Garrett, Robert Max. "The Lay of Sir Gawayne and the Grene Knight." *Journal of English and Germanic Philology,* 24 (1925), 125–34.

Gerhardt, Mia I. *The Art of Story-Telling: A Literary Study of the Thousand and One Nights.* Leiden: E. J. Brill, 1963.
Gérold, Théodore. *La Musique au moyen âge.* Paris: Librairie Ancienne, Honoré Champion, Editeur, 1932.
Gerould, G. H. "The Gawain-Poet and Dante: A Conjecture." *PMLA,* 51 (1936), 31–36.
Gesta Romanorum. Ed. Sidney J. H. Herrtage. *Early English Text Society,* Extra Series 33 (1879).
Gesta Romanorum. Trans. Charles Swan, rev. and ed. Wynnard Hooper. New York: Dover Publications, 1959.
al-Ghazzālī, Abū-Ḥāmid. *al-Durra al-Fākhira, La Perle précieuse,* trans. Lucien Gautier. Geneva: H. Georg Libraire-Editeur, 1878.
Gibb, H. A. R. *Arabic Literature.* London: Oxford Univ. Press, 1926.
Gist, Margaret Adlum. *Love and War in the Middle English Romances.* Philadelphia: Univ. of Pennsylvania Press, 1947.
Goldstein, David, trans. *Hebrew Poems from Spain.* New York: Schocken Books, 1966.
Gollancz, Israel, ed. *Pearl.* London: Oxford Univ. Press, 1921.
———, ed. *Pearl, Cleanness, Patience and Sir Gawain. Early English Text Society,* 162 (1923; rpt. 1931 and 1971).
Gower, John. *Confessio Amantis,* trans. Terence Tiller. Baltimore: Penguin Books, 1963.
———. *Confessio Amantis of John Gower,* ed. Reinhold Pauli. 3 vols. London: Bell and Daldy, 1857.
Greene, Walter Kirkland. "*The Pearl*—A New Interpretation." *PMLA,* 40 (1925), 814–27.
Grunebaum, Gustave E. von. *Medieval Islam: A Study in Cultural Orientation.* Chicago: Univ. of Chicago Press, 1946.
al-Ḥalū, Selīm. *al-Muwushshaḥat al-Āndalusīa.* Beirut: Librairie al-Hayat, 1960.
Hardison, O. B., Jr. *Christian Rite and Christian Drama in the Middle Ages.* Baltimore: The Johns Hopkins Press, 1965.
Hart, Elizabeth. "The Heaven of Virgins." *Modern Language Notes,* 42 (1927), 113–16.
Hartmann, Martin. *Das arabische Strophengedicht: I. das Muwashshaḥ.* Semitische Studien. Weimar: Emil Felber, 1897.
Haskins, Charles Homer. *The Renaissance of the Twelfth Century.* Cambridge, Mass.: Harvard Univ. Press, 1927.
———. *The Rise of Universities.* New York: Henry Holt & Co., 1923.
———. *Studies in the History of Medieval Science.* 2nd ed., 1927; rpt. New York: Ungar Publishing Co., 1960.
Hibbard, Laura A. *Medieval Romance in England.* Rev. ed. New York: Burt Franklin, 1960.

Highfield, J. R. L. "The Green Squire." *Medium Ævum,* 22 (1953), 18–23.

Hillman, Sister Mary Vincent. "Some Debatable Words in *Pearl* and Its Theme." *Modern Language Notes,* 60 (1945), 241–48.

Hills, David Farley. "Gawain's Fault in *Sir Gawain and the Green Knight.*" *Review of English Studies,* 14 (1963), 124–31.

Hitti, Philip K. *History of the Arabs.* 4th ed., rev. London: Macmillan & Co., 1949.

———. *Islam and the West.* Princeton: D. Van Nostrand Co., 1962.

Hodapp, Marion F. "Two Fourteenth-Century Poets: Geoffrey Chaucer and the Archpriest of Hita." *Dissertation Abstracts,* 29 (1968), 1897A (Univ. of Colorado).

Hoffman, Stanton de Voren. "The *Pearl:* Notes for an Interpretation." *Modern Philology,* 58 (1960), 73–80.

Holmes, Urban Tigner, Jr. *A History of Old French Literature: From the Origins to 1300.* Chapel Hill: Robert Linker, 1937.

Hopper, Vincent Foster. *Medieval Number Symbolism.* New York: Columbia Univ. Press, 1938.

Howard, Donald R., and Christian Zacher, eds. *Critical Studies of Sir Gawain and the Green Knight.* Notre Dame: Univ. of Notre Dame Press, 1968.

Hulbert, J. R. "Syr Gawayne and the Grene Knyȝt." *Modern Philology,* 13 (1916), 433–62, 689–730.

Hull, Eleanor. "The Silver Bough in Irish Legend." *Folk-Lore,* 12 (1901), 431–45.

Huppé, Bernard F., and D. W. Robertson, Jr. *Fruyt and Chaf.* Princeton: Princeton Univ. Press, 1963.

Ibn-ᶜArabī. *Sufis of Andalusia: The Rūḥ al-Quds and al-Durrat al-Fākhirah,* trans. R. W. J. Austin. London: George Allen and Unwin, Ltd., 1971.

Ibn-Ḥazm, ᶜAlī Ibn-Aḥmad. *A Book Containing the Risāla Known as The Dove's Neck-Ring about Love and Lovers,* trans. A. R. Nykl. Paris: Librairie Orientaliste Paul Geuthner, 1931.

Ibn-al-Khaṭīb, Lisān al-Dīn. *Jaish al-Taushiḥ,* ed. Hilal Najī and Muḥammad Maḍhūr. Tunis: al-Manār Press, 1967.

Irving, Thomas B. "How Arab Learning Reached Western Europe." *Islamic Literature,* 16 (August, 1970), 453–62.

Jackson, W. T. H. *Medieval Literature: A History and a Guide.* New York: Collier Books, 1966.

Jeanroy, Alfred. *Les Origines de la poésie lyrique en France au moyen âge.* 4th ed., rev. Paris: Librairie Ancienne, Honoré Champion, Editeur, 1965.

———. *La Poésie lyrique des troubadours.* 2 vols. Paris: Henri Didier, 1934.
Jones, C. Meredith. "The Conventional Saracen of the Songs of Geste." *Speculum,* 17 (1942), 201–25.
Jones, H. S. V. "The Cléomadès and Related Folk-Tales." *PMLA,* n.s. 16 (1908), 557–98.
———. "The *Cléomadès,* the *Méliacin,* and the Arabian Tale of the 'Enchanted Horse.'" *Journal of English and Germanic Philology,* 6 (1907), 221–43.
———. "Some Observations upon the *Squire's Tale.*" *PMLA,* n.s. 13 (1905), 346–59.
Kean, Patricia M. *The Pearl: An Interpretation.* New York: Barnes & Noble, Inc., 1967.
Keene, Donald. "The Hippolytus Triangle, East and West." *The Yearbook of Comparative and General Literature,* No. 11, Supplement (1962), 162–71.
Keller, John Esten. *Alfonso X, el Sabio.* Twayne's World Authors Series, No. 12. New York: Twayne Publishers, 1967.
Kennedy, Sally P. "Vestiges of Rule Ritual in *Sir Gawain and the Green Knight.*" Ph.D. dissertation, University of Tennessee, 1968.
Kiteley, J. F. "The *De Arte Honeste Amandi* of Andreas Capellanus and the Concept of Courtesy in *Sir Gawain and the Green Knight.*" *Anglia,* 79 (1961), 7–16.
Kittredge, George Lyman. *A Study of Gawain and the Green Knight.* Cambridge, Mass.: Harvard Univ. Press, 1916.
Krappe, Alexander Haggerty. "Who *Was* the Green Knight?" *Speculum,* 13 (1938), 206–15.
Kritzeck, James. *Peter the Venerable and Islam.* Princeton: Princeton Univ. Press, 1964.
Kyng Alisaunder, Part I: Text. Ed. G. V. Smithers. *Early English Text Society,* 227 (1952).
Kyng Alisaunder, Part II: Introduction, Commentary, and Glossary. Ed. G. V. Smithers. *Early English Text Society,* 237 (1953).
Langland, William. *Piers the Ploughman,* trans. J. F. Goodridge. Baltimore: Penguin Books, 1959.
Lasater, Alice E. "Wolfram's 'Flegetanis.'" *The Southern Quarterly,* 11 (January, 1973), 157–66.
Lee, A. Collingwood. *The Decameron: Its Sources and Analogues.* New York: Haskell House, 1966.
Lévi-Provençal, E. *La civilisation arabe en espagne: vue générale.* Paris: G. P. Maisonneuve & Co., 1948.
———. *Histoire de l'espagne musulmane.* Rev. ed. 2 vols. Paris: G. P. Maisonneuve & Co., 1950.

Lewis, C. S. *The Allegory of Love.* New York: Oxford Univ. Press, 1958.

Lidzbarski, Mark. "Wer ist Chadhir?" *Zeitschrift für Assyriologie und Verwandte Gebiete,* 7 (1892), 104–16.

Loomis, Roger Sherman, ed. *Arthurian Literature in the Middle Ages.* Oxford: Oxford Univ. Press, 1959.

———. *Celtic Myth and Arthurian Romance.* New York: Columbia Univ. Press, 1926.

———. *The Development of Arthurian Romance.* London: Hutchinson Univ. Library, 1963.

———. "Gawain in the *Squire's Tale.*" *Modern Language Notes,* 52 (1937), 413–16.

———. *The Grail: From Celtic Myth to Christian Symbol.* New York: Columbia Univ. Press, 1963.

———. "More Celtic Elements in *Gawain and the Green Knight.*" *Journal of English and Germanic Philology,* 42 (1943), 149–84.

———. "Morgain la Fée and the Celtic Goddesses." *Speculum,* 20 (1945), 183–203.

———. *Wales and the Arthurian Legend.* Cardiff: Univ. of Wales Press, 1956.

Lorris, Guillaume de, and Jean de Meun. *The Romance of the Rose,* trans. Harry W. Robbins, ed. Charles W. Dunn. New York: E. P. Dutton & Co., 1962.

Lowes, John Livingston. "The Squire's Tale and the Land of Prester John." *Washington University Studies,* 1 (October, 1913), 3–18.

Lull, Raymond. *The Book of the Ordre of Chyualry,* ed. Alfred T. P. Byles. *Early English Text Society,* 168 (1926).

Madeleva, Sister M. *Pearl: A Study in Spiritual Dryness.* New York: D. Appleton, 1925.

Mandeville's Travels. Ed. M. C. Seymour. Oxford: Oxford Univ. Press, 1967.

Mason, Eugene, trans. *Aucassin and Nicolette and Other Mediaeval Romances and Legends.* New York: E. P. Dutton & Co., 1958.

McAlindon, T. "Magic, Fate, and Providence in Medieval Narrative and *Sir Gawain and the Green Knight.*" *Review of English Studies,* 16 (1965), 121–39.

Medieval Epics. New York: The Modern Library, 1963.

Mekinassi, A. *Léxico des las palabras Españolas de origen Arabe.* Tetuán: Editorial Cremades, 1963.

Menéndez Pidal, Ramón. *Poesía arabe y poesía europea.* 5th ed. Madrid: Colección Austral, Espasa-Calpe, 1963.

Mérimée, Ernest. *A History of Spanish Literature,* trans. S. Griswold Morley. New York: Henry Holt & Co., 1930.

Migne, Jacques Paul, ed. *Patrologiae Cursus Completus, Series Latina,* CLXXXIX. Paris: Apud Garnier Fratres, Editores, 1890.

Moon, Douglas M. "The Role of Morgain la Fée in *Sir Gawain and the Green Knight.*" *Neuphilologische Mitteilungen,* 67 (1966), 31–57.

Moorman, Charles. *The Pearl-Poet.* Twayne's English Authors Series. New York: Twayne Publishers, 1968.

———. "The Role of the Narrator in *Pearl.*" *Modern Philology,* 53 (1955), 73–81.

Morris, Richard, ed. *Early English Alliterative Poems. Early English Text Society,* 1 (1864).

———, ed. *Sir Gawayne and the Green Knight: An Alliterative Romance-Poem (1320–30 A. D.). Early English Text Society,* 4 (1864).

Murray, Margaret A. "The Egyptian Elements in the Grail Romance." *Ancient Egypt,* ed. Flinders Petrie. New York: Macmillan & Co., 1916.

Mustard, Helen M., and Charles E. Passage, trans. *Parzival,* by Wolfram von Eschenbach. New York: Vintage Books, 1961.

Nazi, Shaheer. "The Identification of al-Khidr." *The Muslim Digest,* 21 (November, 1970), 97–100.

Nicholson, Reynold A. *A Literary History of the Arabs.* Cambridge: Cambridge Univ. Press, 1969.

Nitze, William A. "Is the Green Knight Story a Vegetation Myth?" *Modern Philology,* 33 (1936), 351–66.

Northrup, Clark S. "Recent Studies of *The Pearl.*" *Modern Language Notes,* 22 (1907), 21–22.

Nykl, A. R. *Hispano-Arabic Poetry and Its Relations with the Old Provençal Troubadours.* Baltimore: J. H. Furst Co., 1946.

O'Leary, De Lacy. *Arabic Thought and Its Place in History.* Rev. ed. New York: E. P. Dutton & Co., 1939.

Osgood, Charles G., ed. *The Pearl; A Middle English Poem.* Belles Lettres Series. Boston: D. C. Heath & Co., 1906.

Palencia, Angel Gonzáles. *Historia de la literatura arábigo-española.* Barcelona: Editorial Labor, 1928.

———. *Tarīkh al-Fikr al-Āndalusī,* trans. Ḥusayn Muʾnis. Cairo: University of Cairo, 1955.

Paris, Gaston. *La Littérature française au moyen âge.* 5th ed. Paris: Librairie Hachette, 1914.

Pastor, Antonio. *The Idea of Robinson Crusoe.* Watford: Gongora, 1930.

Patch, Howard Rollin. *The Other World According to Descriptions in Medieval Literature.* Cambridge, Mass: Harvard Univ. Press, 1950.

———. "Some Elements in Mediaeval Descriptions of the Otherworld." *PMLA,* n.s., 26 (1918), 601–43.

Patience. Ed. J. J. Anderson. 1969; rpt. Manchester: Manchester Univ. Press, 1972.

Patience: A West Midland Poem of the Fourteenth Century. Ed. Hartley Bateson. Manchester: Victoria Univ. of Manchester Press, 1912.

Paton, Lucy Allen. *Studies in the Fairy Mythology of Arthurian Romance.* 2nd ed. New York: Burt Franklin, 1960.

The Pearl. Ed. Sara deFord and others. New York: Appleton-Century-Crofts, 1967.

Polo, Marco. *The Adventures of Marco Polo,* ed. Milton Rugoff. New York: New American Library, 1961.

Procter, Evelyn S. *Alfonso X of Castile: Patron of Literature and Learning.* Oxford: Oxford Univ. Press, 1951.

———. "The Scientific Works of the Court of Alfonso X of Castile: The King and His Collaborators." *Modern Language Review,* 40 (1945), 12–29.

The Prose Life of Alexander. Ed. J. S. Westlake. *Early English Text Society,* 143 (1913).

Purity: A Middle English Poem. Ed. Robert J. Menner. *Yale Studies in English,* 61 (1920; rpt. 1970).

Raffel, Burton, trans. *Sir Gawain and the Green Knight.* New York: New American Library, 1970.

Randall, Dale B. J. "Was the Green Knight a Fiend?" *Studies in Philology,* 57 (1960), 479–91.

Renwick, W. L., and Harold Orton, eds. *The Beginnings of English Literature to Skelton 1509.* 3rd ed. London: The Cresset Press, 1966.

Robertson, D. W., Jr. "The 'Heresy' of *The Pearl.*" *Modern Language Notes,* 65 (1950), 152–55.

———. "The Pearl as a Symbol." *Modern Language Notes,* 65 (1950), 155–61.

———. "Why the Devil Wears Green." *Modern Language Notes,* 69 (1954), 470–72.

Róheim, Géza. *Animism, Magic, and the Divine King.* London: Kegan Paul, Trench, Trubner, & Co., 1930.

Rougemont, Denis de. *Love Declared,* trans. Richard Howard. Boston: Beacon Press, 1963.

———. *Love in the Western World.* Rev. ed., trans. Montgomery Belgion. New York: Pantheon Books, 1956.

Ruiz, Juan. *The Book of Good Love*, trans. Rigo Mignoni and Mario A. Di Cesare. New York: State Univ. of New York Press, 1970.

Sánchez Albornoz, Claudio. *La españa musulmana: Según los autores islamitas y cristianos medievales*. 2 vols. Buenos Aires: Libreria y Editorial "El Ateneo," 1946.

Sands, Donald B., ed. *Middle English Verse Romances*. New York: Holt, Rinehart, & Winston, 1966.

Sarton, George. *Introduction to the History of Science*. 3 vols. Washington: Carnegie Institute, 1927–48.

Savage, Henry Lyttleton. "Chaucer and the 'Pitous Deeth' of 'Petro, Glorie of Spayne.'" *Speculum*, 24 (1949), 357–75.

———. *The Gawain-Poet: Studies in His Personality and Background*. Chapel Hill: Univ. of North Carolina Press, 1956.

Scarpa, Roque Esteban. *Lecturas medievales españolas*. Santiago, Chile: Zig-Zag, 1949.

Schack, Adolfo Federico. *Poesia y arte de los arabes en españa y sicilia*, trans. Juan Valera. Buenos Aires: Editorial Arabigo-Argentina "El Nilo" de Aḥmed Abboud, 1865.

Schnyder, Hans. *Sir Gawain and the Green Knight*. Bern: A. Francke Verlag, 1961.

Schoeck, Richard J., and Jerome Taylor, eds. *Chaucer Criticism*. 2 vols. Notre Dame: Univ. of Notre Dame Press, 1960.

Schoepperle, Gertrude. *Tristan and Isolt: A Study of the Sources of the Romance*. 2 vols. London: David Nutt, 1913.

Schofield, William Henry. "The Nature and Fabric of *The Pearl*." *PMLA*, 19 (1904), 154–215.

———. "Symbolism, Allegory and Autobiography in *The Pearl*." *PMLA*, 24 (1909), 585–675.

The Seven Sages of Rome. Ed. Killis Campbell. New York: Ginn & Co., 1907.

Shorter Encyclopedia of Islam. Ed. H. A. R. Gibb and J. H. Kramers. Leiden: E. J. Brill, 1965.

Silverstein, Theodore. "Andreas, Plato, and the Arabs: Remarks on Some Recent Accounts of Courtly Love." *Modern Philology*, 47 (1949), 117–26.

Singer, Samuel. *Germanisch-Romanisches Mittelalter*. Leipzig: Max Neihans Verlag, 1935.

Sir Gawain and the Green Knight. Ed. J. R. R. Tolkien and E. V. Gordon. 2nd ed. London: Oxford Univ. Press, 1967.

Smithers, G. V. "What *Sir Gawain and the Green Knight* Is About." *Medium Ævum*, 32 (1963), 171–89.

Solá-Solé, J. M. "Nuevas kharjas mozárabes." *Kentucky Romance Quarterly*, 17 (1970), 29–46.

Southern, R. W. *Western Views of Islam in the Middle Ages.* Cambridge, Mass.: Harvard Univ. Press, 1962.

Speirs, John. *Medieval English Poetry: The Non-Chaucerian Tradition.* London: Faber and Faber, 1957.

———. *"Sir Gawain and the Green Knight." Scrutiny,* 16 (1949), 274–300.

Spitzer, Leo. "The Mozarabic Lyric and Theodore Frings' Theories." *Comparative Literature,* 4 (1952), 1–22.

Stern, S. M. "^{c}Āshiqayn I^{c}tanaqā: An Arabic Muwashshaḥ and Its Hebrew Imitations." *Al-Andalus,* 28 (1963), 155–70.

———. *Les Chansons mozarabes.* 1953; rpt. Oxford: Bruno Cassirer, 1964.

———. "Miscelánea internácional sobre las jarchas mozárabes." *Al-Andalus,* 18 (1953), 133–48.

———. "Studies on Ibn-Quzmān." *Al-Andalus,* 16 (1951), 379–425.

Stevens, Martin. "Laughter and Game in *Sir Gawain and the Green Knight." Speculum,* 47 (1972), 65–78.

Stevick, Robert D., ed. *One Hundred Middle English Lyrics.* New York: Bobbs-Merrill Co., 1964.

Thompson, James Westfall, and Edgar Nathanial Johnson. *An Introduction to Medieval Europe 300–1500.* Rev. ed. New York: W. W. Norton & Co., 1965.

Thorndike, Lynn. *A History of Magic and Experimental Science.* 4 vols. New York: The Macmillan Co., 1923.

Thorndike, Lynn, and Pearl Kibre. *A Catalogue of Incipits of Mediaeval Scientific Writings in Latin.* Rev. ed. Cambridge, Mass.: The Mediaeval Academy of America, 1963.

Ticknor, George. *History of Spanish Literature.* 3 vols. Boston: James R. Osgood & Co., 1872.

Toynbee, Paget. "Dante's Obligations to Alfraganus in the *Vita Nuova* and *Convivio." Romania,* 24, No. 95 (July, 1895), 413–32.

Trachtenberg, Joshua. *The Devil and the Jews: The Medieval Conception of the Jew and Its Relation to Modern Antisemitism.* New

The Très Riches Heures of Jean, Duke of Berry. Ed. Jean Longnon

Haven: Yale Univ. Press, 1943.

and Raymond Cazelles, trans. Victoria Benedict. New York: George Braziller, 1969.

Trounce, A. McI. "The English Tail-Rime Romances." *Medium Ævum,* 1 (1932), 87–108, 168–82; 2 (1933), 34–57, 189–98.

Tunison, J. S. *The Graal Problem: From Walter Map to Richard Wagner.* Cincinnati: Robert Clark Co., 1904.

Turnbull, Eleanor, ed. *Ten Centuries of Spanish Poetry.* New York: Grove Press, 1955.

Ullah, Najib. *Islamic Literature: An Introductory History with Selections.* New York: Washington Square Press, 1963.

Waddell, Helen. *The Wandering Scholars.* Rev. ed., 1934; rpt. London: Constable & Co., 1947.

Wagner, Charles Philip. "The Sources of *El Cavallero Cifar.*" *Revue Hispanique,* 1 (1903), 4–104.

Waite, Arthur Edward. *The Holy Grail: The Galahad Quest in the Arthurian Tradition.* New York: University Books, 1961.

Warren, F. M. "The Troubadour *Canso* and the Latin Lyric Poetry." *Modern Philology,* 9 (1912), 469–87.

The Wars of Alexander. Ed. Walter W. Skeat. *Early English Text Society,* Extra Series 47 (1886).

Warton, Thomas. *History of English Poetry,* ed. W. Carew Hazlitt. 4 vols. London: Reeves & Turner, 1871.

Watt, W. Montgomery. *A History of Islamic Spain.* Islamic Surveys, No. 4. 1965; rpt. Edinburgh: R. & R. Clark, 1967.

Wells, John Edwin. *A Manual of the Writings in Middle English, 1050–1400.* With 9 supplements. New Haven: Yale Univ. Press, 1916–52.

Weston, Jessie L. *From Ritual to Romance.* New York: Doubleday Anchor Books, 1957.

———. *The Legend of Sir Perceval.* 2 vols. London: David Nutt, 1906 and 1909.

———. *The Quest of the Holy Grail.* London: G. Bell and Sons, 1913.

Whicher, George F., trans. *The Goliard Poets: Medieval Latin Songs and Satires.* Privately printed, 1949.

White, Robert B., Jr. "A Note on the Green Knight's Red Eyes." *English Language Notes,* 2 (1965), 250–52.

Wiener, Leo. *Contributions toward a History of Arabico-Gothic Culture.* 4 vols. Vols. 1 and 2, New York: Neale Publishing Co., 1917 and 1919. Vols. 3 and 4, Philadelphia: Innes and Sons, 1920 and 1921.

Williams, Margaret, trans. *The Pearl-Poet: His Complete Works.* New York: Vintage Books, 1970.

Yohannan, John D., ed. *Joseph and Potiphar's Wife.* New York: New Directions Publishers, 1968.

Zangwill, Israel, trans. *Selected Religious Poems of Solomon Ibn Gabirol.* Philadelphia: The Jewish Publication Society of America, 1923.

Zimmer, Heinrich. *The King and the Corpse.* New York: Pantheon Books, 1948.

index